T0329659

Novel Beings

ELGAR LAW, TECHNOLOGY AND SOCIETY

Series Editor: Peter K. Yu, *Drake University Law School, USA*

The information revolution and the advent of digital technologies have ushered in new social practices, business models, legal solutions, regulatory policies, governance structures, consumer preferences and global concerns. This unique book series provides an interdisciplinary forum for studying the complex inter-actions that arise from this environment. It examines the broader and deeper theoretical questions concerning information law and policy, explores its latest developments and social implications, and provides new ways of thinking about changing technology.

Titles in the series include:

The Making Available Right
Realizing the Potential of Copyright's Dissemination Function in the Digital Age
Cheryl Foong

The Regulation of Social Media Influencers
Edited by Catalina Goanta and Sofia Ranchordás

Fundamental Rights Protection Online
The Future Regulation of Intermediaries
Edited by Bilyana Petkova and Tuomas Ojanen

Judges, Technology and Artificial Intelligence
The Artificial Judge
Tania Sourdin

Regulating Online Behavioural Advertising Through Data Protection Law
Jiahong Chen

The Future of Copyright in the Age of Artificial Intelligence
Aviv H. Gaon

Pandemic Surveillance
Privacy, Security, and Data Ethics
Edited by Margaret Hu

Regulating Social Network Sites
Data Protection, Copyright and Power
Asma Vranaki

Novel Beings
Regulatory Approaches for a Future of New Intelligent Life
Edited by David R. Lawrence and Sarah Morley

Novel Beings

Regulatory Approaches for a Future of New Intelligent Life

Edited by

David R. Lawrence

Durham Law School, Durham University, UK

Sarah Morley

Newcastle Law School, Newcastle University, UK

ELGAR LAW, TECHNOLOGY AND SOCIETY

Edward Elgar
PUBLISHING

Cheltenham, UK • Northampton, MA, USA

Published by
Edward Elgar Publishing Limited
The Lypiatts
15 Lansdown Road
Cheltenham
Glos GL50 2JA
UK

Edward Elgar Publishing, Inc.
William Pratt House
9 Dewey Court
Northampton
Massachusetts 01060
USA

A catalogue record for this book
is available from the British Library

Library of Congress Control Number: 2022946679

This book is available electronically in the **Elgar**online
Law subject collection
http://dx.doi.org/10.4337/9781800889262

ISBN 978 1 80088 925 5 (cased)
ISBN 978 1 80088 926 2 (eBook)

Printed and bound by CPI Group (UK) Ltd, Croydon, CR0 4YY

For Margot, Mimi, and Otto

Contents

Contributors

Alan Dignam is King's Counsel (Hon) and Professor of Corporate Law at Queen Mary University of London.

Colin Gavaghan is Professor of Digital Futures, University of Bristol Law School.

John Harris is Professor Emeritus in Bioethics at the University of Manchester; Honorary Professor in Medical Law and Ethics at the Centre of Medical Law and Ethics, Kings College London; and a Distinguished Research Fellow in the Oxford University Uehiro Centre for Practical Ethics.

Mike King is Senior Lecturer in the Bioethics Centre of the University of Otago.

David R. Lawrence is Assistant Professor in Biolaw at Durham Law School.

Aisling McMahon is Professor of Law at the School of Law and Criminology at Maynooth University.

Sarah Morley is Lecturer in Law at Newcastle University Law School.

Muireann Quigley is Professor of Law, Medicine, and Technology at the University of Birmingham Law School.

Joseph T.F. Roberts is Research Fellow in Law and Philosophy at the University of Birmingham Law School.

Daniel Tigard is a Senior Research Associate in the Institute for History and Ethics of Medicine, School of Medicine, Technical University of Munich. As of autumn 2022, he will be Assistant Professor of Philosophy at the University of San Diego.

Acknowledgements

The editors wish to thank all of the many colleagues who have taken the time to participate in and contribute to the various activities of the wider Novel Beings Network of researchers, who inspired this collection.

Introduction

The law as it stands is woefully insufficient to regulate emerging scientific advances, and in particular those that will stem from the creation of new morally valuable technologies. Gene science, advanced pharmaceuticals, robotics and cybernetics, the internet, breakthroughs in artificial intelligence (AI) and yet more technologies more usually associated with science fiction have in recent years risen to the forefront of science. Not the least of these developments is the potential for the emergence of new types of intelligent being – which we term 'novel beings' – and their precursor technologies. We use the term 'novel beings' to include any entity created through artifice and which might warrant some degree of moral status and contingent protection.[1] Novel beings, here, could range from already (partially) synthetic animal models to artificial general intelligence, or even biotechnological replicas of human beings. This essential artificiality does not necessarily imply a different inherent value to a naturally occurring equivalent. However, sapient, reasoning creatures that we artificially create may deserve their own protections and freedoms; even to share human rights. We may already be seeing new sentiences created that can suffer harms, such as brain organoids.[2] Further developments are likely to yield models better able to emulate human neural processes, increasing the possibility of emulating cognitive functions. Similarly, in-silico animal simulations are only limited by time and computing power before more cognitively complex organisms can be replicated.

We are already used to seeing a number of precursor technologies, such as genomics, synthetic biology, and neurotechnologies; as well as in the profusion of 'expert systems' – algorithms and simple (or 'narrow') artificial intelligences (AI) that interlace our everyday lives, from smart assistants, to the financial markets, to social media. All these technologies, and more, are collectively and individually poised to present great and fundamental challenges for society and for the law. We have already experienced the disruptive

---

[1]   For further discussion of the nature of 'Novel Beings', see the papers included in the special issue: David R. Lawrence and Sarah Morley (eds), 'Regulating consciousness: the challenge of consciousness in new forms of life' (2021) 30(3) *Cambridge Quarterly of Healthcare Ethics*.

[2]   Andrea Lavazza and Marcello Massimini, 'Cerebral organoids: ethical issues and consciousness assessment' (2018) 44(9) *Journal of Medical Ethics* 606.

potential of the emergence of these technologies through the deployment and use of expert systems in politics, policing, and economics.[3] As the stewards of scientific progress, we are beholden to protect all parties – both existing persons, and the beings we may create through research in both AI and biology.

Novel beings is a new and developing area of scholarship. Whilst the consideration of morally valuable technology is in itself an established topic, it has not received significant academic or policy-related attention outside a relatively small – but growing – literature of 'robot rights',[4] which is often centrally focused on philosophical abstracts rather than practical legal solutions. There is a strong literature on emerging technology law,[5] although much of it fails to advocate sufficiently farsighted protective action due to uncertainty; and that which is taken focuses primarily on human or environmental health.[6] Aspects of responsibility around novel beings have been studied, albeit in different or narrower contexts. This includes legal work on the responsible deployment of expert systems[7] or general ethical work on related concepts such as the posthuman,[8] AI,[9] and the relationship between rights and moral status;[10] as well as literature regarding regulatory dimensions of emerging bio

---

[3]   Digital Culture, Media and Sport Committee, 'Disinformation and "fake news"' (Final Report, HC 1791, 2019); Alex Hern, 'Cambridge Analytica Scandal "Highlights Need For AI Regulation"' (*The Guardian*, 16 April 2018) <https://www.theguardian.com/technology/2018/apr/16/cambridge-analytica-scandal-highlights-need-for-ai-regulation> accessed 15 April 2022; Adam Liptak, 'Sent to Prison by a Software Program's Secret Algorithms' (Nytimes.com, 1 May 2018) <https://www.nytimes.com/2017/05/01/us/politics/sent-to-prison-by-a-software-programs-secret-algorithms.html> accessed 15 April 2022; Tshilidzi Marwala and Evan Hurwitz, *Artificial Intelligence and Economic Theory: Skynet in the Market* (Springer 2017).

[4]   E.g. Wendell Wallach and Colin Allen, *Moral Machines* (Oxford University Press 2010); David J. Gunkel, 'The other question: can and should robots have rights?' (2017) 20 *Ethics and Information Technology* 87–99.

[5]   Roger Brownsword, Eloise Scotford and Karen Yeung (eds), *The Oxford Handbook of Law, Regulation and Technology* (Oxford University Press 2017).

[6]   Deryck Beyleveld and Roger Brownsword, 'Emerging technologies, extreme uncertainty, and the principle of rational precautionary reasoning' (2012) 4 *Law, Innovation and Technology* 35.

[7]   Marion Oswald *et al.*, 'Algorithmic risk assessment policing models: lessons from the Durham HART model and "Experimental" proportionality' (2018) 27 *Information & Communications Technology Law* 223–250.

[8]   David R. Lawrence, 'The edge of human? The problem with the posthuman as the "beyond"' (2017) 31 *Bioethics* 171–179.

[9]   Stuart Russell and Peter Norvig, *Artificial Intelligence: A Modern Approach* (4th edn, Pearson 2021).

[10]   Charles Taylor, 'The concept of a person', in Charles Taylor (ed.), *Philosophical Papers, Volume 1* (Cambridge University Press 1985); Peter Singer and Paola Cavalieri (eds), *The Great Ape Project: Equality Beyond Humanity* (St. Martin's 1993).

and computer technologies,[11] and work highlighting the fundamental legal problems of new sapient life.[12] In the courts, great ape rights have been considered[13] (demonstrating the unique challenges inherent in extending personhood, which is poorly defined in law), though there has been no specific consideration of granting rights and/or protections to new sapient (or sentient) beings.[14] This existing theoretical literature presents a useful foundation upon which to build the beginnings of practical recommendations for policy and legislative development.

This edited collection emerges from a successful Wellcome Trust-funded pilot study.[15] It explored the role of companies in the development and regulation of new morally significant technologies. The project additionally brought together and established a substantial network of leading researchers in bioethics, legal theory, and company law, some of whom are the contributing authors to this collection. In this earlier work, cited in recommendations of the House of Lords AI Report (2018),[16] we offered philosophical analysis of the legal status of corporations (established 'artificial' persons in legal terms), and studied regulatory levers including shareholder primacy and responsibility for the deployment and disposal of the technologies. Our research showed that more fundamental questions needed thorough investigation, including a hierarchy of moral value, resultant status, and consequent responsibilities and obligations, i.e. whether greater moral status implies higher responsibility, and whether once a certain capacity threshold is passed beings acquire their own legal obligations. Lower moral status may equate to less responsibility for the being and greater obligations for the developer or owner. For example, current forms of AI would have no legal responsibility, this falling to the developer,

---

[11]   Colin Gavaghan, 'Lex machina: techno-regulatory mechanisms and "rules by design"' (2017) 15(1) *Otago Law Review* 123–145.

[12]   David R. Lawrence and Margaret Brazier, 'Legally human? "Novel beings" and English law' (2018) 26 *Medical Law Review* 309–327.

[13]   Including, for example, the chimpanzees Tommy (*The Nonhuman Rights Project, Inc., On Behalf of Tommy, v Patrick C. Lavery*. 998 N.Y.S.2d 248 (App. Div. 2014)); and Hercules and Leo (*Matter of Nonhuman Rights Project, Inc. v Stanley*. N.Y. Slip Op 31419, State of New York Supreme Court (2015)).

[14]   See David R. Lawrence and Sarah Morley, 'Regulating the Tyrell Corporation: the emergence of novel beings' (2021) 30(3) *Cambridge Quarterly of Healthcare Ethics* 421.

[15]   Wellcome Trust: WT 208871/Z/17/Z, 'Regulating the Tyrell Corporation: Company Law and the Emergence of Novel Beings'.

[16]   Parliament, House of Lords (2018) AI in the UK: ready, willing and able? (HL100, 2018) paras 315, 317, 318, 379 (footnotes 427, 438, 439, 522).

whereas a being equivalent to human adult capacities could have commensurate rights and obligations.[17]

Moreover, we found deficiencies in legislative proposals that relate to AI, and in existing biolaw.[18] We have, over several years, been the primary proponents of research into the question of novel beings, advocating thorough and systematic re-evaluation of our legal assumptions in order to sufficiently prepare for the advent of these new morally significant technologies.[19] Existing policy and regulation are ill-prepared for this brave new world of novel beings or their precursors. The question, then, is how can we enforce this responsible approach broadly within the law, through regulatory instruments, to ensure responsible development and operation of this new technology? Any new suggested regulation is generally piecemeal and problem-specific, with recently proposed documents addressing only existing technologies such as self-driving cars and latterly facial recognition software.[20]

Debates surrounding the regulation of new technology (or at least how to navigate its impacts) are *not* new – we are intimately familiar with arguments over the cotton gin, printing presses, automobiles, the internet and more recently AI technology. Within these debates there are commonly two sides, either advocating action to mitigate issues in advance of wide public use of the new technology or for responsive action to remedy harms by utilising and adapting existing regulations. Anecdotally, our prior research into novel beings suggests a similar divide as regards regulation for novel beings and

---

[17] At the time of writing, elements of this notion had recently been the subject of discussion in a series of patent cases regarding the 'inventor' of AI, DABUS: *Thaler v Comptroller General of Patents Trade Marks and Designs* [2021] EWCA Civ 1374; *Thaler v Hirschfeld* [2021] No. 1:20-cv-903, 2021 WL 3934803; *Thaler v Commissioner of Patents* [2021] FCA 879.

[18] For a full accounting of these deficiencies, see: Lawrence and Morley, n. 14.

[19] See, for instance: Lawrence, n. 8; David R. Lawrence, 'More human than human' (2017) 26(3) *Cambridge Quarterly of Healthcare Ethics* 476–490; David R. Lawrence, 'Amplio, ergo sum' (2018) 27(4) *Cambridge Quarterly of Healthcare Ethics* 686–697; David R. Lawrence, 'Robotic intelligence – philosophical and ethical challenges', in Simona Giordano (ed.), *Bridging the Gap between Science and Society* (Manchester University Press 2018); Lawrence and Brazier, n. 12; Lawrence and Morley, n. 14, as well as the papers included in n. 1.

[20] See, for example, Regulation of the European Parliament and of the Council Laying Down Harmonised Rules on Artificial Intelligence (Artificial Intelligence Act) and Amending Certain Union Legislative Acts, COM/2021/206 Final; High-Level Expert Group on Artificial Intelligence, 'Ethics guidelines for trustworthy AI' (B-1049 Brussels April 2019); Parliament, House of Lords, 'AI in the UK: ready, willing and able?' (2018, HL100); Liaison Committee, 'AI in the UK: No Room for Complacency' (2020, HL196).

morally valuable technologies.[21] Consequently it seems appropriate that this collection reflects this split, and is arranged in two parts, on proactive regulation and reactive regulation respectively.

Part I, on 'Proactive Regulation' (featuring contributions from Dignam, Harris, Lawrence, Morley and Tigard), focuses on potential ways in which we might mitigate the positive, and secure against the negative impacts of the technologies of interest on arrival, given our privilege of prediction. The pace of law-making being necessarily slow, it can be argued that there is an onus to act early in order to be ready and not merely trust in self-regulation by technology developers. This may mean the creation of new regulatory instruments based on some degree of speculation, or the updating of existing law and guidance codes, as well as further acts of forethought. The broad argument for this approach holds that it is essential to begin this process now, as any regulatory action will take a long time to develop and implement. In doing so, we can learn from other scientific and technological areas (e.g. regarding addressing the content and reach of the internet, or the scramble to produce effective regulations for mitochondrial replacement therapy, which had long been a clear and present issue for biotechnologists[22]) and seek to identify and mitigate potential harm.

Part II, on 'Reactive Regulation' (featuring contributions from Gavaghan, King, McMahon, Quigley and Roberts), includes chapters advocating or contemplating the more commonly seen regulatory response to technology, wherein a technology can be confirmed as a real and present issue generating specific concerns to be addressed. This can then be approached in a systematic fashion that may involve the reinterpretation and expansion of existing legislation, responsive action, or the generation of new instruments after the fact. These instruments would have the likely advantage of increased specificity over anything speculatively designed. This may be advantageous given that it is difficult to predict how these technologies will develop and in what form.

---

[21] Conducted with the support of a Wellcome Trust award: WT 208871/Z/17/Z. See n. 15.
[22] The Human Fertilisation and Embryology (Mitochondrial Donation) Regulations 2015.

PART I – PROACTIVE REGULATION

Embedded Ethics as Preparatory Regulation of Technology: A New Solution to the Collingridge Dilemma?

Dr Daniel Tigard

In his chapter, Tigard argues that a collaborative and collegial mode of proactive regulation should be taken. It is, he suggests, possible to influence the design and development of emerging technology in ways that can minimise the potentially harmful social, moral and political effects it could have. He posits that in doing so we might overcome the Collingridge Dilemma, a formulation of the core challenge approached by this collection: that regulating too early means a lack of knowledge of detail and regulating too late means that measures cannot be truly effective. Tigard makes the case that we must not wait for traditional regulatory methods, like new laws or corporate white papers, to be implemented after technologies are deployed; for at that point, the potentially negative effects may already be felt. Rather, we must try to make a positive impact at a much earlier stage. Using an ongoing project, 'Responsible Robotics', he explores the process of 'embedded ethics' – the merging of ethics and social sciences into technology development teams, in an effort to identify and address ethical issues before they become entrenched problems.

Repugnance, Denial, and Fear: Societal Challenges for Regulation of Novel Beings

Dr David R. Lawrence

In his chapter, Lawrence explores the likely reaction to the emergence of novel beings and argues that gut instinct and public opinion may not be a satisfactory basis for decision-making where there are potentially significant risks in so epochal an event. He suggests that previous examples, such as hysterical news features on genetically modified children and the frequent headlines associating AI with sci-fi genocides, are damaging to the public discourse on emerging science. The fear and indulgence of the 'wisdom of repugnance' has previously had stark impact on policy discussions, such as in the media storm over mitochondrial replacement therapy – the so-called 'three-parent baby' – and it seems likely that the same would take place in debates over novel beings. Given this, and combined with the glacial pace of regulatory development, Lawrence argues that we cannot afford to wait until public opinion – and therefore political and legislative will – are taken over by a 'good headline' that offers no consideration to those other than ourselves who could be harmed. Equally, he says, if we seek to avoid controversy by not attempting to regulate in advance, we make it more likely that fears about emerging technologies will be realised. Lawrence concludes that it may be necessary to act in the face of public opinion in the now, in order to institute useful legislation to protect that public in the future.

Morally Significant Technology: A Case Against Mere Corporate Self-Regulation

Dr Sarah Morley

Morley's chapter explores how the current regulation of morally significant technology (MST) is inadequate. At present no regulation exists that specifically and directly addresses the responsibility of companies in the development, operation and disposal of emerging technologies. This means that corporations are left to regulate themselves, without clear channels for accountability and government intervention. The chapter discusses the shortcomings for self-regulation as a regulatory strategy, which is often referred to as corporate social responsibility or CSR. She argues that, whilst CSR will always have a role to play in a regulatory regime, its effectiveness in encouraging companies to behave well *on its own* is limited and lacking in any real enforcement mechanisms. This is concerning considering that MST has the potential to cause significant harm to society (politically, economically and even physically) and challenges what we consider as sentient or sapient creatures, worthy of their own protections. She concludes that the existing CSR standards are fragmented and inappropriate for those corporations developing MST and that we cannot, in good faith, trust companies to self-regulate in an area so morally significant as the emergence of this new type of technology. The chapter concludes that without an enquiry into proper, proactive, hard regulation, we may unwittingly grant corporations too much control without appropriate redress for harm.

Beware Oz the Great and Powerful: Sci-Fi Determinism, Flawed Artificial Intelligence and Emerging Regulatory Frameworks

Prof. Alan Dignam

Dignam considers two aspects of the regulatory challenge around artificial intelligence (AI) – determinism versus values and the flaws of the first generation of commercial AI. The chapter first identifies a problematic technology-sector approach to regulation which is built on, he argues, an empirical sci-fi libertarian culture that addresses AI technology in a deterministic way. This, he states, considers humans as subjects of technology, rather than treating technology as a social construction shaped by humans. Dignam reasons that in the determinist conception, regulation is either unnecessary or deregulatory, while in a social construct conception regulation plays a role in shaping technology. The second part of the chapter identifies core problematic issues with the first generation of commercial AI, focused on human bias, explainability, self-interested AI, trust and AI's potential to undermine broad legal norms. Dignam concludes that the preparatory regulation of AI is warranted, given the problematic experience of the first wave of AI, and assesses the different emerging models of regulation used by China, the EU, UK and US.

Newer Technologies, Older Attitudes, and Retrograde Regulation

Dr David R. Lawrence and Prof. John Harris

Lawrence and Harris' chapter revisits an earlier work in which they advocated a more rational approach to evaluating controversial emerging biotechnologies. Several years later, with the advent of novel beings becoming increasingly likely, they say, there has been a singular failure to adjust approaches to biotechnology regulation and a continuation of the same illogical leaps and the same subsequent harms. The new and future technologies that will contribute to the development of novel beings are building on ones we are familiar with, are likely to be subject to similar hostility in certain quarters and will be similarly controversial in their permissibility under the range of differing moralities presented by international biolaw regimes. They argue that we have always acted in arrears and suffered the consequences when matters outpace and outreach our regulatory capacities. Lawrence and Harris go on to highlight the likely deleterious effects of allowing regressive attitudes to continue as new morally significant technologies become reality, and make a case for evolving our thinking about most effective ways to regulate for them. They conclude that there is a moral imperative to do so, and to no longer stick to the old ways of dealing with new technologies.

PART II – REACTIVE REGULATION

Being Novel? Regulating Emerging Technologies under Conditions of Uncertainty

Dr Joseph T.F. Roberts and Prof. Muireann Quigley

In their chapter, Roberts and Quigley are cautious about the emergence of novel beings and the extent to which they may exist, if ever. The uncertainty around advances in technology guides their consideration of the way in which we might develop future regulation. They argue that because we do not know what type of beings will materialise (their physical nature or cognitive characteristics), we lack the context in which to propose preparatory regulation that will be informed and effective – a sentiment many academics and scientists share. One regulatory strategy that could be taken, they state, is to simply 'wait and see'. However, they reason that this also has significant limitations and that preparatory regulation could be adopted. Yet, the epistemic uncertainty surrounding novel beings, they argue, means a principles-based approach may be the most fruitful for both regulators and regulatees. As such, Roberts and Quigley outline normative principles that can be used to guide the regulation of precursor technologies (and, in particular, artificial general intelligence), which should not impact upon our ability to appropriately regulate emerging technology in the future.

The 'Ethical' Regulation of 'Novel Being' Technologies: The Potential Role for Patents as Ethical Drivers, Blockers and Guiders?

Prof. Aisling McMahon

McMahon observes that since the advent of biotechnologies, patenting of life forms has come under increasing scrutiny, particularly around the extent to which certain life forms should or should not be patentable. This is because a patent allows the patent-holder an exclusive right to stop others using the technology. Intellectual property rights (IPRs) can facilitate rightsholders, for example, in obtaining an exclusionary right over a technology for the duration of the right. McMahon argues that this enables those rightsholders to act as gatekeepers, allowing them to shape or dictate how technologies are developed, used and accessed by others downstream. IPRs could therefore play a key role in regulating novel beings, and other emerging technology, as a driver, blocker and ethical guide for technological development and use. However, McMahon concludes that in order for IPRs to be a useful regulatory tool, a broader consideration of what patents are needs to be addressed first. She argues that patents are not and should not merely be for economic purposes. Patents have more extensive and nuanced functions – and they need to be viewed as such. Only then can they be useful for shaping and steering technological developments in a range of contexts, including novel beings.

A Phased Approach to Protection of Artificial Beings

Prof. Colin Gavaghan and Dr Mike King

In their contribution, Gavaghan and King suggest that while there is an obvious moral impetus to protect future entities with moral status, there is a distinction between how we ought to manage those whose status is certain and those whose is not. They identify two 'phases' of artificial beings, with a line between things without moral status (phase one), and those which could conceivably qualify (phase two). They call for caution over blurring this line too much, suggesting that premature regulatory action that risks ascribing qualities to things that we know have no direct moral claim – even if they may be designed to attempt to convince us otherwise – might inflame our tendency to anthropomorphise such things as robotic 'pets' or military drones. Instead, Gavaghan and King advance a gradualist approach, balancing epistemic and moral considerations in a tripartite framework that provides a method of evaluating entities that will not necessarily resemble those we recognise today. Their approach – concerned with epistemic certainty or uncertainty over a subject's status, moral 'badness' of possible harm, and the cost of any intervention – is a means to avoid misattributing existing entities with a status they do not warrant and engaging in regulatory overreach.

PART I

Proactive regulation

1. Embedded ethics as preparatory regulation of technology: a new solution to the Collingridge Dilemma?

Daniel Tigard[1]

1   INTRODUCTION

Emerging technologies, such as automated robotics and artificial intelligence (AI) systems that rely on big data, are affecting us in socially, morally and politically meaningful ways. With this growing recognition across academic and public arenas, we see the need to develop new modes of regulation in order to assure our continued well-being in a world increasingly occupied by novel beings.[2] It seems that we must not wait for traditional regulatory methods, like laws or corporate self-regulation, to be implemented after technologies are deployed; for at that point, the potentially negative effects may already be felt.[3] Largely in response to this line of concern, a recent trend in research and practical interdisciplinary collaboration—known as 'embedded ethics'—aims to make a positive impact starting from early stages of development.

Embedded ethics is a process of merging ethics and social sciences into technology development teams, whether in educational or commercial settings, in an effort to identify and address ethical features of emerging technologies

---

[1]   The author acknowledges support from the Bavarian Research Institute for Digital Transformation on the project 'Responsible Robotics: Tracing Ethical and Social Aspects of AI-Based Transformations in Healthcare Work and Knowledge Environments' at the Technical University of Munich. Gratitude is also owed to project partners and colleagues, including Maximilian Braun, Svenja Breuer, Alena Buyx, Amelia Fiske, Sami Haddadin, Stuart McLennan, Ruth Müller, Abdeldjallil Naceri, and members of the Munich Institute of Robotics and Machine Intelligence.
[2]   David Lawrence and Sarah Morley, 'Regulating the Tyrell Corporation: The Emergence of Novel Beings' (2021) 30 *Cambridge Quarterly of Healthcare Ethics* 421–434.
[3]   Sarah Morley, 'Morally Significant Technology: A Case Against Corporate Self-Regulation' (see Chapter 3).

throughout their development.[4] Yet this approach is not entirely new, nor is it without significant hurdles. In this chapter, I explain some of the merits and challenges of this process, with a current project called 'Responsible Robotics' serving as a case study. This three-year interdisciplinary research project is intended to create a collaborative, collegial atmosphere, where the design and development of technology will be influenced in ways that might minimize the potentially harmful social, moral and political effects. Although the long-term effectiveness of embedding ethics will remain an open question for the foreseeable future, considering its ideals and present state of development, as I argue, the embedded ethics approach can be seen as a novel preparatory mode of regulation.

In order to make the case for embedded ethics as preparatory regulation of technology, it must first be made clear exactly what is meant when speaking of preparatory modes of regulation. This task naturally raises the widely discussed Collingridge Dilemma, the problem of regulating technology too early, before we have sufficient knowledge of its impact, or too late for regulation to be truly effective. Accordingly, in section 2, I will establish this conundrum alongside a definition of preparatory regulation, as a foundation for the account that follows. I will then, in section 3, turn to an outline of the Responsible Robotics project, which harnesses and builds upon the embedded ethics approach. Here I also enumerate some ways in which embedded ethics is like earlier interdisciplinary sociotechnical research, and I suggest several points of distinction. In section 4, I then discuss some merits and challenges of the embedded ethics approach and I show why, despite its focus on collaboration over regulation, embedded ethics can nonetheless be seen as a preparatory mode of regulation. I conclude in section 5, with some thoughts on how embedded ethics may stand to overcome the difficulties of the Collingridge Dilemma.

---

[4]   Barbara Grosz et al., 'Embedded Ethics: Integrating Ethics Across CS Education' (2019) 62 *Communications of the ACM* 54–61; Stuart McLennan et al., 'An Embedded Ethics Approach for AI Development' (2020) 2 *Nature Machine Intelligence* 488–490; Stuart McLennan et al., 'Embedded Ethics: A Proposal for Integrating Ethics into the Development of Medical AI' (2022) 23 *BMC Medical Ethics* 1–10. See also Louise Bezuidenhout and Emanuele Ratti, 'What Does It Mean to Embed Ethics in Data Science? An Integrative Approach Based on Microethics and Virtues' (2020) *AI & Society* 1–15; Amelia Fiske, Daniel Tigard, Ruth Müller et al., 'Embedded Ethics Could Help Implement the Pipeline Model Framework for Machine Learning Healthcare Applications' (2020) 20 *American Journal of Bioethics* 32–35.

2   PREPARATORY REGULATION AND THE
         COLLINGRIDGE DILEMMA

To begin, consider a working definition of preparatory modes of regulation. In essence, preparatory regulation plausibly refers to an attempt to mitigate in advance the potentially negative impacts of technology, and to secure the potentially positive impacts, based upon prediction or an ongoing awareness of technology's emergence.[5] At first glance, this sort of strategy would appear advantageous, particularly in cases involving widely used devices and programs which are highly likely to have a variety of far-reaching and possibly severe effects. Indeed, depending upon the technology in question, preparatory modes of regulation may turn out to be the *only* form of effectively staving off at least the initial negative impact. That is, reactive modes, by contrast, will often be too late to help, as these more traditional forms of regulation—such as new laws or amendments—take time to create and implement. By the time reactive measures go into effect, the impacts of new technology, for better or worse, are already being felt. Considering the long-term perspective of this trend, it may well seem that the pace of technology's development is continually outrunning the pace of traditional legal developments, and so we are regularly confronted with innovations which have yet to be regulated.[6]

In many ways, the contrast between preparatory and reactive modes of regulation reflects the key difficulties of the Collingridge Dilemma, a conundrum now widely discussed in science and technology studies, particularly in literature on technology assessment and 'responsible innovation'.[7] Yet, despite

---

[5]   This useful definition was suggested by David Lawrence and Sarah Morley. See also Daniel Sarewitz, 'Anticipatory Governance of Emerging Technologies' in Daniel Sarewitz, *The Growing Gap Between Emerging Technologies and Legal–Ethical Oversight* (Springer 2011) 95–105.

[6]   Cf. Risto Karinen and David H. Guston, 'Toward Anticipatory Governance: The Experience with Nanotechnology' in M. Kaiser, M. Kurath, S. Maasen and C. Rehmann-Sutter (eds), *Governing Future Technologies* (Springer 2009) 217–232; Sarah R. Davies and Cynthia Selin, 'Energy Futures: Five Dilemmas of the Practice of Anticipatory Governance' (2012) 6 *Environmental Communication: A Journal of Nature and Culture* 119–136; Evan Michelson, *Assessing the Societal Implications of Emerging Technologies: Anticipatory Governance in Practice* (Routledge 2016).

[7]   E.g. Alfred Nordmann, 'A Forensics of Wishing: Technology Assessment in the Age of Technoscience' (2010) 7 *Poiesis & Praxis* 5–15; Wolfgang Liebert and Jan C. Schmidt, 'Collingridge's Dilemma and Technoscience' (2010) 7 *Poiesis & Praxis* 55–71; Sarewitz, 'Anticipatory Governance of Emerging Technologies' (n. 5); David H. Guston, 'Understanding "Anticipatory Governance"' (2014) 44 *Social Studies of Science* 218–242. See also Barbara Ribeiro et al., 'Introducing the Dilemma of Societal Alignment for Inclusive and Responsible Research and Innovation' (2018) 5 *Journal of Responsible Innovation* 316–331; Audley Genus and Andy Stirling, 'Collingridge and

its popularity, a straightforward summary of the nature of this supposed dilemma—sometimes referred to as technology's 'control dilemma'—is rather elusive. In its original formulation, David Collingridge described attempts to control technology as difficult, since 'during its early stages, when it can be controlled, not enough can be known about its harmful social consequences to warrant controlling its development; but by the time these consequences are apparent, control has become costly and slow'.[8] Presumably, then, at any given time we have the ability to impose some sort of regulation on emerging technology, but we cannot be sure how to regulate it (or how it should be regulated), since we do not yet know its societal impact. Notably, an underlying assumption here seems to be that regulation of technology without such knowledge may be unwarranted, and this assumption might be readily rejected, particularly by those adopting a more precautionary stance.[9] In any case, the future is also problematic, since then we will know enough to form a basis of regulation, but it will be too late to stave off at least the initial harms.

With Collingridge's influential statement we see the motivation to work toward preparatory or anticipatory forms of regulation, but also that such modes are often simply impossible. We also see, on a conceptual level, what is commonly interpreted as the two *horns* of the dilemma. For example, in a recent account, Olya Kudina and Peter-Paul Verbeek establish that, on the one hand, 'at an early stage of development, it is still possible to influence the direction of [technology's] development, but we do not yet know how it will affect society'.[10] On the other hand, 'when the technology has become societally embedded, we do know its implications, but it is very difficult to influence its development'.[11] Indeed, Collingridge's difficulty is naturally framed as two distinct horns of a dilemma.[12] Still, while the basic tension is

---

the Dilemma of Control: Towards Responsible and Accountable Innovation' (2018) 47 *Research Policy* 61–69.

[8]   David Collingridge, *The Social Control of Technology* (Pinter and St. Martin's Press 1980) 19.

[9]   E.g. Hans Jonas, *The Imperative of Responsibility: In Search of an Ethics for the Technological Age* (University of Chicago Press 1984).

[10]   Olya Kudina and Peter-Paul Verbeek, 'Ethics from Within: Google Glass, the Collingridge Dilemma, and the Mediated Value of Privacy' (2019) 44 *Science, Technology, & Human Values* 291–314.

[11]   Ibid., 292.

[12]   Genus and Stirling, 'Collingridge and the Dilemma of Control' (n. 7); Marvin J. Croy, 'Collingridge and the Control of Educational Computer Technology' (1996) 1 *Society for Philosophy and Technology Quarterly Electronic Journal* 107–115.

clear and seemingly problematic, upon inspection it is not obvious how exactly we are faced with a true dilemma.[13]

In an underappreciated work on educational computer technology, Marvin Croy provides a helpful analysis of Collingridge as a *constructive dilemma*.[14] Here, a clear disjunction is made explicit in the first premise, namely that technology is either in an early developmental stage where we cannot know what changes to make since its effects are unknown, or in a later stage where change is costly and difficult. If the former, then regulation is not possible. But if the latter, then regulation is not feasible, since the technology in question has already become entrenched in society. Thus, it follows that regulation is either not possible or not feasible. I will later refer to this as the 'impossibility formulation' of the dilemma. When framed in these terms, it is hard to deny the challenges of regulation. Further, on Croy's account, the Collingridge problem shows us that *any* regulatory approach is doomed to fail. To see this, consider a second version of the constructive dilemma, which I will refer to as the 'failure formulation'. First, we can attempt to regulate either by early predictions of technology's effects, or by reacting to the effects.[15] If the former, then regulation fails because of our predictive unreliability. But if the latter, then regulation still fails, because of technology's rigidity—that is, technology has become 'societally embedded', as Kudina and Verbeek put it. Thus, it follows that regulatory efforts will fail, either because of our predictive unreliability or because of technology's rigidity.

Considering these two formulations of the problem, we begin to see how one might arrive at a general skepticism of all regulatory efforts, or perhaps even how corporate self-regulation—however disingenuous it may be[16]—could be left as the only viable route to minimizing technology's negative effects and securing its positive effects. Nonetheless, it is important to note that, at least on the failure formulation of the constructive dilemma, we may well be faced

---

[13] Considering the literature on *moral* dilemmas, it can be argued that the Collingridge problem is not of this sort, since moral dilemmas are typically understood as situations in which an agent is simultaneously confronted with two possible actions, both of which are required, but where doing both is somehow impossible. For a thorough overview, see Terrance McConnell, 'Moral Dilemmas' in Edward Zalta (ed.), *Stanford Encyclopedia of Philosophy* (Stanford University 2018) <https://plato.stanford.edu/entries/moral-dilemmas/> accessed 3 August 2021.

[14] Croy, 'Collingridge and the Control of Educational Computer Technology' (n. 12). I refer to this work as 'underappreciated' due to the little attention it has received relative to its age; specifically, a total of 13 citations (found by Google Scholar) since its publication in 1996; and only one citation in the past five years. Also, note that I am framing Croy's interpretation of 'control' in terms of regulation.

[15] Ibid., 108.

[16] Cf. Morley, 'Morally Significant Technology' (n. 3).

with a *false* dilemma. Specifically, the 'reactive horn' is quite straightforward in the sense that reactive modes of regulation, such as new laws and amendments, are built and implemented as reactions to technology's effects, once those become apparent. However, the 'preparatory horn' need not be seen only as an attempt to *predict* technology's effects. Surely there are other ways of preparing ourselves for the future that do not rely solely on making predictions of the possible effects of technology.

Predictions alone would appear to leave us fixed to a given conception of how technology will be implemented and incorporated into society, by whom, for what reasons, and so on. As some theorists—including Collingridge[17]— argue, we must assume that our predictive abilities are at least somewhat fallible, and perhaps highly fallible when considering the emergence of newfound technologies. As such, it should be expected that our attempts to regulate by means of early predictions will often fail. For example, it now seems clear that few regulators predicted the increasing influence Facebook would have on wider social and political domains.[18] While this could be counted as an obvious failure, prediction is by no means the only approach to preparatory regulation. Rather than relying on fixed predictions, we can construct and promote flexible approaches, and in fact, Collingridge himself endorsed flexibility and corrigibility as promising pathways. Below, I discuss a notion of flexibility that is characteristic of the embedded ethics model. But first, I sketch the motivations and structure of this emerging approach to collaborative technology development.

3   EMBEDDED ETHICS AS A DISTINCT PREPARATORY PATHWAY

In order to help illustrate the use of embedded ethics, I begin this section by sketching the Responsible Robotics project. I will also outline some of the ways in which embedded ethics is similar to earlier interdisciplinary research, and some ways that it remains distinct.

Responsible Robotics is a three-year collaboration among researchers in ethics, social science, and robotics and machine-learning technologies. One of the key motivations, particularly on the technical side of the project, is the apparent need to introduce novel systems in various healthcare settings, such as caring for elderly populations and conducting medical practice remotely via

---

[17] Collingridge, *The Social Control of Technology* (n. 8). See also Croy, 'Collingridge and the Control of Educational Computer Technology' (n. 12).

[18] E.g. Sara M. Smyth, 'The Facebook Conundrum: Is it Time to Usher in a New Era of Regulation for Big Tech?' (2019) 13 *International Journal of Cyber Criminology* 578–595.

telemedicine and digital twinning. With the growing awareness that elderly populations around the world are starting to increase relative to younger, working age populations, it seems that new caring solutions are clearly called for. Likewise, the problems associated with providing healthcare to underserved populations, as well as social distancing guidelines amidst the recent pandemic, have shown that distance-enabling telemedical systems and tools like digital twins could fill a variety of important needs.[19] Still, while novel technologies give some reason for optimism, there are of course numerous concerns being raised, such as the inability of robotic devices to attend to the social and emotional needs of the elderly, or the difficulty of properly representing a person with a digital twin.[20]

Innovative technological systems employed in care settings undoubtedly pose a host of social, ethical and political questions. A range of regulatory issues arises, such as who (or what) can be held liable, or how to locate responsibility, when AI systems cause harm?[21] To be clear from the outset, the aim of Responsible Robotics is not to satisfy these sorts of challenges in an effort to proceed with development and implementation. Rather, the project adopts a broader objective of working to identify, understand, and address the range of social and ethical aspects of technology that may arise, starting at the design phases and carrying on into the anticipated implementation settings. Unlike overarching principle-based paradigms,[22] with our work we aim to incorporate ethics and social considerations from the ground up, by forging strong interdisciplinary collaborations, drawing upon diverse expertise, and allowing ethical and social inquiries to arise naturally as an everyday part of development. Our work includes regular meetings among the various researchers, site visits to laboratories and ethnographic observations of user studies, and qualitative

---

[19] For a recent discussion, see Jordan Parsons, 'The Telemedical Imperative' (2021) 35 *Bioethics* 298–306.

[20] Robert Sparrow and Linda Sparrow, 'In the Hands of Machines? The Future of Aged Care' (2006) 16 *Minds and Machines* 141–161; Matthias Braun, 'Represent Me: Please! Towards an Ethics of Digital Twins in Medicine' (2021) 47 *Journal of Medical Ethics* 394–400.

[21] Cf. Hannah R. Sullivan and Scott J. Schweikart, 'Are Current Tort Liability Doctrines Adequate for Addressing Injury Caused by AI?' (2019) 21 *AMA Journal of Ethics* 160–166; Helen Smith and Kit Fotheringham, 'Artificial Intelligence in Clinical Decision-Making: Rethinking Liability' (2020) 20 *Medical Law International* 131–154; Daniel Tigard, 'Artificial Moral Responsibility: How We Can and Cannot Hold Machines Responsible' (2021) 30 *Cambridge Quarterly of Healthcare Ethics* 435–447.

[22] E.g. European Commission, 'Ethics Guidelines for Trustworthy AI' (2019) <https://ec.europa.eu/futurium/en/ai-alliance-consultation/guidelines.1.html> accessed 13 August 2021; Luciano Floridi and Josh Cowls, 'A Unified Framework of Five Principles for AI in Society' (2019) 1 *Harvard Data Science Review*.

peer-to-peer interviews with developers and various healthcare professionals.[23] Ultimately, we intend for our observations and the results of working alongside developers to be formulated into various tools, such as workshops and multimedia guides, which can then be fed back into the development process and utilized by future development teams.

Importantly, what we aim to 'embed' is not simply an *ethicist* or even a team of ethicists. On first glance at the emerging model, it may be tempting to suppose one could hire researchers in ethics and place them in a relevant development project. Perhaps this would represent a step forward in raising awareness of ethical and social aspects, whether in technical education or industry settings.[24] Yet, it becomes increasingly evident that embedded ethics must be more substantive and more meaningful—particularly for those on the technical side of such collaborations—that is, *if* we are to openly identify and truly address the host of social and ethical features of technology, such as fairness, potential biases and product transparency. Without genuine collaboration between researchers in ethics and social science, on one hand, and developers working on novel systems, on the other, the real-life scenarios and questions that arise would not be adequately defined or addressed. In fact, where ethics and related research is only loosely involved but not thoroughly incorporated, concerns may reasonably be raised that the partnership is little more than a publicity campaign or an effort at 'ethics washing', where companies or institutions merely promote ethical awareness or principles to create a favorable public opinion and thereby profit.[25] Instead, what we find must be embedded

---

[23]   Cf. Ruth Müller and Martha Kenney, 'Agential Conversations: Interviewing Postdoctoral Life Scientists and the Politics of Mundane Research Practices' (2014) 23 *Science as Culture* 537–559. See also McLennan et al., 'An Embedded Ethics Approach for AI Development' (n. 4); Fiske et al., 'Embedded Ethics Could Help Implement the Pipeline Model Framework for Machine Learning Healthcare Applications' (n. 4).

[24]   One worry with placing ethicists and encouraging them to become immersed in development settings is that they will 'go native', losing their critical sensibilities and positioning as external observers. While a full reply would require more discussion than is possible here, briefly it can be said that this points to the importance of ethicists and social scientists maintaining a sense of neutrality and critical distance. See, for example, Arie Rip and Douglas K.R. Robinson, 'Constructive Technology Assessment and the Methodology of Insertion' in Neelke Doorn, Daan Schuurbiers, Ibo van de Poel and Michael E. Gorman (eds), *Early Engagement and New Technologies: Opening Up the Laboratory* (Springer 2013) 37–53. I thank an anonymous reviewer for drawing attention to this concern.

[25]   See Luciano Floridi, 'Translating Principles into Practices of Digital Ethics: Five Risks of Being Unethical' (2019) 32 *Philosophy & Technology* 185–193; Elettra Bietti, 'From Ethics Washing to Ethics Bashing: A View on Tech Ethics from within Moral Philosophy' (2020) *Proceedings of the 2020 Conference on Fairness, Accountability, and Transparency* 210–219.

is a sincere sensitivity in developers themselves, an ability to recognize and effectively think through the social and ethical features of the systems under development. I will return to the idea of sensitivity in the following section, but first it should be briefly noted how the approach outlined here is similar to—and how it differs from—other interdisciplinary paradigms for infusing ethics into technology.

First, one clearly related approach to the model we invoke is the 'embedded ethiCS' program advanced by Barbara Grosz and colleagues.[26] Here, ethics is being integrated into the educational curriculum, by adding short ethics-based modules into existing computer science courses. This approach shows students that 'ethical issues permeate almost all areas of computer science; it familiarizes them with a variety of concrete ethical issues ... and it provides them repeated experiences of reasoning through those issues'.[27] As Grosz and her colleagues explain, the creation of ethics modules was in part a response to student requests for opportunities to discuss ethical issues arising with today's technology. With this, it may seem that the only difference is in the domain of application, namely technical education as opposed to research and development, and perhaps a corresponding dissimilarity in the interest expressed by students compared to that of more established developers—a potential challenge I address below. Nonetheless, unlike the 'embedded ethiCS' program, our approach has at its foundation the peer-to-peer integration and ongoing involvement of the various fields. From there, we work together to build practical tools, including thought experiments and workshops, which are then further tailored to incorporate the ideas raised specifically by the participating development teams. In these ways, our approach addresses the goals and concerns that are in fact arising within each technical project, rather than prescribing cases and tools that may be applicable in the future professional work of computer science students.[28]

Relatedly, an early sociotechnical framework known as 'ethics parallel research' has undertaken similar objectives of investigating social and ethical aspects of applied sciences and engineering, also with a bottom-up approach to grasping the relevant issues.[29] Like our use of embedded ethics, the ethics

---

[26] See Grosz et al., 'Embedded Ethics: Integrating Ethics Across CS Education' (n. 4). Also, note that the 'CS' in embedded ethics is stylized as such by Grosz and colleagues.

[27] Ibid., 56.

[28] For encouraging me to clarify this distinction, I thank an anonymous reviewer.

[29] E.g. Simone van der Burg, 'Taking the "Soft Impacts" of Technology into Account: Broadening the Discourse in Research Practice' (2009) 23 *Social Epistemology* 301–316; Ibo van de Poel and Neelke Doorn, 'Ethical Parallel Research: A Network Approach For Moral Evaluation (NAME)' in Neelke Doorn, Daan Schuurbiers, Ibo

parallel model promotes long-term collaborations, encouraging ethicists to think 'like partners in a team' rather than as external consultants or temporary coaches who will soon move on from the project.[30] Indeed, we share with this approach a commitment to inspiring reflexivity about the issues that arise directly in the laboratory. Still, we find it important to emphasize that collaborative work with ethics should be thoroughly integrated and extends beyond the educational curriculum, as well as beyond technical research, well into development, even (and perhaps *especially*) within industry settings. As we have found, for many developers in robotics and machine-learning systems, research is only secondary and often entirely peripheral to the immediate project.

A further point of distinction is that, as partnered ethicists and social scientists, we take our role to be exploratory and assistive to those on the technical side of the project, and in no way does our role involve *monitoring* development.[31] In this way, by eschewing activities seen as forms of monitoring, embedded ethics distinguishes itself from well-established accounts of responsible innovation, midstream modulation, and constructive technology assessment.[32] In fact, it seems that open dialogues, which prove to be crucial to the success of embedded ethics, will occur fluidly only when we assure that our presence is not intended to monitor, govern, or regulate the development processes. However, this feature of the embedded ethics approach may seem to raise a puzzle with respect to its prospects of serving as some form of regulation. That is, if embedded ethics is explicitly *not* a form of monitoring, assessing, or regulating technology, how exactly can it be seen as a preparatory mode of regulation? I address this question next, in discussing some of the merits and challenges of embedded ethics.

---

van de Poel and Michael E. Gorman (eds), *Early Engagement and New Technologies: Opening Up the Laboratory* (Springer 2013) 111–136; Karin Jongsma and Annelien Bredenoord, 'Ethics Parallel Research: An Approach for (Early) Ethical Guidance of Biomedical Innovation' (2020) 21 *BMC Medical Ethics* 1–9.

[30]   Van der Burg, n. 29, 312.

[31]   The task of monitoring is discussed as an objective of the STW funding institute in the Netherlands, and espoused as a related goal of 'ethics parallel' research. See van der Burg, n. 29, 311.

[32]   E.g. Jack Stilgoe, Richard Owen and Phil Macnaghten, 'Developing a Framework for Responsible Innovation' (2013) 42 *Research Policy* 1568–1580; Erik Fisher, Roop Mahajan and Carl Mitcham, 'Midstream Modulation of Technology: Governance from Within' (2006) 26 *Bulletin of Science, Technology & Society* 485–496; Arie Rip, Johan Schot and Thomas Misa, 'Constructive Technology Assessment: A New Paradigm for Managing Technology in Society' in Arie Rip, Johan Schot and Thomas Misa, *Managing Technology in Society: The Approach of Constructive Technology Assessment* (Pinter 1995) 1–12.

4   REGULATING WITHOUT REGULATION

The embedded ethics approach as deployed by the Responsible Robotics project shares some common features of earlier sociotechnical paradigms and of the recent 'embedded ethiCS' educational program. Yet, it also bears several points of distinction from other models, including its continuously team-oriented nature, inclusion of development and industry, and emphasis on exploration and assistance rather than monitoring or governance of the technical work.[33] That being said, projects aiming to 'embed' ethics and social considerations into other fields will face significant challenges. I clarify some of them in this section, then I proceed to discuss the merits of our approach. The latter will help to make clear a particular notion of flexibility, which in turn can be used to address the difficulty set out by Collingridge.

First, as with many research endeavors and development projects, whether academic or driven by industry, one of the key practical challenges for efforts to 'embed' ethics is the question of resources. Unless one finds and manages to employ ethicists willing to work pro bono, hiring and fully incorporating the relevant experts will require time and funds. Since those resources are naturally limited, some might be reluctant to pursue such projects or may settle for less rigorous models of embedding ethics, such as temporary external consultations. However, it appears in recent times that the relevant funding opportunities are on the rise—evidently, there are a growing number of institutions and grants aimed specifically at addressing social and ethical aspects of emerging technology.[34] Granted, some funding schemes call for a degree of caution, particularly when the sources can be traced to the very domain under scrutiny.[35] Nevertheless, it may come as encouragement to see recent increases in attention to AI ethics and prominent appeals to fund multidisciplinary work on AI research.[36]

---

[33]   It is worth noting that the distinctions may be subtle, and indeed some will likely contest the idea that our use of embedded ethics is importantly different from related approaches. To the extent that the aforementioned frameworks all bear key points of resemblance, it can nonetheless be argued that embedded ethics, and perhaps related models too, can serve as preparatory modes of regulation. Again, I thank an anonymous reviewer for comments here.

[34]   For an example of a database collecting such funding applications, see Explore AI Ethics <https://www.exploreaiethics.com/tag/funding/> accessed 12 August 2021.

[35]   See Oscar Williams, 'How big tech funds the debate on AI ethics' (2019) *New Statesman* <https://www.newstatesman.com/science-tech/technology/2019/06/how-big-tech-funds-debate-ai-ethics> accessed 12 August 2021.

[36]   For a useful overview of guidelines for AI ethics, see Anna Jobin, Marcello Ienca and Effy Vayena, 'The Global Landscape of AI Ethics Guidelines' (2019) 1 *Nature Machine Intelligence* 389–399. For an example of calls for multidisciplinary funding,

Relatedly, with the growth of multidisciplinary development projects, we may often see challenges in terms of motivation. Specifically, one might be concerned that corporate settings and technical research in academic institutes are unlikely to adopt embedded ethics programs unless the incorporation of broader social and ethical perspectives is explicitly mandated, either externally or via corporate self-regulation. Here again, it seems that there would be a risk of corporations and technical research 'ethics washing' the public.[37] With this concern in mind, we see the importance of ethicists and social scientists working to retain a neutral, external position, and being committed enough to make effective use of the opportunity. That is, even if industry and technical projects are motivated by, say, commercial interests to incorporate embedded ethics programs, the non-technical members of the resulting collaborations can still work to make the integration of ethics more meaningful than the industry stakeholders intended it to be. Furthermore, by imparting a keen sensitivity to social and ethical features upon developers themselves, ethicists and social scientists integrated into technical projects can aim to share the critical reflective work, rather than allowing the bulk of it to be shifted onto themselves alone.[38]

Next, as alluded to above, a potential receptivity challenge may arise depending upon the domain of application for embedded ethics. Specifically, some groups or projects will naturally be more interested in incorporating social and ethical considerations than others. Likewise, within distinct teams or projects there will likely be noticeable variation in individuals' ability or desire to engage with ethics and social science researchers. For some, it will simply be practical matters, such as time constraints, that determine the ability to think through aspects which are not strictly technical, and so may be seen as unnecessary. Yet, here also, it seems there are reasons for optimism, namely in

---

see Future of Life Institute, Asilomar AI Principles (2017) <https://futureoflife.org/ai-principles/> accessed 13 August 2021. Naturally, we should retain a critical eye for funding and projects that purportedly incorporate multidisciplinary perspectives. But even if technical development is driven by ulterior motives (e.g. commercial interests) to incorporate non-technical work, these may still represent opportunities for committed ethicists to make a meaningful impact.

[37] Floridi, 'Translating Principles into Practices of Digital Ethics: Five Risks of Being Unethical' (n. 25); Bietti, 'From Ethics Washing to Ethics Bashing: A View on Tech Ethics from within Moral Philosophy' (n. 25); Daniel Tigard, 'Responsible AI and Moral Responsibility: A Common Appreciation' (2021) 1 *AI and Ethics* 113–117.

[38] Indeed, this worry should be taken seriously throughout sociotechnical research, as the interdisciplinary collaborations may turn out to defeat their key purposes, namely by allowing technical experts to further outsource reflection upon social, ethical, and political impacts. Again, I'm grateful to an anonymous reviewer and admit that the concern deserves more attention than I can offer here.

considering computer science students' requests to discuss ethics.[39] In fact, in development settings with more advanced technology experts too, our efforts have likewise been met with a positive reception. However, the extent to which embedded ethics programs make a discernible impact on future technologies and users—how and in what ways the social, moral, and political aspects are addressed—will require measurements and evaluations which can be made only after such programs are well established. Even so, it is possible to assess the challenges and the merits of embedded ethics, based upon the ideals, objectives, and current state of implementation among such projects.

The growth of funding opportunities and positive reception for embedding ethics into technology is not entirely surprising, and it seems that the contemporary approach indeed carries potential benefits for a range of stakeholders. Consider, by analogy, that clinical ethics rose to prominence with the increasing ethical concerns in medicine in the latter decades of the 20th century, leading to the permanent residence of clinical ethicists in medical schools and various healthcare institutions worldwide.[40] With the increasing social, ethical, and political concerns about technology, what we see today may well be a similar movement toward the regular integration of ethics expertise in the development and use of novel technological systems. Still, it is important to make clear exactly what sorts of benefits we can expect from the emerging embedded ethics approach.

In closing my initial discussion of the Collingridge problem, I claimed that at least one version of the difficulty—which I called the failure formulation—rests upon a false dilemma. That is, prediction is not the only means by which we could pursue the preparatory pathway. Thus, we can grant that prediction and reaction will both lead to failures in regulation, but this does not leave us altogether doomed to fail in our efforts to regulate novel systems. Following Collingridge's own proposal, I suggested that our preparatory efforts can include the construction and promotion of flexibility, namely in those who work to design and develop emerging technologies. But the notion of flexibility I have in mind differs from the idea seen in Collingridge. On his account, flexibility entails maintaining an openness to future options.[41] In this way, developers as well as users can maximize their problem-solving capabilities by being able to choose between various technical solutions or various features of a given system. Collingridge lends further support to this idea by later referring to flexibility as 'ease of control of small units'.[42]

---

[39]   Grosz et al., 'Embedded Ethics: Integrating Ethics Across CS Education' (n. 4).
[40]   Albert Jonsen, *The Birth of Bioethics* (Oxford University Press 2003).
[41]   Collingridge, *The Social Control of Technology* (n. 8) 38.
[42]   Ibid., 115.

Undoubtedly, this notion of flexibility has its appeal, particularly as a potential preparatory mode of regulation. In short, we could work to ensure that a multitude of future options and the ease of control are left open, and thereby mitigate the undesirable impacts of any one technical solution simply by choosing another, one that appears better equipped to secure the more desirable impacts. Notice, however, that in order to evade the failure formulation of the dilemma, we would need to avoid relying on prediction as a means of securing the desirable impacts of technical systems. In other words, if we must predict even a wide range of options to be left open, it seems we are no better off in resolving the initial difficulty, since one of the key problems was our inability to make reliable predictions.[43] Thus, an alternative notion of flexibility is needed, and it seems that the approach to embedded ethics described here is equipped to provide one.

Consider again Collingridge's concern for our natural fallibility. Granted that we will not be able to reliably predict the most effective systems for securing the positive impacts and mitigating the negative, we would do well to fully consider why this may be the case. One reason, perhaps the most obvious, is that we simply cannot know the ways in which a given technology—and the use of it by ourselves and others—will affect us. For example, when starting a new social media account, I cannot be sure that it will enable desirable interactions. Likewise, I cannot know the extent or the ways in which it might cause harm. But these and related considerations are only one sort of fallibility which we may be forced to admit in our use of future technologies. Another is that we do not yet know exactly what we will find to be a positive or negative impact. In considering our use of emerging systems, and the unknown ways in which they will affect us and the world around us, we must also bear in mind that our evaluations too will undergo change. That is, what we consider desirable and undesirable, how we perceive personal benefits and harms—these factors will likewise be affected by the new systems in use, regardless of the number of options from which we can choose. The point to emphasize here is that the wider social and political environments that help to bring emerging technologies into everyday life will affect how we perceive and evaluate them.[44] How, then, does embedding ethics into the development of novel systems help to address this wide range of uncertainty?

One of the key goals of the embedded ethics approach, as outlined above, is helping developers to recognize socially, morally, and politically relevant

---

[43]   A related critique is seen in Croy, 'Collingridge and the Control of Educational Computer Technology' (n. 12).

[44]   For a thorough defense of this sort of position, see Tsjalling Swierstra, 'Nanotechnology and Technomoral Change' (2013) 15 *Etica & Politica* 200–219. See also Kudina and Verbeek, 'Ethics from Within' (n. 10).

aspects of technology; helping to instill an attunement simply to the questions that arise and the variety of stakeholder perspectives to consider. Through everyday collaboration, and with more structured interactions, we aim to foster a sensitivity to what the anticipated users—and what society at large—might perceive and what they might care about with the potential emergence of the system in development. In this way, sensitivity provides the sort of benefit, a truly robust sense of flexibility, that is required to remedy our fallibility concerning both the impacts of technology and what its prospective users may come to value in the future. After all, flexibility must be much more than an openness to future options, since we cannot know what those will or should be. In sum, it should be openly recognized that any anticipated options, along with our perceptions of them, are vulnerable to change. Flexibility, then, is not just a matter of having multiple options and retaining sufficient control over them; it is an ability to adapt to newfound circumstances and newly discovered perspectives and values brought about by our use of technology.[45] As such, becoming sensitive to these sorts of changes would go much farther in terms of addressing the impacts of technology than merely ensuring a multitude of options.

The very features that make embedded ethics distinct as an interdisciplinary practice, such as the focus on collaborative exploration, help to build competencies in developers for identifying and addressing non-technical features of their work. No doubt, these sorts of skills would be far more challenging to convey—dialogues would be closed off, genuine collaboration would stall— where developers have a sense that the ethics and social science teammates are deployed with the intent to monitor or regulate technical progress. In this way, by assuring that embedded ethics is not a process of imposing regulation, we can thereby contribute to the effort to mitigate potentially negative impacts and secure potentially positive impacts of emerging systems. In other words, while it may appear somewhat paradoxical, it is by *not* regulating technology that embedded ethics can serve as a preparatory mode of regulation.

---

[45] Again, see Kudina and Verbeek, 'Ethics from Within' (n. 10). See also Peter-Paul Verbeek, 'Obstetric Ultrasound and the Technological Mediation of Morality: A Postphenomenological Analysis' (2008) 31 *Human Studies* 11–26; Tsjalling Swierstra, Dirk Stemerding and Marianne Boenink, 'Exploring Techno-Moral Change: The Case of the Obesitypill' in Paul Sollie and Marcus Düwell (eds), *Evaluating New Technologies* (Springer 2009) 119–138.

5   CONCLUSION

In a recent editorial on the EU's 2021 Artificial Intelligence Act,[46] Luciano Floridi states that the 'challenge is no longer digital innovation but the governance of the digital'.[47] Indeed, just as we continue to advance in our technological capabilities, it seems clear that we must likewise advance in our ability to regulate technology. Still, the work of Collingridge and the continuing attention to the difficulty he identified are testaments to the fact that we have long grappled with the challenges of regulating emerging technologies. In conclusion, then, it seems fitting to ask: To what extent does the contemporary embedded ethics approach help to overcome Collingridge's dilemma?

On the first version—which I called the impossibility formulation—the problem appeared to arise from a rather static perspective within each timeframe. That is, at the early stage of development, regulation is not possible, since we do not know technology's effects and thereby what to change. But at later stages, technologies are presumably so entrenched in society that regulation is unfeasible then too. Yet, by pointing out the static perspective that each of these *horns* assumes, we can begin to see how a more dynamic, flexible approach to development might work to transcend the two timeframes. Specifically, where we build competencies in developers for anticipating and understanding the possible perspectives of others, both current and future users and stakeholders, it seems that at the early developmental stages we do not need to know exactly how technology will affect us in order to mitigate the negative impacts and promote the positive. With the sort of sensitivity that can be fostered by embedded ethics projects, we see a path to building precisely these competencies. In this way, embedded ethics helps to address the impossibility formulation of Collingridge, namely by bridging the two timeframes, essentially denying the first key premise of the constructive dilemma.

On the second version, however—the failure formulation—we encountered the problem that any attempt to regulate in the present or in the future will fail. And so, it may appear that even if we bridge the two timeframes, we are nonetheless doomed to live with unregulated technological innovations. Yet, here too, the sense of flexibility outlined above, a sensitivity instilled in developers, provides reason for optimism. In particular, by becoming attuned to the soci-

---

[46]   European Commission, 'Proposal for a regulation of the European Parliament and the Council laying down harmonised rules on Artificial Intelligence (Artificial Intelligence Act) and amending certain Union legislative acts' (2021) <https://eur-lex.europa.eu/legal-content/EN/TXT/?uri=CELLAR:e0649735-a372-11eb-9585-01aa75ed71a1> accessed 13 August 2021.

[47]   Luciano Floridi, 'The European Legislation on AI: A Brief Analysis of Its Philosophical Approach' (2021) *Philosophy & Technology* 1–8.

etal impacts and to our potential changes in perspective, those who design and build emerging technologies show that there are indeed ways to identify and address social and moral aspects. Importantly, by encouraging sensitivity to future users and society generally, we need not rely on *predictions* of technology's possible impacts. Accordingly, the embedded ethics approach defended here allows us to see that the choice between failure by our fallibility or failure by the rigidity of technology is a false dilemma.

Admittedly, these are merely two ways of construing the now classic Collingridge Dilemma; albeit two highly forceful and widely adopted formulations. There are surely other ways of framing the challenge of regulation such that we may be forced into accepting one of several undesirable pathways. In this way, the difficulty becomes a tragic choice of trying to choose the least of all evils. Given the novelty of today's embedded ethics programs, it will take time to determine whether or not the interdisciplinary approach leaves us truly better off with future technologies. If nothing else, perhaps embedding ethics will help us to appreciate simply that dilemmas, by their nature, cannot be fully resolved.

2. Repugnance, denial, and fear: societal challenges for regulation of novel beings

David R. Lawrence

It is unlikely that the integration of novel beings into society will be smooth. This is not due to any necessarily inherent issues with these entities; rather, we are not a species particularly welcoming of change, or indeed of anything 'other'. Repugnance, denial, and fear are the first reactions to many new bioscientific developments, and it seems highly likely the same responses will happen here.

Public opinion is likely to be a major consideration in the development and institution of any future legislation that might act to regulate the development and emergence of novel beings or their precursor technologies. In recent times we have seen several wide public debates over emerging biotechnological and artificial intelligence (AI)-related issues, including the idea of electronic personhood and the research licensing of genome editing in human embryos. These arguments, often heated, have influenced policy discussions and in some cases their outcomes. Frequently these debates are highly emotive and reactionary, fuelled by the so-called 'wisdom of repugnance', a common naturalistic fallacy, or misunderstanding. So significant a societal change as would be the introduction of novel beings, and the potential extension of natural personhood for those that qualified, is likely to spark similar reactions. The regulation of novel beings also faces other challenges familiar to emerging technology law, be they from prioritisation of more immediate concerns, reluctance to act on an unknown, or simple indolence in the face of a significant task. If it is a role of regulation to ensure that the public feel secure about emerging technologies, then their concerns cannot be ignored. However, if novel beings warrant natural rights, they too will require protection. In this chapter I will argue that it may be necessary to act in the face of public opinion in order to institute effective or useful legislation, to protect that public – and novel beings themselves – in the future.

FILM, FICTION, AND FRIGHTENING IMAGERY

Novel beings – albeit not having 'arrived' yet – are hardly the first bioscientific development (likely) to cause uproar. Examples from recent decades are many: so-called 'three-parent babies', human cloning, genetically modified organisms (GMOs), the He Jiankui affair,[1] even in-vitro fertilisation (IVF); all caused significant hand-wringing and media debate. We see yet more in clinical contexts; withdrawal of treatment cases such as that of Charlie Gard[2] being particularly sensational. It is difficult to say if the outcry around these examples was entirely organic, stemming from some fear or revulsion deeply felt by the general public, or if it was at least in part ignited by sensationalism in the news media.

Media controversy over science and technology development is no real indicator as to how we ought to act. As the saying goes, 'never let the truth get in the way of a good story', and it is rare to see a media piece on an emerging biotechnology (or otherwise, AI being a particularly egregious area for this) that doesn't invoke some dystopian vision from film and literature to stir up debate. Such stories are not prone to providing reasoned or thoughtful analysis. The same is not (usually) true of genuine scientific controversy, which is a fundamental contributor to knowledge production. Lasting disagreements in science tend, through iteration, comparison, refinement of position, and further exploration, to find a resolution that is not only a middle ground but usually empirically true (which is always promising). 'Criticism is an essential part of everyday science. Controversies often represent extended periods of that critical process.'[3] This truth is often lost in media presentations of scientific debate. The most prominent examples, perhaps, in recent times are in the climate change debate, and following a very similar pattern, the various arguments over the science of mask wearing, social distancing, or vaccine use during the COVID-19 pandemic – arguments that show no sign of ending anytime soon. However, these are not real scientific controversies. In the case of climate change, there is an overwhelming weight of consensus on the one side, and the opponents – those who deny it is real, or that it will have deleterious effects – are mostly arguing in bad faith, co-opting the deliberative scientific process

---

[1]   Henry T. Greely, 'CRISPR'D Babies: Human Germline Genome Editing in the "He Jiankui Affair"' (2019) 6 *Journal of Law and the Biosciences* 111.

[2]   John Harris and David R. Lawrence, 'Ethical Expertise and Public Policy', in Annabelle Lever and Andrei Poama (eds), *Routledge Handbook of Ethics and Public Policy* (Routledge 2018) 76–88.

[3]   Michael R. Dietrich, 'What Is the Nature of Scientific Controversies in the Biological Sciences?', in Kostas Kampourakis and Tobias Uller (eds), *Philosophy of Science for Biologists* (Cambridge University Press 2020) 235–254.

to do so. Repeatedly unearthing lines of inquiry that have been conclusively, evidentially answered is not a legitimate form of debate; it is instead a tactic used to cast doubt about the validity of research in public forums.[4]

Similarly, film and fiction are deployed – almost weaponised – quite deliberately by commentators to try and shape how viewers or readers perceive emerging technologies. This is not inherently bad; it is a useful method of communication, to analogise and to connect an unfamiliar idea with one the audience might recognise. Academics do this frequently: I am no exception, both when teaching and in print.[5] Given the prevalence of biotechnology and AI or robotics as the focus in film and fiction, it is no surprise that it is very common to use them as examples when discussing emerging technologies of the type of interest here. Indeed, very frequently science fiction deals with much the same questions as we may have regarding novel beings; the editors of this volume have frequently invoked the film *Blade Runner* when discussing them, even going so far as to title grants and papers after the fictional corporation that develops the technology.[6]

To take one such technology of interest in the context of novel beings that frequently features in the news, gene editing, it is nearly impossible to escape mention of Aldous Huxley's most famous work. Articles such as 'The Brave New World of Gene Editing'[7] and the front-page newspaper headline, 'Dawn of the Brave New World Baby',[8] are typical, and the novel is commonly referenced in bioethical literature.[9] The film *Gattaca* is another very frequent

---

[4]   Justin B. Biddle and Anna Leuschner, 'Climate Skepticism and the Manufacture of Doubt: Can Dissent in Science Be Epistemically Detrimental?' (2015) 5 *European Journal for Philosophy of Science* 261.

[5]   E.g. David R. Lawrence, 'The Edge of Human? The Problem with the Posthuman as the "Beyond"' (2016) 31 *Bioethics* 171.

[6]   Such as David R. Lawrence and Sarah Morley, 'Regulating the Tyrell Corporation: The Emergence of Novel Beings' (2021) 30 *Cambridge Quarterly of Healthcare Ethics* 421; and, indeed, the title of the grant that this volume continues the work of: Wellcome Trust: WT 208871/Z/17/Z, 'Regulating the Tyrell Corporation: Company Law and the Emergence of Novel Beings'.

[7]   Matthew Cobb, 'The Brave New World of Gene Editing', *The New York Review of Books* (13 July 2017) <https://www.nybooks.com/articles/2017/07/13/brave-new-world-of-gene-editing/> accessed 3 May 2022.

[8]   Sam Greenhill and Jenny Hope, 'Dawn of the Brave New World Baby', *Daily Mail* (11 January 2009).

[9]   John Lynch, 'Bioethics and Brave New World: Science Fiction and Public Articulation of Bioethics' (2019) 2 *Rhetoric of Health & Medicine* 33.

feature in scientific[10] and ethical[11] papers – and anecdotally, I have never seen an undergraduate 'genethics' course that did not feature some mention. Similarly, it seems impossible to discuss human enhancement technologies – another potential precursor to the novel being – without invoking Mary Shelley's *Frankenstein*, often accompanied by the image of Boris Karloff in his seminal portrayal of the monster.[12]

The increase in news stories about AI in the last decade has revealed something of a paucity of imagination in the fictional examples used. Overwhelming all others, references to the Terminator franchise abound, with titles such as 'The Pentagon's "Terminator Conundrum"',[13] 'Terminator-like AI movie death scenarios are just "one to two decades away"'[14] or 'Elon Musk Warns of Terminator Tech'.[15] One particularly egregious example comes from a *Popular Science* article – an outlet that we might expect to be beyond such stunts – describing a robot capable of advanced spatial reasoning and visual–motor coordination. They title it 'A Ping-Pong Playing Terminator'.[16] All these uses of a 1980s' movie franchise may say more about the subeditors' ages or perhaps the expected reader demographic, but the message is unmistakeable: these technologies might be in some way hostile.

---

[10]   Pierre Baldi *et al.*, 'Countering GATTACA: Efficient and Secure Testing of Fully-sequenced Human Genomes' (CCS '11: Proceedings of the 18th ACM Conference on Computer and Communications Security, Chicago, 2011) <https://doi .org/10.1145/2046707.2046785> accessed 3 May 2022.

[11]   Bert Gordijn and Henk ten Have, 'Science Fiction and Bioethics' (2018) 21 *Medicine, Health Care and Philosophy* 277.

[12]   Michael Cook, '"Frankenstein" Organs Proposed for Human Enhancement', *BioEdge* (23 November 2013) <https://bioedge.org/enhancement/frankenstein-organs -proposed-for-human-enhancement/> accessed 3 May 2022; and 'Halloween+: Frankenstein and Transhumanism', *h+ Magazine* (30 October 2015) <https:// hplusmagazine.com/2015/10/30/halloween-the-shelley-godwin-archives-launch -frankenstein-and-transhumanism/> accessed 3 May 2022.

[13]   Matthew Rosenberg and John Markoff, 'The Pentagon's "Terminator Conundrum": Robots that Could Kill on Their Own', *NY Times* (25 October 2016) <https://www.nytimes.com/2016/10/26/us/pentagon-artificial-intelligence-terminator .html> accessed 3 May 2022.

[14]   Phoebe Weston and Joe Pinkstone, 'Killer Terminator-Style AI Is Only "One to Two Decades Away"', *Mail Online* (1 March 2018) <https://www.dailymail.co .uk/sciencetech/article-5449117/Terminators-style-AI-one-two-decades-away.html> accessed 3 May 2022.

[15]   Paul Rodgers, 'Elon Musk Warns of Terminator Tech', *Forbes* (5 August 2014) <http://www.forbes.com/sites/paulrodgers/2014/08/05/elon-musk-warns-ais-could -exterminate-humanity/> accessed 18 April 2022.

[16]   Brooke Borel, 'A Ping-Pong-Playing Terminator', *Popular Science* (2010) <http://www.popsci.com/technology/article/2010-02/ping-pong-playing-terminator> accessed 3 May 2022.

The phenomenon has not gone unremarked; in his Reith Lectures, Stuart Russell recently implored journalists 'to stop using [The Terminator's] image for every single article about autonomous weapons'.[17] He goes on to describe the false beliefs that the propagation of this image instils – most dangerously that such weapons are fiction, when they are available today and are understood (by the United Nations) to have killed already.[18] He quotes the US Deputy Secretary of Defense as saying that 'there is no risk of accidentally creating Skynet'[19] in reference to the rogue AI that creates the Terminators. This – apparently serious – reference demonstrates how deeply this unhelpful image has become embedded in our thinking, even pervading the arguments of senior politicians. Similarly, the 'use and misuse' of *Brave New World* in discussion of gene editing has been criticised.[20]

It is striking that almost all this use of science fictionxamplees when presenting stories about new technology is done to portray matters in a negative light. The stories and films – and it is overwhelmingly film references, presumably because this provides a useful source of a frightening image for the newspaper – are usually depicting a world we do not want to live in or to come to pass, some kind of dystopia or apocalypse. None of us would relish living in a world haunted by skeletal killer robots, and this is precisely the threat presented in these articles. Little wonder, then, that people might be wary. It should be acknowledged, too, that this is not a topic that it would be easy to strike a balance in. Stories of bright, perfect futures are fundamentally not overly interesting, utopian science fiction is far less common than dystopian (at least in the popular consciousness), save where it is ultimately revealed to hide some totalitarian regime or other sinister plot. Utopias do make a bit more of an appearance in technology marketing and liberal bioethics – promised worlds of human enhancement or where disease is eradicated, for example – but most of this fails to penetrate the zeitgeist. Frightening worlds such as those invoked in the media articles being more popular scenarios makes sense – good stories need injustice to be overcome, an antagonist to be defeated, and good stories stick in the mind and make for good reference points for journalists and editors on a deadline.

---

[17]   Stuart Russell, 'AI in Warfare', BBC Radio 4 (18 February 2022) <https://www.bbc.co.uk/programmes/m0012719> accessed 2 May 2022.
[18]   UN Security Council, 'Letter dated 8 March 2021 from the Panel of Experts on Libya established pursuant to resolution 1973 (2011) addressed to the President of the Security Council', 8 March 2021, S/2021/229.
[19]   Russell (n. 17).
[20]   Derek So, 'The Use and Misuse of *Brave New World* in the CRISPR Debate' (2019) 2(5) *CRISPR Journal* 316.

STEERING PERCEPTIONS

It is no real surprise then that people are, very often, afraid of emerging biotechnologies. Some part of this may be a product of the wisdom of repugnance,[21] to which I will return below. Another major factor, though, must be this media presentation of 'controversial' science. A constant association of emerging technologies with negative – even horrific – imagery, usually entirely unwarranted and even with a very tenuous link, comes from newspapers, television news, and leisure media. A documentary on the many new prosthetic and supportive technologies that could combine to be parts of a 'bionic man', broadcast by the UK's Channel 4, is an excellent example.[22] Supposedly a showcase for emerging technologies that had great promise for assisting the disabled, for treating disease, for improving lives, the programme was pervaded by quasi-gothic fonts, dark lighting, and creepy music whenever a scientist or futurist spoke of the possibilities. The programme was not intended to cause fear of technology, and the script was full of praise for it – so why this presentation? There is no evident reason other than that it was perhaps an attempt at drawing viewers in by appealing to a morbid curiosity. This documentary is far from alone in doing so, and given how common this is, it would be stranger if some unconscious negative association did not form around emerging technology, than that it seems to.

Scientists (to generalise) are well aware of the optics of their work, the risk of popular condemnation, and the power of capturing the popular consciousness. When human ova were first successfully fertilised in vitro by Robert Edwards, Patrick Steptoe, and Barry Bavister, in 1969,[23] there was a range of negative newspaper headlines calling the work 'disturbing',[24] including speculation of totalitarian states raising armies 'without the advent of a mother'.[25] To head off calls for tight regulation of biological research, Edwards and Steptoe made significant efforts over the next decade to 'portray … IVF as a medical

---

[21] Leon Kass, 'The Wisdom of Repugnance' (1997) 216(22) *The New Republic* 17.
[22] At the time of writing, the documentary film itself no longer appears to be easily available for viewing, but many articles and images are available online. 'How to Build a Bionic Man', Channel 4 (23 January 2013) <https://www.channel4.com/press/news/how-build-bionic-man> accessed 3 May 2022.
[23] R. G. Edwards, B. D. Bavister and P. C. Steptoe, 'Early Stages of Fertilization in Vitro of Human Oocytes Matured in Vitro' (1969) 221 *Nature* 632.
[24] Duncan Wilson, 'In Vitro Fertilization, Infertility, and the "Right to a Child" in 1970s and 1980s Britain', in Gayle Davis and Tracey Loughran (eds), *The Palgrave Handbook of Infertility in History: Approaches, Contexts and Perspectives* (Palgrave Macmillan 2017) 565.
[25] Jon Turney, *Frankenstein's Footsteps* (Yale University Press 2000) 172.

procedure that met the "needs" of infertile couples".[26] Edwards argued that their goal was 'to make it possible for some infertile patients to have their own children wherever we believe our help to be valid and meaningful';[27] and that 'the primary motivation for our work stems from a fundamentally humanitarian view'.[28] These views were not kept solely to the scientific sphere, and by the time of the birth of Louise Brown in 1978 there was little criticism of IVF – with even tabloids proclaiming her, famously, 'Superbabe'.[29] There was some later backlash as fears arose around what would happen to the traditional family unit, a moral panic partly driven by rising conservatism in Thatcherite England, but this largely focussed on parental relations and propriety, rather than any idea of the children themselves as 'unnatural'.[30]

Wherever we have poor media reactions to technologies, we must also consider the benefits a technology can bring. Over 8 million babies born worldwide via IVF (up to 2018 – with a possible 500,000 deliveries per year since, global pandemic notwithstanding)[31] owe their existence to biotechnology and science and in particular to the work of Edwards and Steptoe, as well as their many predecessors in decades of research. We may hope that a very large proportion of these children are glad to be alive and glad their births were not prevented by the suppression from repugnance or fear of the science that made them possible.

It should be noted, however, that such hard work need not always be done to avoid media opprobrium. An interesting example played out during the production of this volume. In September 2021, David Bennet Sr received a xenotransplantation of a heart and thymus from a pig that had been genetically modified using the CRISPR-Cas9 technique to remove certain enzymes involved in the causation of hyperacute organ rejection.[32] There was a reasonable amount of media attention but perhaps not as much as might be expected of such a procedure, and it was notably positive – or at least factual and neutral – in tone.[33]

---

[26] Wilson (n. 24).

[27] Robert G. Edwards, 'Aspects of Human Reproduction', in Watson Fuller (ed.), *The Social Impact of Modern Biology* (Routledge 1971) 110.

[28] Ibid., 100.

[29] As on the front page of: 'Meet Louise, the World's First Test-tube Arrival: Superbabe' *London Evening News* (27 July 1978).

[30] Wilson (n. 24).

[31] Bart C. J. M. Fauser, 'Towards the Global Coverage of a Unified Registry of IVF Outcomes' (2019) 38 *Reproductive BioMedicine Online* 133.

[32] Talha Burki, 'Pig-Heart Transplantation Surgeons Look to The Next Steps' (2022) 399 *The Lancet* 347.

[33] 'Man Gets Genetically-Modified Pig Heart in World-First Transplant', BBC News (11 January 2022) <https://www.bbc.co.uk/news/world-us-canada-59944889> accessed 3 May 2022; Rivka Galchen, 'The Medical Miracle of a Pig's Heart in

This could be considered somewhat surprising given that xenotransplantation has not been especially commonplace, certainly in the popular consciousness, and also because previous attempts at cardiac xenotransplantation had not been successful. This included the death of an infant girl implanted with a baboon heart,[34] and a highly controversial case of pig organ transplant in Assam, India.[35] The only popular media example available, a 1997 children's novel and later television drama series (my own first exposure to the concept of xenotransplantation), *Pig-Heart Boy*, centred on the titular transplant recipient being pilloried and cast out for being 'infected'.[36] The violation of a human body like this, by implantation of foreign material from another species, seems to fit the description of 'unnatural' that is so often deployed against bioscience, and yet Bennet Sr's case was uncontroversial. Very little further discussion occurred in the mainstream media until Bennet Sr eventually died, and even then, there was very little negative reflection on the technique. Coverage was even positively inflected in that much was made of the fact he had lived longer with the heart than any previous xenotransplant recipient.[37]

The reason outrage was quelled in this case cannot be because it is a life-saving practice. We can think of mitochondrial replacement therapies (MRTs) which do the same (the 'non-identity problem' notwithstanding), and the venom about so-called 'three-parent babies' was pernicious, as discussed below. Quite why this story didn't receive negative headlines is a mystery – I will speculate that it may have been because of other bioscience-related concerns at the time, such as the ongoing global COVID-19 pandemic. A positive story is occasionally welcome.

REPUGNANCE, DENIAL, AND FEAR

Perhaps the general attitude displayed to emerging bio-/AI technologies should be expected. We live in strange times – our future is ever more uncertain. Quite aside from geopolitical and economic unrest, we face changes to 'truths' we have known since time immemorial. Human beings, embodied as *Homo*

---

a Human Body', *The New Yorker* (21 February 2022) <https://www.newyorker.com/magazine/2022/02/28/the-medical-miracle-of-a-pigs-heart-transplant-in-a-human-body> accessed 3 May 2022.

[34] David K. C. Cooper, 'A Brief History of Cross-Species Organ Transplantation' (2012) 25 *Baylor University Medical Center Proceedings* 49.

[35] Dinesh C. Sharma, 'Indian Xenotransplant Surgeon Seeks Damages from Government' (1999) 353 *The Lancet* 48.

[36] Malorie Blackman, *Pig-Heart Boy* (HarperCollins 1997).

[37] For example: Roni Caryn Rabin, 'Patient in Groundbreaking Heart Transplant Dies', *NY Times* (9 March 2022) <https://www.nytimes.com/2022/03/09/health/heart-transplant-pig-bennett.html> accessed 3 May 2022.

sapiens, have been the dominant species on Earth for as long as we have existed, if we set aside some uncertainty in prehistory caused by our hominid relatives.[38] The prospect of novel beings might conceivably threaten this high position,[39] and it is no real surprise that subsidiary technologies, 'controversial' sciences as mentioned, would be viewed with suspicion – even with fear and revulsion. Whereas media opponents of AI proliferation tend to return to the same scaremongering discussed above, critics espouse a range of well-worn reasons why we might want to avoid performing emerging bioscience. Some hold that it would be freakish or unnatural to undergo procedures that might alter our own bodies from the so-called 'norm',[40] or even that it would fly in the face of God to raise man to that station by creating new kinds of life.[41] More argue that we should fear the unknown consequences of our actions, or that we would be embarking on the proverbial 'slippery slope'.[42] Other quarters warn of the corruption of 'human dignity' or the destruction of our own identities as humans;[43] and still more commentators rail against the risks they perceive of creating a genetic divide, a subclass of 'natural' persons oppressed by the emerging 'posthuman'.[44]

As vociferous as some of these criticisms may be, they are also frequently difficult to defend, or are based on fallacy. The 'natural' is far from being the same as the good, and is something of a meaningless term in any case – just as it is something of a smokescreen to hide behind what is 'normal', or the concept of dignity. Obeying the fear of the unknown is a sure path to stagnation, and although precaution is often to be lauded, excessive precaution[45] in the face of evidence to the contrary is simply an attempt to retain what is often an ugly status quo. The novel being is an idea about which we have no good reason to make such assumptions as listed above; and it is hard to deny that we,

---

[38] David R. Lawrence, 'Amplio, Ergo Sum' (2018) 27 *Cambridge Quarterly of Healthcare Ethics* 686.

[39] Lawrence (n. 5).

[40] Norman Daniels, 'Normal Functioning and the Treatment–Enhancement Distinction' (2000) 9 *Cambridge Quarterly of Healthcare Ethics* 309.

[41] Harvey Flaumenhaft, 'The Career of Leon Kass' (2003) 20 *Journal of Contemporary Health Law and Policy* 3.

[42] Eliezer Yudkowsky, 'Artificial Intelligence as a Positive and Negative Factor in Global Risk', in Nick Bostrom and Milan M. Ćirković (eds), *Global Catastrophic Risks* (Oxford University Press 2008) 303.

[43] For example: Leon Kass, *Life, Liberty, and the Defense of Dignity* (Encounter Books 2002).

[44] Bill McKibben, *Enough: Staying Human in an Engineered Age* (Times Books 2003).

[45] See discussion in David R. Lawrence and John Harris, 'Newer Technologies, Older Attitudes, and Retrograde Regulation', Chapter 5 in this volume.

in a sense, play God on a regular basis through such reproductive technologies as are commonly accepted (for instance, IVF, MRTs and pre-implantation genetic diagnosis).

Yet, the technologies in question do inspire revulsion among many. For some, this may be a product of the 'yuck' factor, and some may simply fear what they see and what – in their perception – it may cost them in terms of their own privileges. The presentation of the information, as discussed above, surely heavily influences this reaction. This distaste – also known as the wisdom of repugnance[46] – is a questionable defence and very rarely a sound basis for judgment, despite the arguments of Leon Kass and his adherents.[47]Although Kass defends it, claiming that 'in crucial cases … repugnance is the emotional expression of deep wisdom, beyond reason's power fully to articulate it',[48] it has no evidentiary or theoretical backing and as such cannot be taken seriously in debate as a legitimate rationale. It is within our nature to resist the unknown or the different, but what marks us as human (and what is a hallmark of that which we consider to be civilisation) is our ability to act against base instinct, to evaluate and reason, and to determine the best course of action to arrive at the greatest good. Repugnance, and the reactions it inspires, are a poor substitute for exercising this capacity.

The potential advent of novel beings is, it might be reasonable to suggest, likely to inspire more direct repugnance in the shape of xenophobia. A novel being will not be *Homo sapiens*, even if it might be possible to describe it as 'human' in a philosophical sense, based on its characteristics,[49] and given our apparent inability to tolerate other members of our own species, it seems dubious that something so 'other' would be welcomed with open arms. This fear, too, is hardly significant; it is a product of some animal instinct, the same that leads to racism and extreme nationalism today. Reasonable people do not allow such opinions to colour their views on other races, cultures, or creeds with whom we may share everything save one insignificant factor. The same ought to hold true for novel beings, particularly those who warrant this kind of discussion.

We claim as a society to believe in equality, and yet indulge so frequently in stigma and hostility in defence of our own 'normality'. This type of fear is usually presented as moral disapproval. Wherever a group seems to deviate from the norm they are stigmatised and portrayed as a threat to keenly held moral values (even if those values were rarely mentioned before the group

---

[46]   Kass (n. 21).
[47]   Ibid.
[48]   Ibid.
[49]   David Lawrence, 'More Human than Human' (2017) 26 *Cambridge Quarterly of Healthcare Ethics* 476.

became visible). That threat is, as above, generally non-existent. Instead, the desire of the dominant group is to protect itself and secure its dominance; an instinct that might be understandable if we are to believe the portrayal of novel beings – related emerging technologies out to 'terminate' us – or at least remove us from our top spot.

Emerging biotechnologies and AI technologies developing ever faster is the new reality, and it would be wilful ignorance to deny that the world and the human experience are being forever changed by it (in such places as the discrepancies of developed and developing world have allowed). So far, we might be able to say that this phenomenon has been broadly positive, some-thing which has brought great benefits to our ways of living, without denying the many endemic problems with certain deployments of AI. Very few people are true Luddites; almost everyone with access and the means partakes of these technological developments and enjoys the fruits, enjoys the conveni-ences, and enjoys the ease they bring. However, it seems to be comfortable to consider 'humans' as a finished product occupying the position they deserve, to deny that any good can come from transformation or that emerging (bio) technologies are anything but inimical to our station. It may be comforting to imagine that our technological elevation has stopped outright, with our evo-lution stopped, though of course this is merely a function of our own limited perceptions, and it continues at the same glacially slow pace as ever. We are afraid of the idea of further change, or the emergence and evolution of any-thing that can challenge our dominance, because we dislike the idea of having further self-development to undertake. Once we finally reach adulthood, that is supposed to be the end of the road, the final stage, and it feels brutally unfair that we might have yet more to do to justify our place in the world.

If our collective feelings can be so easily influenced by the promotion of repugnance, denial, and fear, we ought perhaps to be concerned. These attitudes, whether legitimate or poorly founded, do infiltrate policymaking. Policymakers and politicians listen – or like to tell us that they do – to the mood of the public, and in the context of regulating to reflect public attitudes to science, that is a very fine line to walk. The groundswell of support in the UK for the use of MRTs around 2014–15 is an example of that. A great division was visible in the UK press's stances on MRT, ranging from the creation of the questionably accurate 'three-parent baby' label, used to suggest that any such child would be unnatural, somehow fundamentally wrong, to articles in clear support, showing the stories of those who could be helped.[50] It is difficult to

---

[50] For instance, Tim Stanley, 'Three Parent Babies: Unethical, Scary and Wrong', *The Telegraph* (3 February 2015) <http://www.telegraph.co.uk/news/health/11380784/Three-parent-babies-unethical-scary-and-wrong.html> accessed 2 May 2022; as

say outright that this popular backing swayed the decision by the legislature to legalise the use of MRTs, but it seems very likely that had the majority of the debate not been in favour, it would not have gone the way it did.

The 'three-parent baby' rhetoric is even used in the title of at least one official Hansard entry,[51] which perhaps demonstrates how this term, and its associations, overshadowed the whole issue. It is not entirely clear when the term 'three-parent babies' in the context of MRTs first appeared, as it appears to have been used in press coverage[52] of a conceptually similar IVF technique[53] that first led to a birth in 1997, and up to 50 more by the early 2000s, of children that may or may not have DNA material from three 'parents'.[54] The term was initially used reasonably innocuously to make a complex scientific procedure easily understandable, much like the use of the science fiction examples already discussed. During the surge of interest in MRTs, as the UK began to seriously consider legalisation, the term became widespread, despite its inaccuracy. As I have argued elsewhere on this topic,

> the third-party DNA contained in the donated mitochondria comprises much less than 1% of the total genetic contribution, and does not transmit any of the traits that confer the usual family resemblances and distinctive personal features in which both parents and children are interested.[55]

Furthermore, the term ignores the difference between a parent and a mere progenitor. Fundamentally, it gives an evocative but fundamentally false picture of the technology. When we consider the 'wisdom of repugnance' discussed above, the fear of the 'unnatural' combined with the adverse connotations piled

---

opposed to Polly Toynbee, 'This Isn't About Three-Parent Babies. It's About Saving Families Needless Misery', *The Guardian* (3 February 2015) <https://www.theguardian.com/commentisfree/2015/feb/03/three-parent-babies-families-religious-mps-vote-mitochondrial-replacement> accessed 3 May 2022.

[51]   HC Deb 12 March 2014, vol. 577, cols 164–173 (Mitochondrial Transfer (Three-Parent Children)).

[52]   Richard Alleyne, '"Three Parent Babies" Take A Step Closer To Reality', *The Telegraph* (12 November 2009) <https://www.telegraph.co.uk/news/health/news/6546448/Three-parent-babies-take-a-step-closer-to-reality.html> accessed 3 May 2022.

[53]   Jason A. Barritt *et al.*, 'Cytoplasmic Transfer in Assisted Reproduction' (2001) 7 *Human Reproduction Update* 428.

[54]   Shane Kula, 'Three-Parent Babies Have Been Here Since the Late '90s', *Slate Magazine* (18 February 2016) <https://slate.com/technology/2016/02/three-parent-babies-have-been-here-since-the-late-90s.html> accessed 3 May 2022.

[55]   John Harris and David R. Lawrence, 'New Technologies, Old Attitudes, and Legislative Rigidity', in Roger Brownsword, Eloise Scotford and Karen Yeung (eds), *Oxford Handbook on the Law and Regulation of Technology* (Oxford University Press 2017) 915.

on the term by connecting it to the spectre of, for instance, 'designer babies'[56] or even 'mutants',[57] it is unsurprising that it took on a negative overtone. Some of the more fanciful – and concerning – impacts of this can be seen from the aforementioned debate, in which one Conservative MP queried whether 'if someone does not know who the third or fourth person who created them is, through sheer chance they may well find themselves marrying their brother or sister'.[58] I will not dwell on the further discussion of whether the procedure would affect the embryo's 'soul'.

Cooler heads ultimately prevailed, and the UK did legalise the use of MRT.[59] But this example is instructive – prejudices can very easily infect science policy and legislation. I cannot put it better than did Martha Nussbaum:

> The law, most of us would agree, should be society's protection against prejudice. That does not imply that emotions play no legitimate role in legal affairs, for often emotions help people to see a situation clearly, doing justice to the concerns that ought to be addressed.[60]

In some ways, this position echoes that of Kass in favour of repugnance – that it is in some cases an expression of 'deep wisdom'.[61] If a technological development is so abhorrent to us, even if we cannot quite articulate the reasons why, then there is perhaps good reason to be cautious. Our bodies and minds do act to preserve us, after all, and 'Emotions are not intrinsically opposed to reason, for they involve pictures of the world and evaluations.'[62]

As Nussbaum goes on to note, disgust (much like repugnance) is in some cases the reason for something to be illegal. She uses the example of obscenity law, and we could imagine that the reasoning there could be applied to particularly outlandish or risky sciences. However, this logic is fallible. Disgust has been used to justify (or to try to justify) the criminalisation of homosexuality; a position that is clearly untenable in the modern world – and which relies on

---

[56] Hitika Sharma, Drishtant Singh, Ankush Mahant, S. Sohal, A. Kesavan and S. Samiksha, 'Development of Mitochondrial Replacement Therapy: A Review' (2020) 6 *Heliyon* e04643.

[57] Mia De Graaf, 'Doctors Defend "Mutant" Three-Parent DNA Babies as Revolutionary', *Mail Online* (5 August 2017) <https://www.dailymail.co.uk/health/article-4762744/Doctor-told-stop-marketing-3-person-baby-technique.html> accessed 3 May 2022.

[58] HC Deb 12 March 2014, vol. 577, cols 165–166.

[59] The Human Fertilisation and Embryology (Mitochondrial Donation) Regulations 2015.

[60] Martha Nussbaum, 'Danger to Human Dignity: The Revival of Disgust and Shame in the Law' (2004) 50(48) *The Chronicle Review* B6.

[61] Kass (n. 21).

[62] Nussbaum (n. 60).

the idea that it is alright to deny freedoms just because they may offend sensibilities. Repugnance is therefore not, as Kass might claim, a reliable guide in times of social change. Unfortunately, much like changing attitudes to race and to sexuality, it seems likely that novel beings will need to go through some process of gradual acceptance into society.

NOVEL BEINGS, NOT-SO-NOVEL ATTITUDES

The premise of this volume is that we face, in the reasonably near future, the creation of novel entities that possess some degree of moral validity and status, potentially equivalent to our own. Given all the above context for our probable common societal reactions to emerging controversial technologies, it seems likely that the novel being will elicit a similar response. After all, a 'three-parent' baby or a gene-edited child, altered only in one, non-visible, apparently beneficial way, is enough to raise such condemnation; so one can only imagine the strength of feeling a sapient AI or a synthetic sentient animal would engender. It is incumbent on us to decide how we will manage this emergence, and there are strong reasons to prefer an approach that recognises and protects the moral status – or probable moral status – that they might have.

I have explored at some length elsewhere the reasons why a novel being – be it an android, a sapient synthetic biological creature, or a disembodied artificial general intelligence – would warrant moral status and the corresponding legal protections that should bring.[63] Where we consider legal protections for a group it is because we see that group as possessing whatever level of moral value is worthy of that protection. The qualifying requirement to enjoy the level that we consider ourselves to possess seems to be personhood. However, as with other beings we have previously encountered throughout history – i.e. citizens of foreign nations – personhood is no guarantee of non-aggression or of automatic friendship, and this is reflected in the xenophobic tendencies towards scientific advances we see in many public responses. Beyond these knee-jerk prejudices, though, we know that we ought not generally assume hostility from other persons. Rather, shared moral status should give us grounds for understanding. Conflict generally arises where there are incompatible motivations, and there is no good reason to assume that things would be fundamentally different with a sapient novel being. In fact, we can make certain assumptions about their basic motivations: they are very likely to be similar to our own. We

---

    63   David R. Lawrence and Margaret Brazier, 'Legally Human? "Novel Beings" and English Law' (2018) 26 *Medical Law Review* 309; Lawrence (n. 5); Lawrence (n. 49).

want to be safe, secure, free, and so on – it seems reasonable to assume that those requirements would underlie the existence of any novel being as well.[64]

However, whether through repugnance or xenophobia, and whether promulgated by media reports and popular debate or not, that shared ground is not likely to be easily recognised. The kinds of right that we tend to think of under the banner of 'human' rights, including fundamental rights to life, to protection against torture or degrading treatment, or to liberty – these rights apply, or are generally thought of as applying, only to human beings. While we do provide certain protections to other animals (and there have been attempts to extend human-equivalent rights to certain species[65]), it isn't obvious that rights law will be directly applied to any novel being that we might imagine could warrant it. The examples of cases in non-human animals only took place (and were, for the most part, unsuccessful) after years of activism and gradual shifts in policymaker attitudes,[66] as well as high-profile initiatives such as the 'Great Ape Project'.[67] This is not to say that a novel being worthy of the name (as we have chosen to use it in this volume, i.e. any entity created through artifice and which might warrant some degree of moral status) should not automatically have rights and protections commensurate with their degree of moral status; quite the opposite. However, it does seem unlikely that this would occur without resistance from the courts and legislature,[68] or public outcry.

A RESPONSIBILITY TO BE PROACTIVE

When we consider the potential stakes – new, lab-grown posthumans, or the birth of AGI that could think and reason like a human, with wants and needs and moral rights of its own – there is probably comfort in repugnance, denial, and fear. We might understand the reticence to welcome even morally deserving novel beings with open arms. We are weak creatures ourselves, vulnerable to the 'other', or so we tend to believe. Anyone trying to usher in that 'other' threatens our safety and security, and it is perhaps natural to lash out against

---

[64]   I have explored this at some length with colleagues in David R. Lawrence, César Palacios-González and John Harris, 'Artificial Intelligence: The Shylock Syndrome' (2016) 25 *Cambridge Quarterly of Healthcare Ethics* 260.

[65]   Notably orang-utans, such as Sandra: Asociacion de Funcionarios y Abogados por los Derechos de Los Animales y Otros Contra GCBA Sobre Amparo, Expte A2174-2015/0; see also: 'Orangutan Granted Controlled Freedom by Argentine Court', CNN (23 December 2014) <http://edition.cnn.com/2014/12/23/world/americas/feat-orangutan-rights-ruling/> accessed 13 April 2022.

[66]   Lawrence and Brazier (n. 63).

[67]   Paola Cavalieri and Peter Singer, *The Great Ape Project: Equality Beyond Humanity* (St Martin's Griffin 1996).

[68]   Lawrence and Brazier (n. 63).

that threat. The media wish to sell a story, but they also wish to be a popular representative – so they are not to be blamed for voicing this fear. We must remember, though, the great benefits that controversial science has brought. Had IVF been suppressed for fear of the unnatural, many millions around the world would not be among us. If there were no 'three-parent babies', families affected by mitochondrial disease would continue to suffer – as they do in many countries. The hostile attitudes displayed towards these technologies are no longer appropriate for nor reflective of the realities of the technologies themselves, or our policymaking needs.

Reactive regulation will, necessarily, be reactive; not to be trite, but it cannot help but take into account the social response to the emergence of a given technology. This social response, as mediated by the media attitudes discussed at length earlier, is very likely to be negative, exclusionary, and conservative. Of course, it is more than possible that those creating the regulation will be critically capable, and able to ignore these biases. Nevertheless, if law is meant, in very broad terms, to reflect the values of the society it protects,[69] then the expressed desires of that society (even if misinformed) will surely hold some degree of influence. Reactive regulation, then, is likely to be overly restrictive, and if we take the reactions calling for moratoria and bans in the wake of developments in genome editing[70] as any kind of precedent, we could perhaps expect the same responses here.

Banning the development of novel beings – or any emerging technology – outright as a paean to fear and repugnance would be damaging. This is true not only for the safe further development of the science, but in how it would cast the lives of those already created through them – children created through MRT, for instance. Moreover, we know that bans and moratoria are ineffective; the birth of the CRISPR twins Lulu and Nana, discussed elsewhere in this volume, is unavoidable evidence.[71] In this sense, it will not matter if novel beings are legally permitted or prohibited in any given place. If they are created in a different jurisdiction, by accident, or simply without regard for regulations, they may come to exist anyway. If the science is possible, we must assume it will be developed somewhere. If so, we will have to engage with it, and determine our response; those in favour of reactive forms of regulation would endorse this.

---

[69]   I am aware this is a very broad-brush statement, but I believe the sentiment to be true enough for this purpose.

[70]   See, for instance: Michael McCarthy, 'Scientists Call for Moratorium on Clinical Use of Human Germline Editing' (2015) *BMJ* 6603; and Eric S. Lander *et al.*, 'Adopt a Moratorium on Heritable Genome Editing', *Nature Comment* (13 March 2019) <https://www.nature.com/articles/d41586-019-00726-5> accessed 15 April 2022.

[71]   Lawrence and Harris, Chapter 5 in this volume.

However, this ignores that we do have the gift of foresight. We are in a position to act ahead of time – to regulate proactively – to try and direct the development of novel beings' technologies in ways we find acceptable. We know that the constituent technologies are extant or in development, and we know that whatever we do, matters will progress. It seems foolhardy to institute bans and thus drive research underground, or to places with less oversight, when it may be possible to provide environs to constructively guide that work 'in the open'. Whilst that would be no guarantee, it may be the best we can realistically do. Further, if we fail to act proactively, emerging technologies or even the novel beings themselves will be left to the mercies of the existing law, until the reactive regulation can be brought to bear however many years down the line – by which time we might expect things to be too late. As far as novel beings go, there is plenty of reason to think that existing law could apply and even include them, but there is just as much to think that such inclusion would be resisted.[72] Existing regulation is not fit for purpose here if it allows for such discrepancy. Once the problems created by this lack of fitness display themselves, we will very much be forced into harmful reactivity, and influenced by the repugnance, denial, and fear that seem sure to surround our premise. Harms already permitted by allowing developments to come to pass in rogue laboratories – we do not yet know the full health implications for Lulu, Nana, or the unnamed child who followed them[73] – will be compounded. We do not have the right to wait and see, to not act first to do what good we can. We cannot afford to wait until public opinion – and therefore political and legislative will – is taken over by a 'good headline' that offers no consideration to those other than ourselves who could be harmed.

This should remind us that there is a deeper story to be told about the weight of scientific advancements. As the stewards of scientific progress, we are beholden to all parties; both to existing persons, and to the beings we may create. The repugnance and fears surrounding novel beings are purely our problems to solve, or to prevent from arising. We can take steps to do so through careful design and implementation of appropriate regulation and policy, to govern their development and ensure both their, and our, protection.

---

[72] Lawrence and Brazier (n. 63).

[73] David Cyranoski, 'What CRISPR-Baby Prison Sentences Mean for Research', *Nature* (3 January 2020) <https://www.nature.com/articles/d41586-020-00001-y> accessed 2 May 2022.

3. Morally significant technology: a case against mere corporate self-regulation[1]

Sarah Morley

1   INTRODUCTION

We are in the midst of a technological revolution that has seen the emergence of new types of morally significant technology (MST). A profusion of 'expert systems' or narrow artificial intelligence (AI) now interweave into our everyday lives, alongside efforts made towards artificial general intelligence (AGI). Recent developments in synthetic biology include the creation of brain organoids (or 'mini brains')[2] and the possibility to write entire synthetic genomes.[3] Whilst these emerging technologies could potentially offer many benefits to society, they inevitably present far-reaching and significant moral implications[4] with some even challenging our perception of what it is to be human.[5]

As Roger Brownsword has observed, 'it is trite that new technologies are economically and socially disruptive'[6] but these new emerging technologies

---

[1]   The author wishes to acknowledge the support of the Wellcome Trust: WT 208871/Z/17/Z 'Regulating the Tyrell Corporation: Company Law and the Emergence of Novel Beings'; I would like to thank Mr Chris Riley, Professor Mathias Siems, Professor Alan Dignam, Professor Daithi MacSithigh and Dr David Lawrence for their advice and comments on earlier drafts of this chapter.
[2]   A. Lavazza and M. Massimini, 'Cerebral organoids: ethical issues and consciousness assessment' (2018) 44(9) *Journal of Medical Ethics* 606.
[3]   See G. M. Church et al., 'Realizing the potential of synthetic biology' (2014) 15 *Nature Reviews Molecular Cell Biology* 289.
[4]   See Government response to House of Lords Artificial Intelligence Select Committee's Report on 'AI in the UK: ready, willing and able?' (CM 9645, June 2018); see also House of Lords, 'AI in the UK: ready, willing and able?' (HL100, 2018) ('AI in the UK: ready, willing and able').
[5]   D. R. Lawrence and M. Brazier, 'Legally human? "Novel beings" and English law' (2018) 26 *Medical Law Review* 309.
[6]   R. Brownsword, 'Law and technology: two modes of disruption, three legal mind-sets, and the big picture of regulatory responsibilities' (2018) 14 *Indian Journal of Law and Technology* 1.

have the ability to significantly interfere with, and impact upon, the economy, policing and democratic elections on a scale previously unknown.[7] Yet governments across the world, and in particular those in the UK and US, continue to facilitate self-regulation by the companies that develop and operate this emerging technology. A sufficient regulatory framework must be established because, as it stands, the law is ill-equipped to deal with the difficult regulatory challenges these new technologies create. How then should the law respond?

There are a number of ways of dividing regulatory strategies to control corporations' behaviour and build systems of accountability. One way is to contrast the use of legal norms with what is often referred to as corporate social responsibility (CSR), meaning essentially a reliance on non-legal norms and incentives to encourage companies to behave well. The choice between these two regulatory strategies has already led to a rich debate in human rights and environmental law regulation.[8] The purpose of this chapter is to address this choice in, and apply this debate to, the context of technology companies' development of MST. Whilst there is an extensive literature concerning CSR, it does not discuss the regulation of emerging technology and – vice versa – literature that does focus on regulating new technology (such as MSTs) does not consider the work of CSR. The original approach taken in this chapter is to apply established and already well-researched ideas surrounding CSR to this new and developing area of research in emerging technology. My argument is that, at least in this context, CSR is likely to be much less effective than its proponents hope or claim, and the law likely to be much more effective, and thus more necessary, than its critics allege. A proactive approach for the regulation of MST, including novel beings, should be adapted and mandatory minimums for regulation (at the very least) should be adopted.

---

[7]   See D. R. Lawrence and S. Morley, 'Regulating the Tyrell Corporation: the emergence of novel beings' (2021) 30(3) Cambridge Quarterly of Healthcare Ethics 421; Digital Culture, Media and Sport Committee, 'Disinformation and "fake news"', Final Report, HC 1791, 2019 (DCMS, 'Disinformation and "fake news"'); T. Marwala and E. Hurwitz, *Artificial Intelligence and Economic Theory: Skynet in the Market* (Springer, 2017).

[8]   See United Nations Global Compact, 'The Ten Principles of the UN Global Compact' <https://www.unglobalcompact.org/what-is-gc/mission/principles> accessed 16 April 2021; see, for example, S. Bijlmakers, *Corporate Social Responsibility, Human Rights and the Law* (Routledge, 2018); F. Wettstein, 'CSR and the debate on business and human rights: bridging the great divide' (2012) 22 *Business Ethics Quarterly* 739; B. Sjäfjell and C. M. Bruner, *Cambridge Handbook of Corporate Law, Corporate Governance and Sustainability* (Cambridge University Press, 2019); A. Crane, A. McWilliams, Dirk Matten, J. Moon and D. S. Siegel (ed.), *The Oxford Handbook of Corporate Social Responsibility* (Oxford University Press, 2008).

I argue that there are five main limitations significant to self-regulation in regard to regulating MST. These are: (i) the lack of an agreed perspective on what is 'good corporate behaviour' in relation to the development of MST; (ii) the lack of credibility of CSR as a regulatory tool; (iii) the vague and unmeasurable content of CSR codes of conduct;[9] (iv) corporations' own failures to properly assess the risk of their activities in regard to MST; and (v) the difficulties in enforcing CSR codes and principles. Taken together, these weaknesses deprive CSR of the structural capacity necessary to govern MST effectively.

The chapter proceeds as follows. Section 2 provides examples of MST and outlines the technological context of the chapter. Section 3 provides background to the public initiatives proposed to date and Section 4 clarifies the conceptualisation of CSR. In Section 5, the chapter turns to its central argument by highlighting the strategic weaknesses of using self-regulation and CSR to regulate MST. The ineffective nature of CSR strategies is further evidenced in Section 6 by demonstrating that other industries more generally do not behave well when the law does not require it. Section 7 concludes.

These technologies generate endless questions as to how we define what would be correct, responsible behaviour for corporations dealing with MST, and what legal regulation should look like, but it is not the purpose of this chapter to attempt to settle any of these more broad and complex issues. It is also important to note that imposing mandatory obligations on corporations is not meant to prevent innovation, but to ensure responsible development of MST and create appropriate mechanisms for redress. It is perhaps corporations who are best placed to develop such technologies – more so for example than the state. Additionally, whilst the chapter tries to identify the appropriate sphere for legal regulation, it is accepted that legal norms cannot capture all responsible behaviour and that there will inevitably be a requirement for a sphere of non-legal responsible behaviour.

2   MORALLY SIGNIFICANT TECHNOLOGY

Morally significant technology is a broad term, coined here to incorporate a spectrum of emerging technologies. At the lower end of the spectrum, we have precursor technologies that we would not describe as sapient or even sentient – which encompasses the technology we currently know and use today – and at the higher end, those technologies that we might categorise as novel beings that may be created in the future. Many of the things that qualify as novel beings fall within the category of MST. The term 'novel being' includes

---

[9]   See, for example, that promulgated by Google: 'AI at Google: our principles' <https://www.blog.google/technology/ai/ai-principles/> accessed 28 June 2020.

any entity *artificially* created (either via biological or non-biological material) that warrants legal protection due to its moral status as a sentient or sapient being – as any animal or human should.

The term 'moral significance' is not used here as a precise concept to differentiate between different types of emerging technology, but rather it is used in a more general way to include those that require regulating because, whilst they are often hugely beneficial, the potential for harm is significant and that of course has moral implications. Examples of these harms are physical injury, financial loss, political threats and broader ethical concerns. Thus, questions of morality will always be raised when considering the behaviour of companies developing and operating this technology and how our regulation should respond. The objective of regulation would be to provide protection against damage and other forms of disruption that may impact our daily lives.

This section describes two types of MST to explain some of the moral challenges they present. The two examples are, first, AI and, second, developments in synthetic biology. To be sure, these two examples do not exhaust the range of MST that currently exists. However, we shall focus on the two selected examples because these are forms of emerging technology that have already become relatively prolific, and because they encompass those technological developments which seem to generate the most recurrent risks.

AI is non-biological, an autonomous product of computer science, potentially ranging from a basic algorithm to a complex, sapient android; whilst synthetic biology is the development of *new biological* systems. Whilst some of the potential risks these technologies produce will be similar, they present inherently different dangers, and consequently there may be differences in how regulation handles these two types of technological developments. However, the critique of CSR's ineffectiveness to regulate these technologies applies equally to both types and accordingly I will address both categories together for the present purposes of this chapter.

2.1   Artificial Intelligence

The explosion of new and powerful AI technology is a pressing issue that has attracted attention from governments,[10] private bodies[11] and the media,[12] and is a growing area of academic research. In bioethics and philosophy literature

---

[10]   'AI in the UK: ready, willing and able?' (n. 4); see also the Alan Turing Institute <https://www.turing.ac.uk/research/research-projects> accessed 4 April 2021.

[11]   Such as the Future of Life Institute <https://futureoflife.org> accessed 4 April 2021; Leverhulme Centre for the Future of Intelligence <http://lcfi.ac.uk> accessed 4 April 2021.

[12]   See Government response to 'AI in the UK: ready, willing and able?' (n. 4).

much of the debate has considered whether it is 'right' or 'moral' to create sentient or sapient beings (and indeed whether this could be possible)[13] and what moral status these beings might have.[14] Computer science and legal literature consider algorithmic fairness,[15] big data ethics[16] and the regulation of the internet.[17] Other legal and philosophical work has concentrated on the regulation of autonomous vehicles[18] and weapons,[19] and the use of AI technology in medicine.[20]

AI has become part of our daily lives, from smartphones powered by machine learning to voice recognition systems we use in our homes, to algo-

---

[13] See C. Pennachin and B. Goertzel, 'Contemporary approaches to artificial general intelligence' in B. Goertzel and C. Pennachin (eds), *Artificial General Intelligence Cognitive Technologies* (Springer, 2007); D. Endy, 'Foundations for engineering biology' (2005) 438 *Nature* 449; A. Christiansen, 'Synthetic biology and the moral significance of artificial life: a reply to Douglas, Powell and Savulescu' (2016) 30 *Bioethics* 372; J. Boldt and O. Müller, 'Newtons of the leaves of grass' (2008) 26 *Nature Biotechnology* 387.

[14] See D. R. Lawrence, 'Amplio, ergo sum' (2018) 27 *Cambridge Quarterly of Healthcare Ethics* 686; D. R. Lawrence, 'More human than human' (2017) 26 *Cambridge Quarterly of Healthcare Ethics* 476; D. R. Lawrence, 'The edge of human? The problem with the posthuman as the "beyond"' (2017) 31 *Bioethics* 171; D. R. Lawrence, C. Palacios-González and J. Harris, 'The Shylock syndrome' (2016) 25 *Cambridge Quarterly of Healthcare Ethics* 250.

[15] See A. Caliskan, J. J. Bryson and A. Narayanan, 'Semantics derived automatically from language corpora contain human-like biases' (2017) 356 *Science* 183; J. Angwin, J. Larson, S. Mattu and L. Kirchner, 'Machine bias', *ProPublica* (23 May 2016) <https://www.propublica.org/article/machine-bias-risk-assessments-in-criminal-sentencing> accessed 28 January 2021.

[16] See S. Barocas and A. D. Selbst, 'Big data's disparate impact' (2016) 104 *California Law Review* 671; N. M. Richards and J. H. King, 'Big data ethics' (2014) 49 *Wake Forest Law Review* 393; B. Mittelstadt, 'The ethics of biomedical "big data" analytics' (2019) 32 *Philosophy and Technology* 17.

[17] See DCMS, 'Disinformation and "fake news"' (n. 7); L. Edwards, *Law, Policy and the Internet* (Hart Publishing, 2018); E. B. Laidlaw, *Regulating Speech in Cyberspace* (Cambridge University Press, 2015); C. Reed and A. Murray, *Rethinking the Jurisprudence of Cyberspace* (Edward Elgar Publishing, 2018); A. Murray, *Regulation of Cyberspace* (Taylor and Francis, 2014).

[18] J. Harris, 'Who owns my autonomous vehicle? Ethics and responsibility in artificial and human intelligence' (2018) 27(4) *Cambridge Quarterly of Healthcare Ethics* 599–609; J. Boeglin, 'The costs of self-driving cars: reconciling freedom and privacy with tort liability in autonomous vehicle regulation' (2015) 17 *Yale Journal of Law and Technology* 171.

[19] See A. Krishnan, *Killer Robots* (Routledge, 2016); A. Leveringhaus, *Ethics and Autonomous Weapons* (Palgrave Pivot, 2016); H. M. Roff, 'The strategic robot problem: lethal autonomous weapons in war' (2014) 13 *Journal of Military Ethics* 211.

[20] S. Chan, 'Research translation and emerging health technologies: synthetic biology and beyond' (2018) 26 *Health Care Analysis* 310.

rithms that personalise our newsfeeds, filter our emails and make recommendations in streaming services, and much more. Whilst these types of AI have significantly improved over the last decade, they are more properly termed as 'expert systems' or 'narrow' AI.[21] The capabilities of such systems 'generally extend to just one task and are centred on making predictions from existing data sets that are input by human developers and programmers'.[22] These systems benefit our lives in many ways and will continue to do so, but if these systems fail or are misused there can be significant consequences.

One way in which AI can fail is due to errors or biases in the information programmed into the technology.[23] This effect is called 'algorithmic bias', the results of which are alarming.[24] For example, software developed by private companies used to sentence individuals convicted of crimes in the USA has been found to incorrectly flag black defendants as likely to re-offend twice as frequently as white defendants.[25] This software is used in nine different states across the USA and has impacted negatively on thousands of individuals. The process of using AI to determine sentence has also been criticised for violating due process, particularly because the algorithm is kept secret and cannot be 'inspected or challenged'.[26] Algorithmic bias is also a concern for software currently in use for medical diagnosis and the treatment of illnesses such as cancer.[27] Harms have additionally arisen from the improper testing of

---

[21] See S. Russell and P. Norvig, *Artificial Intelligence: A Modern Approach* (Prentice Hall, 2nd edn, 2003) 537–581, 863–898.

[22] J. Creighton, 'Machine reasoning and the rise of artificial general intelligences: an interview with Bart Selman', Future of Life Institute (27 July 2018) <https://futureoflife.org/2018/07/27/machine-reasoning-and-the-rise-of-artificial-general-intelligences-an-interview-with-bart-selman/> accessed 30 July 2020.

[23] See A. Caliskan, J. J. Bryson and A. Narayanan (n. 15); the paper concludes that data programmed into artificial intelligence contain imprints of historic biases which are 'problematic' towards race and gender; see also DCMS, 'Disinformation and "fake news"' (n. 7).

[24] See S. Barocas and A. D. Selbst (n. 16); Barocas and Selbst find that an algorithm is only as good as the data it works with and therefore can inherit the prejudices of prior decision makers and reflect the widespread biases that persist in society at large; J. Kleinberg et al., 'Algorithmic fairness' (2018) 108 *American Economic Association Papers and Proceedings* 22.

[25] See J. Angwin et al. (2016) (n. 15); see also J. Kaplan, 'Why your AI might be racist' *Washington Post* (28 December 2018) <https://www.washingtonpost.com/opinions/2018/12/17/why-your-ai-might-be-racist/?utm_term=.0e4bbe909173> accessed 28 January 2021.

[26] A. Liptak, 'Sent to prison by a software program's secret algorithms', *New York Times* (1 May 2018) <https://www.nytimes.com/2017/05/01/us/politics/sent-to-prison-by-a-software-programs-secret-algorithms.html> accessed 26 May 2020.

[27] P. Hannon, 'Researchers say use of artificial intelligence in medicine raises ethical questions', Stanford Medicine, News Center <https://med.stanford.edu/news/all

AI. Automated technologies (such as cars and drones) have already caused physical injury and death. AI can also be misused by companies to acquire personal data from millions of people[28] and there is also potential for AI to cause serious damage to the economies and stability of an entire country.[29] An example of such occurred when the United Nations accused Facebook of playing a determining role in inciting hatred against the Rohingya Muslim minority in Rakhine State, Burma.[30]

The potential for harm will only be exacerbated by developments in 'general' AI ('AGI'). In simple terms, AGI is a type of AI that has all the characteristics of human intelligence and thus could be considered as a sentient or even sapient being.[31] An AGI might be considered sapient if:

> [T]he construction of [its] software program ... can solve a variety of complex problems in a variety of different domains, and ... controls itself autonomously, with its own thoughts, worries, feelings, strengths, weaknesses and predispositions.[32]

Determining when an AGI will truly hold human intelligence and reasoning is beyond this chapter, but it goes beyond the capabilities of the technology we have today.[33] There is some argument that AGI will never be achieved,[34] but 'rapid progress is already being made in machine reasoning'[35] and 'many

---

-news/2018/03/researchers-say-use-of-ai-in-medicine-raises-ethical-questions.html> accessed 28 January 2020.

[28]   A. Hern, 'Cambridge Analytica scandal highlights need for AI regulation', *The Guardian* (16 April 2018) <https://www.theguardian.com/technology/2018/apr/16/cambridge-analytica-scandal-highlights-need-for-ai-regulation> accessed 26 May 2021.

[29]   Marwala and Hurwitz (n. 7).

[30]   Digital Culture, Media and Sport Committee, 'Disinformation and "fake news"' (Interim Report, HC 363, 2018) para. 78; see also 'UN: Facebook has turned into a beast in Myanmar', BBC News (13 March 2018) <https://www.bbc.co.uk/news/technology-43385677> accessed 9 August 2021.

[31]   Lawrence and Brazier (n. 5); see also Russell and Norvig (n. 21); P. Langley, 'The changing science of machine learning' (2011) 82 *Machine Learning* 275.

[32]   Pennachin and Goertzel (n. 13) 1.

[33]   See Lawrence and Morley (n. 7); see also R. Muller, 'Artificial intelligence is not as smart as you (or Elon Musk) think', *TechCrunch* (25 July 2017) <https://techcrunch.com/2017/07/25/artificial-intelligence-is-not-as-smart-as-you-or-elon-musk-think/?guccounter=1> accessed 30 July 2020.

[34]   P. Allen, 'The singularity isn't near', *MIT Technology Review* (12 October 2011) <https://www.technologyreview.com/s/425733/paul-allen-the-singularity-isnt-near/> accessed 27 May 2020.

[35]   Creighton (n. 22).

researchers assert that human-level cognition will be achieved across a number of metrics in the next few decades'.[36]

There are a number of companies developing what are known as deep learning systems. Deep learning was 'inspired by the structure and function of the brain, namely the interconnecting of many neurons'.[37] One of the deep learning programmes currently available is Cyc – a 'software [that] combines an unparalleled common sense knowledge base with powerful inference engines and natural language interfaces to deliver human-like understanding'.[38] AlphaGo Zero is an often-referenced deep learning machine, which won a game of Go by beating the world's best human player in 2017.[39] To achieve the win, AlphaGo Zero had been 'teaching itself winning strategies', rather than relying on the input of data or human knowledge.[40] Although these achievements in AI are impressive, winning a difficult strategy game falls short of what would be considered as real human intelligence. This is because AlphaGo Zero is not 'programmed to do anything else other than play Go'.[41] However, artificial 'neural networks' that 'acquaint themselves with the world via trial and error, as toddlers do, might in turn develop something like human flexibility'.[42] If this point is reached in the future, there will be extremely difficult challenges for regulating these novel beings, such as if or how AGI might be responsible for its own decisions. If there is already a regulatory framework in place then these challenges will be more easily faced and the potential for harms significantly reduced.

---

[36]   'Experts predict when artificial intelligence will exceed human performance', *MIT Technology Review* (31 May 2018) <https://www.technologyreview.com/s/607970/experts-predict-when-artificial-intelligence-will-exceed-human-performance/> accessed 7 August 2020.

[37]   R. D. Hof, 'Deep learning', *MIT Technology Review* <https://www.technologyreview.com/s/513696/deep-learning/> accessed 31 July 2020.

[38]   Cycorp <http://www.cyc.com> accessed 25 July 2020.

[39]   J. Russell, 'Google's AlphaGo AI wins three-match series against the world's best Go player', *TechCrunch* (25 May 2017) <https://techcrunch.com/2017/05/24/alphago-beats-planets-best-human-go-player-ke-jie/> accessed 7 August 2020.

[40]   A. McAfee and E. Brynjolfsson, 'Where computers defeat humans, and where they can't', *New York Times* (16 March 2018) <https://www.nytimes.com/2016/03/16/opinion/where-computers-defeat-humans-and-where-they-cant.html?_r=0> accessed 27 July 2020.

[41]   Muller (n. 33).

[42]   G. Lewis-Kraus, 'The great A.I. awakening', *New York Times Magazine* (14 December 2016) <https://www.nytimes.com/2016/12/14/magazine/the-great-ai-awakening.html> accessed 24 July 2020.

2.2   Synthetic Biology

There is no settled definition of what constitutes synthetic biology, but it can be described as an 'interdisciplinary field which combines molecular biology and engineering to obtain new biological systems'.[43] Scientists in this area have already made significant leaps towards creating artificial life. In 2010, researchers from the J. Craig Venter Institute (JCVI) and Synthetic Genomics, Inc. (SGI) designed and constructed the first minimal synthetic bacteria cell, JCVI-syn3.0.[44] This was the first successful attempt to design and create a new species from man-made genetic 'instructions'. It signified 'a major step toward our ability to design and build synthetic organisms from the bottom up'.[45]

Academic literature and governmental consultations into the development of new technology generally focus on AI and often overlook synthetic biology. This is at best short-sighted. Developments in this area are more likely to create beings of human-level intelligence and reasoning in a shorter timeframe than developments in AI. By doing so, they will raise profound questions about the concept and creation of new biological life forms. Protocell synthetic biology, in particular, aims to produce living organisms from inanimate materials, and if achieved, could be understood as *creating* life.[46]

Much scientific and ethical debate surrounds whether the bacterium created by JCVI is indeed a 'life form' and what moral status this or any similar organism developed from this research could be given. Critics, in particular, question why the creation of synthetic biology is different from other genetic engineering (such as selective breeding) and consequently why different legal strategies should be implemented.[47] There are, however, 'certain ethical implications of synthetic biology [that] go beyond those of genetic engineering',[48] including 'the range and specificity of human control over the organism's properties'.[49]

---

[43]   Endy (n. 13).

[44]   J. Craig Venter Institute, 'First minimal synthetic bacterial cell designed and constructed by scientists at Venter Institute and Synthetic Genomics, Inc.', Press Release (21 March 2016) <https://www.jcvi.org/first-minimal-synthetic-bacterial-cell-designed-and-constructed-scientists-venter-institute-and> accessed 25 July 2020.

[45]   C. Hutchison et al., 'Design and synthesis of a minimal bacterial genome' (2016) 351 *Science* 6253.

[46]   See L. Gómez-Tatay, J. M. Hernández-Andreu and J. Aznar, 'A personalist ontological approach to synthetic biology' (2016) 30 *Bioethics* 397.

[47]   See A. Christiansen, 'Synthetic biology and the moral significance of artificial life: a reply to Douglas, Powell and Savulescu' (2016) 30 *Bioethics* 372.

[48]   J. Boldt and O. Müller, 'Newtons of the leaves of grass' (2008) 26 *Nature Biotechnology* 387.

[49]   Christiansen (n. 47).

Thus, more thought must be given to whether, and under what conditions, it is acceptable to allow companies to produce these biological artificial life forms.[50] The law is currently severely under-equipped to deal with these scenarios and the continuance of self-regulation in this instance would be, to say the least, unwise.[51]

We cannot predict the developmental trajectory of these technologies and therefore the risks and harms posed by all MST are difficult to precisely assess. However, it is incredibly important to consider these challenges before it is too late, in order to develop a sufficient regulatory response.

3   CURRENT REGULATION AND GOVERNMENTAL ENQUIRY

The focus of this chapter is placed on the UK government and regulation strategies for this jurisdiction; however, the issues raised by MST, which includes novel beings, and corporate self-regulation will be problematic for many countries around the world. Though the balance between state and self-regulation may play out differently in different institutional environments, it is clear that, at a transnational level, states will need to have some co-ordination for the regulation of corporations and MST.[52] The issues and harms this technology can cause transcend state borders (demonstrating the need for co-ordination of company and securities laws, corporate governance and disclosure and transparency rules).

Whilst MST has been the subject of UK governmental enquiry it is argued that it has been limited in scope and has done little to reduce the harmful consequences of MST. Specifically, insufficient attention has been given to the development and operation of MST and the current inability to hold corporations accountable. Remarkably, the 178-page report, produced by the House of Lords Artificial Intelligence Select Committee ('the Select Committee'), titled 'AI in the UK: ready willing and able?',[53] did not comment on the limitations of self-regulation. This chapter aims to add clarity to this debate by addressing the gap in this enquiry by outlining the structural defects of the current self-regulating system, which relies on non-regulatory frameworks such as

---

[50]   Ibid.

[51]   See the Opinion of the European Group on Ethics in Science and New Technologies to the European Commission, 'Ethics of Synthetic Biology' (No 25, 2013) 81.

[52]   See R. Brownsword, 'Legal regulation of technology: supporting innovation, managing risk and respecting values' in T. L. Pittinsky (ed.), *Science, Technology and Society: New Perspectives and Directions* (Cambridge University Press, 2019).

[53]   'AI in the UK: ready, willing and able?' (n. 4).

CSR. This is particularly important as without this enquiry we may unwittingly grant corporations too much control without appropriate redress for harm.

The Select Committee was largely concerned, among other things, with transparency in designing AI, productivity (such as the potential impact of AI on the labour market), and how we might mitigate the risks of AI (including legal liability). Whilst the report was well informed and an important first step in considering the impact AI will have on society, like much of academic literature, it largely debated the risks associated with autonomous vehicles and weapons. Crucially, a large number of respondents to the report stated that no new AI-specific regulation was required. Whilst this may be true for the regulation of data, for example,[54] it does not address the current power that corporations have in not only developing and operating AI but also other categories of technology that fall into MSTs. It is crucial that we take account of corporations due to their significant economic power and ability to influence not only governments but also the general public.[55] The government's response to the Select Committee's report was similarly limited; focusing on the topics of data use and investment in AI development and employment. In regard to harms caused by AI, the government stated that it was not clear whether 'new mechanisms for legal liability and redress ... are required, or whether existing mechanisms are sufficient'.[56] It is clear, they noted, that 'clarity is required'.[57]

A later report, 'AI in the UK: No Room for Complacency',[58] produced by the Liaison Committee, examined the progress of the government in implementing the recommendations made by the Select Committee on Artificial Intelligence. Whilst the Liaison Committee commended the steps the government had taken, particularly in establishing a range of expert bodies to advise on AI policy in the long term,[59] they cautioned against complacency and asked for better co-ordination of the advisory bodies and policies.[60] The Liaison Committee additionally stated that current 'regulatory gaps are a cause for

---

[54]   'AI in the UK: ready, willing and able?' (n. 4) paras 69, 101–102, 373, 386 (the report and many respondents note that the data protection framework is already sufficient and that the General Data Protection Regulation would further strengthen that framework).

[55]   See Laidlaw (n. 17) 60.

[56]   'AI in the UK: ready, willing and able?' (n. 4) recommendations 55–56.

[57]   Ibid.

[58]   Liaison Committee, 'AI in the UK: No Room for Complacency' (2020, HL 196).

[59]   For example, the bodies include: the Artificial Intelligence Council, Centre for Data Ethics and Innovation, Ministerial Working Group on Future Regulation, Regulatory Horizon Council, Digital Regulation Navigator and the World Economic Forum.

[60]   'AI in the UK: No Room for Complacency' (n. 58) paras 71–73.

concern'[61] and that a 'solely self-regulatory approach to ethical standards risks a lack of uniformity and enforceability'.[62] The government responses included a recognition that the 'challenges posed by the development and deployment of AI cannot currently be tackled by cross-cutting regulation'[63] and that sector-specific regulators are better placed to identify gaps which could be filled by developing training courses.[64]

In April 2019, the European High-Level Expert Group on Artificial Intelligence went beyond the UK by releasing 'Ethics guidelines for trustworthy AI'.[65] These guidelines call for the respect of fundamental rights, principles and values when developing, deploying and using AI, for developers to continuously evaluate and assess the design and use of AI and provided an assessment list for 'trustworthy AI'.[66] Nevertheless, the guidelines only briefly discuss accountability by stating that organisations should set up their own governance frameworks.[67] This is *not* sufficient due to a lack of enforcement and accountability mechanisms of these types of frameworks,[68] the limitations of which will be addressed in the following sections of this chapter. In April 2021 the European Commission published the proposal of the new EU Artificial Intelligence Act.[69] This is one of the most significant pieces of legislation to regulate the ethical development of AI internationally and broadly imposes tailored obligations on different actors, such as manufacturers, importers, distributors and users. The development of this regulation is in its early stages and aims to ensure the protection of fundamental rights and user safety as well as instilling trust in the development of AI technology.

---

[61] Ibid., para. 56.

[62] Ibid., para. 24.

[63] Department for Digital, Culture Media and Sport, 'Government response to the House of Lords Select Committee on Artificial Intelligence' (CP390, February 2021) paras 60–70.

[64] Ibid.

[65] High-Level Expert Group on Artificial Intelligence, 'Ethics guidelines for trustworthy AI' (B-1049 Brussels April 2019).

[66] Ibid., 2: 'Trustworthy AI has three components ... (1) it should be lawful ... (2) it should be ethical, ensuring adherence to ethical principles and values and (3) it should be robust.'

[67] Ibid., 23; see also High-Level Expert Group on Artificial Intelligence, 'Final Assessment for Trustworthy Artificial Intelligence' (July 2020) <https://digital-strategy .ec.europa.eu/en/library/assessment-list-trustworthy-artificial-intelligence-altai-self -assessment> accessed 28 July 2021.

[68] Ibid., 22 (the guidelines note that regulation may need to be revised, adapted or introduced).

[69] Regulation of the European Parliament and of the Council Laying Down Harmonised Rules on Artificial Intelligence (Artificial Intelligence Act) and Amending Certain Union Legislative Acts, COM/2021/206 Final.

It is not beyond the UK government to introduce legislation to curb self-regulation for technology corporations. In April 2019, the government introduced the world's first online safety laws as part of the Online Harms White Paper.[70] These proposed legislative measures aim to ensure that online platforms remove illegal content, and prioritise the protection of users, especially children, young people and vulnerable adults. The White Paper proposed a statutory duty of care and a new set of codes of practice that will be overseen and enforced by an independent regulator.[71] The regulator will be given appropriate powers to ensure compliance, which may include fines and individual liability.

The proposed regulation comes after much criticism of corporations' attempts at self-regulation.[72] Margot James, who was serving as the Minister for Digital and Creative Industries, expressed her concerns that the response of large platforms had fallen short. She remarked:

> There have been no fewer than fifteen voluntary codes of practice agreed with platforms since 2008. Where we are now is an absolute indictment of a system that has relied far too little on the rule of law.[73]

The White Paper also stated that voluntary initiatives 'have not gone far or fast enough, or been consistent enough between different companies, to keep UK users safe online'.[74] After the public consultation on the White Paper proposals the government produced the final policy position on the online safety regulatory framework and announced that it would be enshrined in law as the Online Safety Bill. The White Paper stated legislation was necessary in order to 'rebuild public confidence and set clear expectations of companies, allowing our citizens to enjoy more safely the benefits that online services offer'.[75] The proposed legislation comes despite efforts from platforms such as Facebook, now Meta, to improve self-regulation following these criticisms.[76]

---

[70]   Home Department by Command of Her Majesty, 'Online Harms' (White Paper, CP57, April 2019).

[71]   Home Department by Command of Her Majesty, 'Online Harms' (White Paper, CP354, December 2020) ('Online Harms White Paper').

[72]   See DCMS, 'Disinformation and "fake news"' (n. 7).

[73]   Margot James speech on Safer Internet Day (gov.uk, February 2019) <https://www.gov.uk/government/speeches/margot-james-speech-on-safer-internet-day> accessed 3 April 2020.

[74]   Online Harms White Paper (n. 71) para. 8.

[75]   Online Harms White Paper (n. 71) para. 1.

[76]   However, in an op ed written for the *Washington Post*, Mark Zuckerberg welcomed attempts to regulate online content. See Mark Zuckerberg, 'The Internet needs new rules. Let's start in these four areas', *Washington Post* (April 2019) <https://www.washingtonpost.com/opinions/mark-zuckerberg-the-internet-needs-new-rules-lets

This proposed regulation is welcomed and demonstrates the failure of corporations to self-regulate on these issues; but the regulation is narrow in scope and therefore does not provide for the development and operation of MST. It is largely aimed at ensuring platforms properly 'police' the content posted by members of the public.

A matter of great concern lies in that no existing legislation appears to have the power to regulate or control the behaviour of these companies in developing and operating MST.[77] As Dignam notes, the governance of 'the leading technology corporations is in general unusually autocratic and unaccountable even in the context of weak private sector accountability'.[78] There are existing Acts which might be pointed to in the realm of digital technology and the computer sciences, but these seem to have little direct applicability to the development of AI, and more crucially, novel beings. The Computer Misuse Act 1990 is chiefly concerned with offences related to unauthorised access to systems and data.[79] The Data Protection Act 2018 places focus on the rights of data subjects, and the responsibilities of controllers in the collection of information; the intention being to ensure that data accrued is both correct, and fit for purpose.[80] As Laidlaw observes, we cannot 'have a system of private governance running alongside the law, with its own rules, often variable and unknown, concerning what is acceptable and not acceptable'.[81]

4   A CONCEPTUALISATION OF CSR

In view of the serious and profound issues raised by MST, it is argued that a non-legal regulatory strategy, such as CSR, is not suitably equipped to ensure the responsible behaviour of corporations. To illustrate this, Section 4 will give a brief conceptualisation of CSR and Section 5 will then identify the strategic weaknesses of this strategy in ensuring corporations develop MST responsibly and transparently.

-start-in-these-four-areas/2019/03/29/9e6f0504-521a-11e9-a3f7-78b7525a8d5f_story .html?utm_term=.9caa6bf5bccb> accessed 3 April 2021.

[77]   See Lawrence and Morley (n. 7); A. Dignam, 'Artificial intelligence, tech corporate governance and the public interest regulatory response' (2020) 13 *Cambridge Journal of Regions, Economy and Society* 37.

[78]   A. Dignam, 'Artificial intelligence: the very human dangers of dysfunctional design and autocratic corporate governance' (2019) Queen Mary University of London Legal Studies Research Paper No 314/2019, 30 <https://papers.ssrn.com/sol3/papers .cfm?abstract_id=3382342> accessed 6 November 2020.

[79]   Computer Misuse Act 1990.

[80]   Data Protection Act 2018.

[81]   Laidlaw (n. 17) 244.

There are at least two different senses in which the concept of CSR is used: the first is a term that describes 'good corporate behaviour' and focuses on outcomes, including ongoing (repeated) practices. This can be illustrated by a corporation going beyond the minimum requirements of the law and acting as a 'good citizen'.[82] Merrick Dodd first discussed this concept in 1932:

> Customers have a right to demand that a concern so large shall not only do its business honestly and properly, but, further, that it shall meet its public obligations and perform its public duties – in a word, vast as it is, that it should be a good citizen.[83]

Dodd contends that, just as other persons have citizenship, so does the corporation, with social responsibilities that may be contrary to its economic objectives.[84] Corporations are therefore expected to exercise their powers in a socially responsible way, having regard to employees, customers and the general public.[85] Definitional work in CSR, in this sense, is therefore a 'normative exercise in setting out what corporations should be responsible for'.[86] The question of how a business should behave dominates this CSR research. Briefly stated, questions of responsibility here go beyond obligations, such as legal duties or formal agreements, and are tied instead to the role corporations may play in creating harm from the development and operation of MSTs. A corporation may also be required to take responsibility for actions that are done or not done. There will be considerable difficulty in pinpointing what 'responsibility for MST' will mean in the corporate domain. When considering what responsible behaviour towards labour means, for example, we can draw from numerous pieces of domestic and international legislation (such

---

[82] E. M. Dodd Jr, 'For whom are corporate managers trustees?' (1932) 45 *Hard Law Review* 1145; there are also those who consider that CSR can take the form of legal obligations, see D. McBarnet, 'Corporate social responsibility beyond law, through law, for law: the new corporate accountability' in D. McBarnet, A. Voiculescu and T. Campbell (eds), *The New Corporate Accountability: Corporate Social Responsibility and the Law* (Cambridge University Press, 2007) (CSR goes 'through the law'); N. Gunningham, 'Corporate environmental responsibility, law and the limits of voluntarism' in D. McBarnet, A. Voiculescu and T. Campbell (eds), *The New Corporate Accountability: Corporate Social Responsibility and the Law* (Cambridge University Press, 2007); R. Janda, M. Kerr and C. Pitts, *Corporate Social Responsibility – A Legal Analysis* (LexisNexis, 2009).

[83] Dodd (n. 82) 1154.

[84] Ibid.

[85] See A. Dignam and J. Lowry, *Company Law* (Oxford University Press, 10th edn, 2018) 385.

[86] A. Crane et al., 'The corporate social responsibility agenda' in A. Crane, A. McWilliams, D. Matten, J. Moon and D. S. Siegel (eds), *The Oxford Handbook of Corporate Social Responsibility* (Oxford University Press, 2008) 6.

as human rights and employment law). This is not the case for MST due to significant gaps in regulation that directly address the accountability for the new challenges that these powerful technologies possess.[87]

A field of research that does consider these issues is the study of responsible research innovation (RRI), which considers how to direct technology and innovation towards socially desirable ends.[88] Parallels can be drawn between CSR and RRI,[89] which is broadly defined as 'a collective commitment of care for the future through responsive stewardship of science and innovation in the present'.[90] Aims of RRI include engaging stakeholders of corporations and the wider public in the early stages of research and development.[91] We cannot, however, rely on RRI to regulate corporations' behaviour alone. Whilst CSR tools can be used to implement RRI, this approach still relies heavily on self-regulation and therefore will not be sufficient.

The strand of CSR that is of importance to the subject of this chapter is that which emphasises a set of *strategies*, which corporations can implement to achieve (what corporations perceive as) socially responsible behaviour. This usage is less concerned with determining the social responsibilities of corporations, but focuses more on identifying the (non-legal) strategies that should be employed. These strategies are usually voluntary practices whereby corporations adopt policies that reflect the corporations' environmental, social and economic objectives. This means that there is a shift away from the state to private governance. Thus the 'voluntary' adoption of strategies by technology

---

[87] Determining what responsibility means in a corporate domain is certainly complex and requires separate consideration, and therefore goes beyond the work in this chapter. See D. Tigard, 'Responsible AI and moral responsibility: a common appreciation' (2021) 1 *AI and Ethics* 113; V. Dignum, *Responsible Artificial Intelligence: How to Develop and Use AI in a Responsible Way* (Springer, 2019).

[88] See R. Owen, J. Stilgoe, P. Macnaghten, M. Gorman, E. Fisher and D. Guston, 'A framework for responsible innovation' in R. Owen, J. Bessant and M. Heintz (eds), *Responsible Innovation: Managing the Responsible Emergence of Science and Innovation in Society* (John Wiley & Sons, 2013).

[89] Several authors have made this connection between RRI and CSR: K. Iatridis and D. Schroeder, *Responsible Research and Innovation in Industry: The Case for Corporate Responsibility Tools* (Springer, 2016); I. Van de Poel, L. Asveld, S. Flipse, P. Klaassen, V. Scholten and E. Yaghmaei, 'Company strategies for responsible research and innovation (RRI): a conceptual model' (2017) 9 *Sustainability* 2045; R. Owen, P. Macnaghten and J. Stilgoe, 'Responsible research and innovation: from science in society to science for society, with society' (2012) 39 *Science and Public Policy* 751, 754, 755; C. Voegtlin and A. Scherer, 'Responsible innovation and the innovation of responsibility: governing sustainable development in a globalized world' (2017) 143 *Journal of Business Ethics* 227.

[90] Owen et al. (2013) (n. 88) 36.

[91] Owen et al. (2012) (n. 89) 755.

firms for the responsible development of MST can be contrasted well to this field of CSR scholarship, because it addresses the use of strategies other than law to incentivise companies to behave well; therefore this strand of CSR study is a type of regulatory strategy.

There are a number of non-legal strategies adopted under the umbrella of CSR that incentivise good corporate behaviour. These strategies can be internal, such as the adoption of CSR initiatives and codes of conduct, and undertaking social responsibility reporting; or external CSR strategies, whereby good behaviour is compelled by the market and the 'social gaze'. These strategies will now be briefly discussed in turn.

Internal 'CSR initiatives' is a broad term that is defined, for the purposes of this chapter, as policies that are adopted by corporations in an operational manner that affect the day-to-day management of the company and implement, in a more practical way, the corporation's overall CSR objectives. These initiatives can be employed in management standards, responsible supply chain management, and the appointment of corporate responsibility officers. Codes of conduct are complementary to CSR initiatives, and may, in more broad terms, state the corporation's CSR policies.

Codes of conduct are adopted by the vast majority of multinational corporations[92] and can be categorised into two types: public and private. Public codes of conduct, such as the UN Global Compact, are developed by international organisations and are then implemented by corporations. The Compact asks corporations to 'align strategies and operations with universal principles on human rights, labour, environment and anti-corruption, and take actions that advance societal goals'.[93] The OECD also published comprehensive codes, which include standards on human rights, transparency, employment, the environment, combating bribery, consumer interests, and competition and taxation.[94] All such approaches draw their theoretical framework from the Universal Declaration of Human Rights.[95]

The second type of codes is those developed by private actors, such as the corporations themselves and civil society actors. Private codes of conduct seek

---

[92]   M. S. Schwartz, 'Universal moral values for corporate codes of ethics' (2005) 59 *Journal of Business Ethics* 27.

[93]   United Nations, Global Compact <https://www.unglobalcompact.org/what-is -gc> accessed 5 December 2020.

[94]   OECD Guidelines for Multinational Enterprises (2011) <http://www.oecd.org/ daf/inv/mne/48004323.pdf?_ga=2.125359306.1173204165.1546596347404115753 .1546596347> accessed 4 January 2021.

[95]   See T. Campbell, 'The normative grounding of corporate social responsibility: a human rights approach' in D. McBarnet et al. (eds), *The New Corporate Accountability: Corporate Social Responsibility and the Law* (Cambridge University Press, 2007) 553–554.

to set benchmarks for a company's own behaviour and often that of their subsidiaries and suppliers. As Matten and Moon note, 'the precise manifestation and direction of [these policies] lie at the discretion of the corporation'.[96] Note that this is usually the strategy taken for policies on MST too.

Social responsibility reporting is also standard practice for large and medium-sized firms around the world. These reports integrate financial and non-financial information, and often link CSR activity with the UN's Sustainable Development Goals,[97] such as cutting carbon emissions. External reporting of companies' non-financial reports began as a response to demands for more transparency and accountability surrounding environmental issues in the 1960s and 1970s. Whilst some CSR reporting is completed voluntarily, it is important to note that the majority of the reports produced are required by regulation. Corporations are, for example, compelled to produce reports under stock exchange rules and there is a continuing growth in disclosures required by governments for environmental and social governance. For instance, the EU Non-Financial Reporting Directive requires disclosure of non-financial information by large companies (though similar legislation already existed in the UK, Germany and Sweden).[98] In the USA companies are also required to carry out climate change-related disclosure in Securities and Exchange Commission (SEC) filings, and the SEC publishes industry-specific Sustainability Accounting Standards, which advise on the CSR disclosures that should be included in the filings.[99]

There are also external pressures on corporations to adopt CSR initiatives. Over the last three decades the public has increasingly demanded greater protection for the environment and better working conditions for labour, which in turn has led to an increased commitment from corporations to these issues. This is known as the 'social gaze', operating as a form of 'soft regulation', which can inform responsible business behaviour without recourse to legal regulation.[100] CSR initiatives can therefore have a 'soft' positive effect by

---

[96] D. Matten and J. Moon, '"Implicit" and "explicit" CSR: a conceptual framework for a comparative understanding of corporate social responsibility' (2010) 33 *Academy of Management Review* 404, 407.

[97] KPMG, 'The Road Ahead: The KPMG Survey of Corporate Responsibility Reporting' (2017) 5.

[98] Directive 2014/95/EU of the European Parliament and of the Council of 22 October 2014 amending Directive 2013/34/EU as regards disclosure of non-financial and diversity information by certain large undertakings and groups Text with EEA relevance.

[99] See Sustainability Accounting Standards Board <https://www.sasb.org> accessed 10 January 2021.

[100] See J. Moon, *Corporate Social Responsibility: A Very Short Introduction* (Oxford University Press, 2014).

recognising a certain level of responsibility and by responding to stakeholder concerns.

5 LIMITATIONS OF CSR AS A REGULATORY FRAMEWORK FOR MST

Whilst CSR has produced a number of positive and noteworthy changes in corporate behaviour,[101] there are a number of strategic weaknesses to using self-regulation or 'voluntarism'. I argue that five limitations are significant in the context of regulating MST. These are: (i) different perspectives on what is 'good corporate behaviour' and in agreeing core universal values for MST; (ii) credibility of voluntarism as a regulatory tool, including the use of voluntarism to appease shareholders and stakeholders ('greenwashing'); (iii) the contents of codes of conduct are often vague and unmeasurable; (iv) corporations can fail in assessing the risk of their activities; and finally, (v) there is an inability to effectively enforce CSR codes and principles. Crucially, these weaknesses demonstrate that CSR alone does not have the structural capacity to properly govern MST.

5.1 Consensus on 'Good Corporate Behaviour'?

Comparative research completed by Matten and Moon found 'remarkable differences' in CSR strategies between corporations in Europe and the USA. One difficulty in standardising CSR practices is that there is no single agreed-upon definition of what CSR is, despite a vast literature discussing this principle.

Differing standards are largely due to the language companies use in describing their involvement in society.[102] This will only be exacerbated when we include MST – the developments are so new and unpredictable that it will be very hard to use language with any specificity from company to company. Divergent corporate practices also arise from the different social and political contexts in which businesses operate, including attitudes to education and labour, and the historical development of regulatory frameworks that shape the national financial and market systems.[103] Thus, the ethical development of these technologies will look different depending on each jurisdiction.

For example, AI companies such as CloudWalk, Yitu and SenseTime have partnered with the Chinese government to roll out targeted facial recognition

---

[101] See D. Vogel, *The Market for Virtue* (Brookings Institution, 2005).

[102] Matten and Moon (n. 96).

[103] See ibid.; P. A. Hall and D. Soskice (eds), *Varieties of Capitalism* (Oxford University Press, 2001); R. Whitley, 'The institutional approach' (1997) 4 *Organization* 289.

and predictive policing. The use of this technology has been instrumental in the imprisonment of minority groups, such as the Uighur Muslims, in detention camps.[104] China defends the use of this AI as necessary in the fight against 'radicalisation', but this amounts to the deliberate targeting of minority groups. This highlights the 'blind spot in expert control laws, and a way in which the Chinese government can leverage overseas expertise in AI'.[105] Similarly, police forces in the Philippines have utilised technology developed by IBM to fight a war on drugs. This has led to thousands being killed in 'extrajudicial executions'.[106]

What is particularly problematic is that 'codes of ethics, by their very definition, imply that they contain normative guidelines for behaviour'.[107] Yet, with regard to MST, there are no accepted standards to draw on. As Mark Schwartz notes:

> [A] corporate code of ethics that is based merely on the desired moral values of the individual CEO, the legal department, or even an ethics consultant, is arguably a relativistic document that merely suits the objectives of the author.[108]

Dignam's detailed account of the ownership structures and connections between the largest technology companies demonstrates that a few powerful men dictate the agenda for the regulation of MST.[109] He observes that:

> Almost all have unusual private-sector governance structures designed in general to give control to a small group of insiders with tight connections to each other and very similar backgrounds and interests.[110]

---

[104] P. Mozur, 'One month, 500,000 face scans: how China is using A.I. to profile a minority', *New York Times* (14 April 2019) <https://www.nytimes.com/2019/04/14/technology/china-surveillance-artificial-intelligence-racial-profiling.html> accessed 8 October 2020; H. Davidson, 'Alibaba offered clients facial recognition to identify Uighur people, report reveals', *The Guardian* (17 December 2020) <https://www.theguardian.com/business/2020/dec/17/alibaba-offered-clients-facial-recognition-to-identify-uighur-people> accessed 6 July 2021.

[105] 'Western AI researchers partnered with Chinese surveillance firms', *Financial Times* (19 April 2019) <https://www.ft.com/content/41be9878-61d9-11e9-b285-3acd5d43599e> accessed 8 October 2020.

[106] C. Fonbuena, 'Philippines police chief and Duterte drug war enforcer resigns in meth scandal', *The Guardian* (14 October 2019) <https://www.theguardian.com/world/2019/oct/14/philippines-police-chief-and-duterte-drug-war-enforcer-resigns-in-meth-scandal> accessed 8 October 2020.

[107] See Schwartz (n. 92).

[108] Ibid., 57.

[109] See Dignam (n. 77).

[110] Dignam (n. 78) 44.

He also warns that the situation where 'autocrats who live, work and hang out together in small geographic locations brings with it an obvious and urgent concern of disproportionate influence and unrepresentative group think',[111] and argues that the industry itself will insert its own private interests, which may directly work against the public interest.[112]

Consequently, CSR initiatives that speak to the responsible and transparent development of MST may lack ethical justification and legitimacy.[113] Furthermore, as Berenbeim argues, if there are no established principles, there is a risk that there will be a 'race to the bottom' with respect to business practices.[114] Even companies acting in good faith may have different perspectives on what is morally or ethically acceptable; which is an inevitability considering the difficulties in agreeing international standards of ethics.[115] The specific problem then, comes where companies each adopt their own standards for MST, or fail to do so. This phenomenon can already be seen in the wildly different CSR standards and initiatives presently in use.[116]

The UK government shares these concerns: in its response to the House of Lords Artificial Intelligence Select Committee's Report on AI in the UK, it noted, 'it is clear that there is a lack of wider awareness and co-ordination'.[117] They have recommended a cross-sector ethical code of conduct, or 'AI code', suitable for implementation across public and private sector organisations which are developing or adopting AI.[118] This, however, does not address several important issues such as whether this code would be required to be adopted and how, or even if, it will be enforced. It is also exclusively related to AI and ignores other important MSTs, such as synthetic biology and our novel beings.

5.2   The Credibility of CSR Strategies

Corporations have been repeatedly criticised for adopting initiatives that are used for marketing purposes in order to 'present a human and caring face of

---

[111]   Ibid., 40.

[112]   Ibid., 25.

[113]   Ibid.

[114]   R. E. Berenbeim, *Global Corporate Ethics Practices: A Developing Consensus* (The Conference Board, 1999) 697.

[115]   See, for example, the creation of the Cairo Declaration on Human Rights in Islam 1990 over disagreements with the moral basis of elements of the Universal Declaration of Human Rights 1948.

[116]   See Moon (n. 100).

[117]   Government response to 'AI in the UK: ready, willing and able?' (n. 4) para. lxviii.

[118]   Ibid., para. lxxiv.

business'.[119] Whilst there are genuine attempts made by corporations to implement better practices, CSR has often been used in response to an issue or event that has shown the company in a poor light. Consequently, CSR strategies are often referred to as 'window dressing' or 'greenwashing'.

Facebook, now Meta, was accused of such behaviour after the Cambridge Analytica scandal.[120] In early 2018, Facebook CEO Mark Zuckerberg testified before Congress about the reports that Cambridge Analytica had obtained personal data on up to 87 million Facebook users, in violation of Facebook's rules.[121] The company then released a short advert in an attempt to win back consumer trust. It stated:

> We came here for the friends … But then something happened. We had to deal with spam, clickbait, fake news, and data misuse. That's going to change. From now on, Facebook will do more to keep you safe and protect your privacy.[122]

Lisa Stratton, a spokesperson for Facebook, stated:

> As you heard from Mark in his congressional testimony, we are taking a broader view of our responsibilities … We hope this campaign will show that we take our responsibility seriously, and are working to improve Facebook for everyone.[123]

Whilst this type of response to social pressure can lead to improved CSR strategies, it can often be meaningless with no real change being implemented. It is difficult, at present, to see what Facebook has changed in order to better protect their users' data. The disinformation and 'fake news' report produced by the Digital Culture, Media and Sport Committee (DCMS) stated, 'Despite all the apologies for past mistakes that Facebook has made, it still seems unwilling to be properly scrutinised.'[124]

Ashkan Soltani, former Chief Technologist to the US Federal Trade Commission (FTC) stated, 'There is that contemptuousness—that ability to feel like the company knows more than all of you and all the policy makers.'[125]

---

[119] Moon (n. 100) 112.
[120] See DCMS, 'Disinformation and "fake news"' (n. 7).
[121] N. Tiku, 'Facebook launches a new ad campaign with an old message', *Wired* (26 April 2018) <https://www.wired.com/story/facebook-launches-a-new-ad -campaign-with-an-old-message/> accessed 7 December 2020.
[122] Facebook, 'Here Together' <https://www.youtube.com/watch?time_continue= 31&v=Q4zd7X98eOs> accessed 7 December 2020.
[123] Tiku (n. 121).
[124] See DCMS, 'Disinformation and "fake news"' (n. 7) para. 27.
[125] Digital, Culture, Media and Sport International Grand Committee, 'Oral Evidence: Disinformation and "fake news"' (Questions 4274–4382, HC 363, November 2018) Q4337 ('DCMS Oral Evidence').

Soltani spoke of an example regarding the California Consumer Privacy Act, which Facebook supported in public, but lobbied against behind the scenes.[126] The DCMS report also stated that the 'management structure of Facebook is opaque to those outside the business and this seemed to be designed to conceal knowledge of and responsibility for specific decisions'.[127] Failures to properly 'police' content on online platforms culminated in the Online Harms White Paper's proposal for new regulation.

Vogel argues that CSR will only be successful if corporations can see added value in their bottom line.[128] Dignam agrees, stating that a huge driver of AI decision-making development is cost.[129] This is also evidenced by the exploitative practices used by a number of multinational corporations, including taking advantage of lower regulatory standards in developing countries for employment law, health and safety, and the enforcement of human rights.[130] This is seen in the examples of the use of facial recognition software. Google too has been guilty of this behaviour: ethics advisors resigned in protest from Google in 2019 due to the development of 'Project Dragonfly'. This involved a plan to develop a censored search engine for China, even though the company had promised just two months earlier not to design or deploy technology that 'contravenes ... human rights'.[131] This practice has been at the root of a number of major legal cases and scandals over recent years, including the suicides at

---

[126] DCMS Oral Evidence (n. 125) Q4330.

[127] DCMS, 'Disinformation and "fake news"' (n. 7) para. 30.

[128] Vogel (n. 101).

[129] See Dignam (n. 77).

[130] See A. O. Adeyeye, *Corporate Social Responsibility of Multinational Corporations in Developing Countries Perspectives on Anti-Corruption* (Cambridge University Press, 2012); G. Knight, 'Activism, risk, and communicational politics: Nike and the sweatshop problem' in S. May, G. Cheney and J. Roper (eds), *The Debate over Corporate Social Responsibility* (Oxford University Press, 2007) 305; O. Amao, 'Corporate social responsibility, multinational corporations and the law in Nigeria: controlling multinationals in host states' (2008) 52 *Journal of African Law* 89.

[131] Madhumita Murgia, 'How Big Tech is struggling with the ethics of AI', *Financial Times* (29 April 2019) <https://www.ft.com/content/a3328ce4-60ef-11e9 -b285-3acd5d43599e> accessed 10 October 2020.

Apple's supplier Foxconn,[132] Shell's oil spill in the Niger Delta,[133] the Rana Plaza collapse,[134] and the Deepwater Horizon disaster.[135]

As Laidlaw describes, Enron too had a code of conduct to prevent corporate crime, but because 'the culture of Enron was geared to increase the price of stock the code was ignored or overridden'.[136] 'Executives aimed instead for the bottom line and relied on legal advice that what they were doing was lawful.'[137] The DCMS report also concluded that the Cambridge Analytica scandal was facilitated by Facebook's own policies.[138]

Whilst CSR can be an effective means of controlling socially irresponsible behaviour by corporations, 'it is an extremely fragile asset'[139] and there may not be incentives for businesses to go beyond business as usual.[140] CSR therefore struggles to overcome the criticism that it is a weak window dressing that may only serve to deflect public opinion and much-needed legislation. This becomes even more problematic when we consider the content of these policies and codes and their application to MST.

---

[132] See M. Moore, 'Mass suicide protest at Apple manufacturer Foxconn factory', *The Telegraph* (11 January 2012) <https://www.telegraph.co.uk/news/worldnews/asia/china/9006988/Mass-suicide-protest-at-Apple-manufacturer-Foxconn-factory.html> accessed 27 May 2021; J. Chan and N. Pun, 'Suicide as protest for the new generation of Chinese migrant workers: Foxconn, global capital, and the state' (2010) 37 *Asia-Pacific Journal* 1.

[133] H. Mustoe, 'Shell being sued in two claims over oil spills in Nigeria', BBC News (2 March 2016) <https://www.bbc.co.uk/news/business-35701607> accessed 29 January 2021.

[134] D. Thomas, 'Why won't we learn from the survivors of the Rana Plaza disaster?', *New York Times* (24 April 2018) <https://www.nytimes.com/2018/04/24/style/survivors-of-rana-plaza-disaster.html> accessed 27 May 2021.

[135] M. A. Cherry and J. F. Sneirson, 'Beyond profit: rethinking corporate social responsibility and greenwashing after the BP oil disaster' (2011) 85 *Tulane Law Review* 983.

[136] Laidlaw (n. 17) 71.

[137] Ibid., citing C. Pitts and J. Sherman, 'Human Rights Corporate Accountability Guide: From Laws to Norms to Values', Working Paper No. 51, Corporate Social Responsibility Initiative (December 2008) 15–16.

[138] See DCMS, 'Disinformation and "fake news"' (n. 7) paras 76–97 ('it is clear that spending substantial sums with Facebook, as a condition of maintaining preferential access to personal data, was part and parcel of the company's strategy of platform development as it embraced the mobile advertising world. And that this approach was driven from the highest level.').

[139] M. L. Pava, 'Why corporations should *not* abandon social responsibility' (2008) 83 *Journal of Business Ethics* 805, 805.

[140] R. Reich, *Supercapitalism: The Transformation of Business, Democracy, and Everyday Life* (Vintage, 2008).

5.3   Content of CSR Policies and Codes

Although a vast majority of multinational corporations have voluntarily
adopted internal CSR strategies, the language used by corporations is often
poor, particularly in regard to codes of conduct.

Google's codes adopted for MST are illustrative of this point. In June
2018, Google announced seven principles for AI that would guide the development of their technology going forward.[141] This announcement was made
shortly after thousands of Google employees protested against the company's
'involvement in a Pentagon program that uses artificial intelligence to interpret video imagery ... [that] could be used to improve the targeting of drone
strikes'.[142] The new code distances Google from drone warfare by promising
that it will not be involved in the design or deployment of AI '[w]eapons or
other technologies whose principal purpose or implementation is to cause or
directly facilitate injury to people'.[143] Google have stated that the principles
'are not theoretical concepts they are concrete standards that will actively
govern our research and product development and will impact our business
decisions'.[144]

It is commendable that Google has taken steps to address the responsible development of this technology; however, the content of the code is
vague, unmeasurable and unenforceable. The 'Objectives for AI Applications'
include Google's belief that AI should be 'socially beneficial', 'accountable
to people' and that it will 'uphold high standards of scientific excellence'.
Yet, these promises made by Google only demonstrate low levels of integrity,
justice and utility, and only reach a basic standard that represents a minimally
acceptable level for each principle. Codes such as Google's are often cleverly
drafted and include selective content, and lack information about the implementation and impact of their policies.[145] This means that it is difficult to attach
any legal weight to these statements, including how to measure performance
against the statements, and making it impossible to detect breaches. Crucially,
because these statements are made voluntarily, and are vague in content, they
are impossible to enforce outside the corporation.

---

[141] 'AI at Google: our principles' (n. 9).

[142] S. S. D. Wakabayashi, '"The Business of War": Google employees protest work
for The Pentagon', *New York Times* (4 April 2018) <https://www.nytimes.com/2018/
04/04/technology/google-letter-ceo-pentagon-project.html> accessed 27 May 2021.

[143] 'AI at Google: our principles' (n. 9).

[144] Ibid.

[145] See C. Raiborn and D. Payne, 'Corporate codes of conduct: a collective conscience and continuum' (1990) 9 *Journal of Business Ethics* 879.

Sethi noted that corporations often present public statements which are 'lofty [in] intent and purpose but lacking specific content'.[146] For instance, Google's principle, 'to be socially beneficial', states that they will 'take account of a broad range of social and economic factors'. It does not expand on what those factors will be or how Google intends to prioritise social and economic interests should there be a conflict. As Laidlaw observes, in regard to regulation of speech on the internet: 'no company states that it is against human rights in general or free speech in particular. The breakdown happens when moving from these generalised commitments to the operationalisation of these commitments.'[147]

The difficulty in balancing competing interests is well documented in corporate stakeholder literature, which considers how companies can create value for stakeholders such as employees, customers and the community[148] (stakeholder identities and interests also vary cross-nationally).[149] Ultimately, the corporate objective, particularly in Anglo-American corporations, is to carry on the business in the interests of the shareholders.[150] This objective is often prioritised over stakeholders' interests and it is difficult to see how Google, or other multinational tech corporations, would put the interests of society or the technology above those of their shareholders – particularly when this is not made clear in the codes or policies.

We need only consider the use of personal data by Facebook and Cambridge Analytica in targeting political campaigns and their use of algorithms to change information made available to their users.[151] Companies, such as Facebook, state that they are passive actors; however, they control what we see on our social media platforms in order to generate revenue from adverts.[152] These companies are more than willing to manipulate their sites in order to drive profit and increase their global market share.[153] Consequently, it is difficult to believe that without regulation, companies would create CSR policies

---

[146] S. P. Sethi, 'Standards for corporate conduct in the international arena: challenges and opportunities for multinational corporations' (2002) 107 *Business and Society Review* 20, 23.

[147] Laidlaw (n. 17) 233.

[148] See R. E. Freeman, J. F. Harrison and S. Zyglidopoulos, *Stakeholder Theory: Concepts and Strategies (Elements in Organization Theory)* (Cambridge University Press, 2018).

[149] Matten and Moon (n 96).

[150] See A. Berle, 'Corporate powers as powers in trust' (1931) 44 *Harvard Law Review* 1049; see also *Greenhalgh v Arderne Cinemas Ltd (No 2)* [1946] 1 All ER 512.

[151] See DCMS, 'Disinformation and "fake news"' (n. 7).

[152] Ibid., paras 14, 19; see also DCMS, 'Disinformation and "fake news"' (Interim Report) (n. 30).

[153] See DCMS, 'Disinformation and "fake news"'(n. 7).

and codes with effective content and put stakeholders' interests, including the technology's own interests (should it gain sentience or sapience), above profit maximisation.

5.4   Assessment of Risk

Even if corporate policies were appropriate and effective it is important to ask whether initiatives or codes drafted by corporations, such as Google and Facebook, should drive the agenda for MST. Google states that they 'will proceed where we believe that the overall likely benefits substantially exceed the foreseeable risks and downsides'.[154] It should not be corporations that decide when benefits outweigh risks to society or assess what is 'a material risk of harm'.[155]

There are numerous high-profile examples of companies failing to properly assess risks that have caused significant harm to the economy and society, such as the failures that culminated in the 2008 financial crisis. These failures prompted further reform in risk assessment and disclosures required under the Corporate Governance Codes.[156]

Failures in risk assessment arose in the pedestrian death caused by an autonomous car operated by Uber.[157] The technical decisions made in testing the car ultimately may have contributed to the pedestrian's death. Although Uber was granted a licence in Arizona to test their autonomous car, decisions around how the testing was carried out and how the technical decisions were made, such as disabling the emergency braking system and not having a system to alert the operator when they were required to intervene,[158] were made without any regulatory oversight.

In order to provide some form of accountability and ensure risks are properly assessed, Google announced it would set up an ethics committee to ensure the company followed its AI principles. However, the committee was quickly dismantled only a week after it was established. Immediate criticism was raised due to Google's controversial appointment of Kay Coles James, the president of right-wing think tank 'The Heritage Foundation'. Google gave

---

[154] 'AI at Google: our principles' (n. 9).
[155] Ibid.
[156] See Corporate Governance Code 2018, para. 28.
[157] T. Lee, 'Report: Software bug led to death in Uber's self-driving crash', *Ars Technica* (7 May 2018) <https://arstechnica.com/tech-policy/2018/05/report-software -bug-led-to-death-in-ubers-self-driving-crash/> accessed 27 May 2021.
[158] America's National Transportation Safety Board, Preliminary Report (Highway HWY18MH010, 24 May 2018) <https://www.ntsb.gov/investigations/ AccidentReports/Reports/HWY18MH010-prelim.pdf> accessed 29 July 2020.

no insight into how it chose its members, but it is speculated that the decision was made in order 'to appease Republican lawmakers and to curry favour in the event of regulation around AI'.[159] Google has also been criticised for firing leaders of its ethics unit for speaking critically of the company.[160]

Microsoft also set up an AI ethics oversight committee, Aether, to assess the risks of its technology. The company noted that 'significant sales' had been cut off because of the group's recommendations. However, no explanation was provided as to why these products were deemed unsafe. It is therefore unclear as to how Microsoft assesses risks and where they 'draw the line on unethical uses of AI ... Only the company itself knows.'[161]

The refusal of these technology giants to provide transparency into their decision-making processes means it is extremely difficult to understand how they actually assess risk. The appointment of ethics boards may also be used to deflect criticism and to appear to provide oversight without the need for substantive change or reflection on the true risks of MST. Without transparency and disclosure, how can these corporations be held accountable?

5.5   Problematic Enforcement

I argued in the previous section that it is unlikely that corporations can provide sufficient internal regulation of their codes and policies; accordingly, these non-legal strategies will rely heavily on market regulation. It is, however, nearly impossible to monitor or check the veracity of claims made by corporations due to the information asymmetry that exists between the corporation and the market. This is troubling due to empirical evidence that suggests that reports, such as sustainability reports, do not always reflect the truth about a company's operations.[162] Access to information will be further exacerbated in MST as this technology is often developed in secret, which makes it extremely difficult for the market to enforce against breaches of codes or a corporation's bad behaviour. Whilst thousands of workers from Amazon, Microsoft – and most notably – Google, have joined protests against these

---

[159]   J. Vincent, 'The problem with AI ethics', *The Verge* (April 2019) <https://www.theverge.com/2019/4/3/18293410/ai-artificial-intelligence-ethics-boards-charters-problem-big-tech> accessed 8 October 2020.

[160]   'Margaret Mitchell: Google fires AI ethics founder', BBC News (20 February 2021) <https://www.bbc.co.uk/news/technology-56135817> accessed 6 July 2021.

[161]   Vincent (n. 159).

[162]   See J. Emel et al., 'Problems with reporting and evaluating mining industry community development projects: a case study from Tanzania' (2012) 4 *Sustainability* 257.

technology giants,[163] we should not have to rely on 'worker activists' to hold their employers accountable.

Even if the market is aware of bad behaviour, 'the public is a fickle disciplinarian'.[164] Grant found that 'although negative publicity has previously chastised companies for taking short-term environmental risks, it often fails to correct longer-term environmental harms'.[165] This is because the public are vulnerable to PR campaigns and 're-branding', which are likely to be 'more effective at alleviating the outrage over less visceral, longer-term environmental harms'.[166] Crucially, the market will be quick to forgive companies in the MST industry because there is only a small handful of technology companies that 'make products that are ostensibly useful'[167] (these corporations include Google, Facebook, Apple, Amazon, Microsoft). The DCMS Committee also highlighted the importance of considering this issue:

> [T]he dominance of a handful of powerful tech companies has resulted in their behaving as if they were monopolies in their specific area – Facebook, in particular, is unwilling to be accountable to regulators around the world. The Government should consider the impact of such monopolies on the political world and on democracy.[168]

Consumers therefore only have so much leverage,[169] and the market in this respect is unlikely to punish these companies, at least not for very long. Despite global backlash against Facebook, it is still one of the largest corporations in the world with over 2.91 billion active users.[170] In 2015 Amazon was criticised for using controversial corporate structures that reduced the amount

---

[163] See J. Bhuiyan, 'How the Google walkout transformed tech workers into activists', *LA Times* (6 November 2019) <https://www.latimes.com/business/technology/story/2019-11-06/google-employee-walkout-tech-industry-activism> accessed 23 June 2020.

[164] N. Grant, 'Mandating corporate environmental responsibility by creating a new directors' duty' (2015) 17 *Environmental Law Review* 252, 257.

[165] Ibid.

[166] Ibid.

[167] T. Hatmaker, 'Facebook, are you kidding?', *TechCrunch* (8 October 2018) <https://techcrunch.com/2018/10/08/facebook-portal-are-you-serious-rn/> accessed 19 November 2020.

[168] DCMS, 'Disinformation and "fake news"' (n. 7) para. 138.

[169] Hatmaker (n. 167).

[170] Statista <https://www.statista.com/statistics/264810/number-of-monthly-active-facebook-users-worldwide/> accessed 29 March 2022.

of their payable tax,[171] but it was the second corporation in the world to become a trillion-dollar company (after Apple).[172]

The ability for the market to enforce against bad behaviour is further eroded by the fact that MST is sailing into uncharted territory that the general public and other stakeholders may not quite understand. How, as lay people, can we properly assess the risks of MST, including how it should be developed and the potential consequences of its use. It is therefore unrealistic to expect the market alone to properly regulate MST, particularly if novel beings do emerge.

5.6   Lack of Liability for Voluntary Statements

Due to the hurdles for market enforcement, is it possible to hold companies liable for voluntary statements made in policies or codes of conduct? As the law currently stands it does not seem likely. Attenborough has, however, suggested that the doctrine of estoppel could be utilised in enforcing voluntary statements. He examined whether companies, in particular, could be held accountable for environmental statements.[173] There are many distinct doctrines under the umbrella of estoppel,[174] the most relevant of which, for these purposes, being promissory estoppel. For estoppel to be established there must, first, be a promise or representation as to future conduct; second, a promise or representation that must have been relied upon; and third it must be inequitable

---

[171]   S. Bowers, 'Amazon to begin paying corporation tax on UK retails sales', *The Guardian* (23 May 2015) <https://www.theguardian.com/technology/2015/may/23/amazon-to-begin-paying-corporation-tax-on-uk-retail-sales> accessed 30 January 2021.

[172]   T. Warren, 'Microsoft is now a $1 trillion company', *The Verge* (25 April 2019) <https://www.theverge.com/2019/4/25/18515623/microsoft-worth-1-trillion-dollars-stock-price-value> accessed 8 October 2019; see also M. Sweney, 'Amazon halved corporation tax bill despite UK profits tripling', *The Guardian* (3 August 2018) <https://www.theguardian.com/technology/2018/aug/02/amazon-halved-uk-corporation-tax-bill-to-45m-last-year> accessed 30 January 2021.

[173]   D. Attenborough, 'An estoppel-based approach to enforcing corporate environmental responsibilities' (2016) 28 *Journal of Environmental Law* 275.

[174]   E. McKendrick, *Contract Law* (Palgrave, 12th edn, 2017) 102 (though as noted by Attenborough (n. 173), 'debate exists as to whether most, if not all, are species of the same genus, or should be regarded as so different in principle as to be wholly independent'), citing: *Waltons Stores (Interstate) Ltd v Maher* [1988] 62 ALJR 110, 123; *Commonwealth of Australia v Verwayen* [1990] 65 ALJR 540, 546; *Gillies v Keogh* [1989] 2 NZLR 327, 331; *Crabb v Arun DC* [1976] Ch 179, 193 (Scarman LJ); *Amalgamated Investment and Property Co. Ltd (In Liquidation) v Texas Commerce International Bank* [1982] QB 84 at 103, 122 (Lord Denning); *Taylor Fashions Ltd v Liverpool Victoria Trustees Co. Ltd* [1982] QB 133, 153 (Oliver J). See also, M Halliwell, 'Estoppel: unconscionability as a cause of action' (1994) 14 *Legal Studies* 15.

for the promisor to go back upon his promise.[175] Crucially, the representation must take the form of a sufficiently clear and unambiguous assertion – take for example one of Google's statements from its principles for AI:

> Technologies that cause or are likely to cause overall harm. Where there is a material risk of harm, we will proceed only where we believe that the benefits substantially outweigh the risks, and will incorporate appropriate safety constraints.[176]

In order for this statement to amount to a representation it must satisfy the principle of certainty, as statements that are vague will not be enforceable. Google's statement is open-ended, and it is difficult to interpret what terms such as 'overall harm' and 'appropriate safety constraints' mean. To make a statement enforceable, a company would have to make one that created intelligible mutual obligations. Even then, courts are reluctant to allow estoppel to be used as a cause of action.[177]

Given the limitations of estoppel, would the law of misrepresentation be useful? A duty is imposed in law not to make any false statements of fact that induce the party to enter into a contract. A misrepresentation may be defined as an unambiguous, false statement of fact which is addressed to the party misled, which is material and induces the contract.[178] This goes beyond a promise and requires a representation, which is a statement that asserts the truth or a given state of facts as opposed to a promise to do or not do something.[179] The statement cannot be one of opinion or belief but the representation must be made with 'reasonable care and skill'[180] (and the expertise of the representor will be taken into consideration).[181]

The representation must be addressed to the party misled; accordingly, it will be difficult for a statement made to the general public to meet this requirement, particularly considering that the statement must also induce the party into entering a contract with the representor.[182] Therefore, the claimant would need to have a contractual relationship with the company. This would be suitable for situations where a customer has bought or used MST and then suffered harm, but this does not address other ethical and moral issues, such as

---

[175] McKendrick (n. 174) 102; see also *Central London Property Trust Ltd v High Trees House Ltd* [1947] KB 130.

[176] 'AI at Google: our principles' (n. 9).

[177] *Combe v Combe* [1951] 2 KB 215; see judgment of Lord Toulson in *Prime Sight Ltd v Lavarello* [2014] AC 436 [30].

[178] McKendrick (n. 174) 246.

[179] *Kleinwort Benson Ltd v Malaysia Mining Corp Berhad* [1989] 1 WLR 379.

[180] *Esso Petroleum Ltd v Mardon* [1976] QB 801.

[181] *Smith v Land and House Property Corp.* [1884] 28 Ch D 7.

[182] See *Museprime Properties Ltd v Adhill Properties Ltd* [1991] 61 P & C 111.

whether the technology should be developed at all or how it should be operated by a company. It will also mean that harm has already been caused, for which the party is seeking redress.

Even if a corporation could be held liable for such a statement, due to the voluntary nature of the statements, it is likely that companies would stop making assurances or continue to give vague statements that are reassuring to the public but are not legally enforceable. The issues these technologies create are just too important to allow companies to self-regulate.

6 SUBSTANTIVE ENGAGEMENT WITH CSR

I have so far argued that CSR strategies, and by extension self-regulation, are ineffective in ensuring good corporate behaviour in regard to the development of MST. The ineffective nature of CSR strategies is further evidenced in other industries, which generally fail to voluntarily behave well when the law does not require it.

It was larger multinational corporations in certain industries, facing a crisis of trust with critical stakeholder groups, which took the lead in CSR initiatives, such as sustainability reporting.[183] Today, it is not just multinational corporations that adopt or engage with CSR, but a wider range of businesses, both small and medium-sized.[184] Nevertheless, because CSR policies are expressions of the corporation's own values, culture and functioning, the industry in which the company operates has significant importance in whether a corporation will engage with regulating their own behaviour. Voluntary codes of conduct, for example, tend to be concentrated in particular sectors and focus on issues raised by those sectors. For instance, labour issues play a more important role in labour-intensive industries, such as clothing, footwear and manufacturing; and the extraction sector places significant focus on environmental standards. Consequently, the content of CSR policies will greatly depend on the production-specific differences in corporations.[185]

Differences in engagement also arise from the particular social pressures that are placed on corporations.[186] Consumer-facing companies are more sen-

---

[183]   Moon (n. 100) 5.

[184]   Ibid.

[185]   See A. Beckers, *Enforcing Corporate Social Responsibility Codes: On Global Self-Regulation and National Private Law* (Hart Publishing, 2015).

[186]   See Organisation for Economic Co-operation and Development, 'Annual Report' (2001) 2; M. Kurkchiyan and D. McBarnet, 'Contractual control: business regulation of business' in D. McBarnet and T. Campbell (eds), New Corporate Accountability: Corporate Social Responsibility and the Law (Cambridge University Press, 2007) 83.

sitive to reputational harm and consumer backlash;[187] accordingly, those companies who have greater exposure to the public are more likely to adopt CSR initiatives. As Grant concludes, a 'private company that is not customer-facing has almost no business incentive to mitigate long-term environmental risks'.[188]

Even so, CSR strategies used by consumer-facing companies can be weak in nature and, whilst the public can focus on real or perceived shortcomings of multinationals, companies have learned to better manage their reputations. Reich contends that it is virtually impossible for corporations to engage in real socially responsible actions.[189] He states that whilst businesses increasingly use CSR and similar terms, they do so only to make themselves appear to the public as if they are socially responsible. Businesses can therefore exploit the shared language of CSR merely to serve shareholders' interests:

> It is easy to understand why big business has embraced corporate social responsibility with such verve. It makes for good press and reassures the public. A declaration of corporate commitment to social virtue may also forestall government legislation or regulation in an area of public concern where one or more companies have behaved badly, such as transporting oil carelessly and causing a major spill or flagrantly failing to respect human rights abroad. The soothing promise of responsibility can deflect public attention from the need for stricter laws and regulations or convince the public that there's no real problem to begin with. Corporations that have signed codes of conduct promising good behaviour appear to have taken important steps towards social responsibility, but the pressures operating on them to lure and keep consumers and investors haven't eased one bit.[190]

The concerns Reich highlights are particularly relevant to the MST industry and mirror the limitations to self-regulation, as outlined in Section 5. Therefore, relying on managerial goodwill and character to motivate CSR is problematic.[191] For instance, Kunn and Deetz argue that personal agendas and 'identity needs' of managers have more influence over product development than stakeholder interests.[192] A report commissioned by the UK government found that the commitment of the leaders of the company was a key driver in engagement with human rights.[193] As Porritt concludes, the changes made

---

[187] See Vogel (n. 101).

[188] Grant (n. 164) 257.

[189] Reich (n. 140).

[190] Reich (n. 140) 170.

[191] T. Kunn and S. Deetz, 'Critical theory and corporate social responsibility: can/ should we get beyond cynical reasoning?' in A. Crane, A. McWilliams, D. Matten, J. Moon and D. S. Siegel (eds), *The Oxford Handbook of Corporate Social Responsibility* (Oxford University Press, 2008) 176.

[192] Ibid.

[193] Twentyfifty, 'The private sector and human rights in the UK' (October 2009) 42.

by corporations to their behaviour are to date modest, slow, inadequate and inconsistent: 'There are still very few companies that have really got to grips with sustainable development; for most the business model remains largely unchanged.'[194] Although Porritt does note that there 'is an upward curve moving in the right direction'.[195]

Despite some evidence of an upward curve, little is being done by the majority of corporations to significantly reduce their impact. There are still substantial ongoing human rights and environmental abuses in developed and developing countries that are committed by corporations. Moreover, allowing corporations to self-regulate in many important areas means progress is moving much too slowly. As Emeseh explains, 'the promise of CSR filling the regulatory vacuum has remained largely unfulfilled',[196] and there is little evidence of the alleviation of these issues, particularly within the environmental context.[197] If we want to ensure corporations practise sufficiently responsible behaviour with MST, we must adopt minimum legal standards. This would guarantee a certain level of corporate behaviour and commitment.

Without a legal framework, as Grant believes, there are minimal incentives for corporations to fully commit to CSR and self-regulation:

> The current structure of English company law closely reflects the principle of shareholder primacy, leaving directors beholden to the shareholders who own their enterprises, and tacitly encouraging the maximisation of shareholder returns while only weakly requesting that directors pay attention to the environmental consequences of their actions.[198]

Grant argues this is compounded by two commercial disincentives: (i) the expense and uncertain return of environmental sustainability, which heavily weigh against investment; (ii) while the equity markets and the ascent of activist shareholders punish any action that does not lead to increased share prices.[199] Even if one is not cynical about management and shareholder motivations, many social problems do require government intervention and action. Andrew Savitz gives an example of food safety standards.[200] With regard to

---

[194] J. Porritt, *Capitalism as if the World Matters* (Taylor & Francis, 2012) 322.
[195] Ibid.
[196] E. Emeseh, 'Social responsibility in practice in the oil producing Niger Delta: assessing corporations and government's actions' (2009) 11 *Journal of Sustainable Development in Africa* 113, 115.
[197] Ibid.
[198] Grant (n. 164) 259.
[199] Ibid.
[200] A. W. Savitz, 'Robert Reich: right on "super capitalism," not so right on CSR', The Triple Bottom Line Blog (2007) <https://www.getsustainable.net/> accessed 31 January 2021.

scientific developments in the UK, we can consider the prohibition of human reproductive cloning,[201] restrictions on gene editing[202] and other restrictions on the use of human embryos.[203]

CSR scholars such as Vogel also believe that there is a greater need for government intervention. He states that 'governments remain essential to improving corporate behaviour'.[204] Quoting from a World Bank report, Vogel writes 'voluntary CSR practices of private enterprise cannot be an effective substitute for good governance'.[205] He concludes 'the definition of corporate social responsibility needs to be redefined to include ... the capacity of governments to require that all firms act more responsibly'. Much like the development of MST, speech regulation in cyberspace has largely been left to self-regulation. Laidlaw explains that decisions by these corporations tend to be outside the legal system of human rights and the result is a system of private governance running alongside the law, without any of the safeguards one normally expects of state-run systems.[206] In the context of internet regulation, CSR has been insufficient for the protection of freedom of expression online.[207]

The notion of CSR is also not terribly helpful in understanding what is desirable or required at the 'business–society interface'.[208] What counts as 'good' or being a 'responsible corporate citizen' is vague and will depend upon the corporations' own stakeholders, which makes managers' tasks even more challenging.[209] It is difficult for corporations, even those with the best intentions, to develop effective strategies without government intervention. It is also important to note that publicly known binding rules are easier to be applied company-wide than if rules are not publicly known.[210]

Whilst CSR can be used as a 'vehicle for promoting transparency [and] more nuanced accountability',[211] self-regulation alone will not work for

---

[201] Human Reproductive Cloning Act 2001.

[202] Genetically Modified Organisms (Contained Use) Regulations 2014.

[203] Human Fertilisation and Embryology Act 1990 (as amended in 2008).

[204] Vogel (n. 101) 170.

[205] Ibid.

[206] Laidlaw (n. 17) xii.

[207] Ibid.

[208] See J. H. van Oosterhout and P. P. M. A. R. Heugens, 'Much ado about nothing: a conceptual critique of corporate social responsibility' in A. Crane, A. McWilliams, D. Matten, J. Moon and D. S. Siegel (eds), *The Oxford Handbook of Corporate Social Responsibility* (Oxford University Press, 2008).

[209] See D. Matten and A. Crane, 'Corporate citizenship: toward an extended theoretical conceptualisation' (2005) 30 *Academy of Management Review* 166.

[210] P. Starr, *The Social Transformation of American Medicine* (Basic Books, 1983). The sentiment is conveyed throughout the book.

[211] Pava (n. 139) 805.

MST. Voluntary codes are based on consensus, so it is difficult to compel companies to abide by codes; and yet companies may free ride off the legitimacy and goodwill that codes create.[212] Thus there cannot be 'effective control of multinational corporations at international, regional or private level without the corresponding development of an effective minimum institutional framework'.[213] CSR initiatives, or codes of conduct, will need to build upon a minimum framework of regulatory standards. Currently, no such existing workable minimum standards exist that address a company's responsibility or liability directly for MST, or consider issues of morality, or appropriate redress for harm. This needs to be addressed immediately.

This is not to say that CSR has no legitimacy[214] or that it has no place in encouraging good corporate behaviour, but ensuring accountability with MST *will* require a legal obligation rather than a voluntary undertaking. If something is important, we should make it a legal rule that can be enforced. What is demonstrably clear is that a corporation should 'not be in a position of marking its own homework'.[215]

7 CONCLUDING REMARKS

MST presents great potential for conferring benefits on our society, but advances in these technologies are also fraught with the potential for harm. It is therefore necessary for a sufficient regulatory framework to be established that targets the companies developing these technologies. There are two different regulatory strategies that can be employed here: one is the use of hard regulation, i.e. the use of legal norms; and the other is a soft regulatory strategy, which is often referred to as CSR. This chapter has argued that, whilst CSR will always have a role to play, its effectiveness in encouraging companies to behave well is often all too limited. The existing CSR standards are fragmented and are often inappropriate.

Reaching a consensus as to 'good corporate behaviour' is often a difficult practice in the normal course of business. To achieve such a consensus with something as complex and broad as MST demands a collaborative approach.

---

[212] Laidlaw (n. 17) 77.

[213] O. Amao, 'Corporate social responsibility, multinational corporations and the law in Nigeria: controlling multinationals in host states' (2008) 52 *Journal of African Law* 89.

[214] See, for example, Reich (n. 140) (who argues that CSR has no use as a regulatory tool because it no longer exists in the contemporary economic realm: its only purpose is a marketing tool).

[215] Quote from Edward Lucas, DCMS, 'Disinformation and "fake news"' (Interim Report) (n. 30) para. 62.

But CSR's credibility as a regulatory tool is also often criticised due to 'green-washing' strategies; tactics which corporations developing MST have already been accused of using. Public support is also more likely to be maintained due to the small number of corporations producing MST; accordingly, relying on the social gaze to encourage good behaviour is extremely problematic. This is exacerbated by the often vague and unmeasurable content of CSR policies and codes of conduct. Such statements are cleverly drafted and include selective content that lacks information about implementation and any impact of their policies. This is true of Google's 'Principles' and it will be increasingly difficult for the public to assess content when it comes to MST. These products will often be developed in secret, and it will be hard to determine if a policy or code has been breached. Most importantly, corporations should not have sole responsibility to assess the risk of activities regarding MST without intervention.

We cannot, in good faith, trust companies to self-regulate in an area so morally significant as the emergence of this new type of technology. Something so important as this is too big to be left to private concerns guided by profit margins and self-interest; rather it should be subject to government intervention. Regulators should not overlook the necessity of hard law in this area. The introduction of any such minimum standards will clearly require significantly more consideration than the present chapter allows, and must ensure that, at the very least, corporations can be held accountable where appropriate.

4. Beware Oz the Great and Powerful: sci-fi determinism, flawed artificial intelligence and emerging regulatory frameworks

Alan Dignam

INTRODUCTION

In 1979, as part of my final year of primary school, our teacher, Mr Bennett, set out to us the challenge of our 'leisure generation'.[1] In essence we would all have to develop hobbies to fill our time as we would only work a three-day week because robots and computer automation would work the rest. Boredom, it seemed, was to be the coming societal problem. Obsessed as I was with science fiction and in particularly the comic *2000AD*, it was clear from official and unofficial sources that the advent of the new millennium would bring sentient robots, hoverboards and awesome trainers. Apart from the awesome trainers, none of this materalized, as the mass labour-relieving effects of automation failed to create the assumed 'leisure generation'. Indeed, we work more than ever, and I have, as a member of the 'leisure generation', been made wary of predictions of the extent and effects of technological change.[2] Things rarely play out as predicted.

In the midst of a pandemic that has suddenly and unexpectedly turned the world upside down, it is probably even more apparent that predicting the future is fraught with danger. The aim of this chapter is simple, so perhaps oddly for a collection of authors who were set the task of considering 'a major forthcoming challenge for policy and regulation to be the potential emergence

---

[1] As Keynes had done for an earlier generation. J. Keynes, 'Economic possibilities for our grandchildren (1930)' in *Essays in Persuasion* (Harcourt Brace, 1932), 358–373.

[2] V. Robin and J. Dominguez, 'Humans once worked just 3 hours a day. Now we're always working, but why?' (2018) https://bigthink.com/big-think-books/vicki-robin-joe-dominguez-your-money-or-your-life.

of new artificial lifeforms, both sapient and not', it argues that one of the key regulatory challenges in the context of the problems manifest in the first commercial wave of weak artificial intelligence is ensuring that a form of science empiricism mixed with a strong science fiction narrative focused on 'novel beings' does not become a trojan horse for technological determinism where humans are passive subjects rather than active shapers of technology within any emerging regulatory framework – at least in democratic, rule of law nations. In essence we must avoid focusing on the illusory Great and Powerful Oz[3] and look behind to understand who is pulling the levers, how they pull the levers, and why, if we are to manage a public interest regulatory response to the emergence of wide-scale use of artificial intelligence (AI) in society.

It proceeds first in Section I to examine the challenge presented by science empiricism and sci-fi libertarian determinism within the AI sphere. In Section II it moves to consider the challenges presented to rule of law democratic jurisdictions by the flaws present in the first wave of commercial AI. It then concludes by examining the emerging regulatory frameworks and the tensions between them.

I   THE 'INEVITABILITY' OF AI?

Types of Artificial Intelligence

AI has two general industry/academic divisions[4] – general/strong AI, meaning sentient human conscious type AI, and narrow/weak AI, meaning basic narrow/weak processes using statistical analysis of data sets and often large-scale computational power to carry out routine tasks or, in more complex models, to identify patterns. General AI is the ultimate science fiction-inspired goal but does not exist, may never exist or at least if it is going to exist, it has not yet emerged.[5] One must also, when dealing with the general AI literature,

---

   [3]   F. Baum, *The Wonderful Wizard of Oz* (Penguin, 1900).
   [4]   Although there is a hybrid version between the two. See B. Goertzel, 'Human-level artificial general intelligence and the possibility of a technological singularity: a reaction to Ray Kurzweil's *The Singularity Is Near*, and McDermott's critique of Kurzweil' (2007) 171(18) *Artificial Intelligence* 1161–1173.
   [5]   Ibid.; R. Yampolskiy and J. Fox, 'Artificial intelligence and the human mental model' in A. Eden, J. Moor, J. Soraker, J. and E. Steinhart (eds), *The Singularity Hypothesis: A Scientific and Philosophical Assessment* (Springer, 2012) 129–145; and R. Fjelland, 'Why general artificial intelligence will not be realized' (2020) 7 *Humanities and Social Sciences Communications* 1–9. See also the 2021 Reith Lectures, https://www.bbc.co.uk/programmes/m001216k and R. Brooks, 'The seven deadly sins of AI predictions', *MIT Technology Review* (6 October 2017) https://www.technologyreview.com/2017/10/06/241837/the-seven-deadly-sins-of-ai-predictions/.

rationally set aside claims that it already exists and we are unknowingly living in the universe it built for us.[6] Weak/narrow AI is the reality and the focus of concern in this chapter.

There is no doubt that some of the activity that weak AI carries out mimics aspects of human intelligence such as speech or facial recognition. Some of its computational ability goes beyond human ability and the more complex statistical AI models can deal with some level of subtlety and nuance, but they are not of a human order of general intelligence.[7] A telescope, for example, is a complex precision tool designed to enhance human observational ability. It is not intelligent, but it has been intelligently designed by a human. A mechanical watch is a complex instrument that measures time, but it does not consciously 'decide' what time it is. Harrison's H4 Marine Chronometer was the Sat-Nav of its day and was an extraordinary piece of human life-enhancing technology, but no one then or since has described the H4 as 'intelligent' or 'sentient', despite its extraordinary complexity.[8] It remains a tool for human use designed by the immense intelligence of John Harrison. Neither the H4 nor the telescope is intelligent in the human sense, just as a statistical model described and sold as AI is not intelligent.[9] They are at best tools designed by humans for other humans to use, and can be flawed, just like humans.

A blurring of general and weak AI by the tech industry and scientists can also create an illusion of and reaction to assumed superior intelligence and, as we will explore, feeds a technological deterministic narrative where humans are passive subjects of the technology, when in fact commercial weak AI is nothing of the order of human intelligence. Chess computers, AlphaGo and IBM Watson's ability to beat humans within a narrow gaming skill set reinforce the illusion that computers are superior at decision-making than humans when the reality of these AI applications is much more limited.[10] That same assumption would not be made about a telescope, even though, applying the tech AI personification logic, a telescope is better at looking at stars than a human is. In reality the telescope simply assists us to make better observations and decisions and indeed might make us marvel at human ingenuity. AI

---

[6] V. Sergievskii, 'Super strong artificial intelligence and human mind' (2020) 169 *Procedia Computer Science* 458–460 and yes, I realize I wouldn't know if I were part of an AI-built universe, but that isn't proof it exists.

[7] G. Ryle, *The Concept of Mind* (Routledge, 2009); S. Russell and P. Norvig, *Artificial Intelligence: A Modern Approach* (Prentice Hall, 2003); M. Ford, *Architects of Intelligence* (Packt, 2018); and B. Goertzel and C. Pennachin, *Artificial General Intelligence* (Springer, 2007).

[8] D. Sobel, *Longitude* (Penguin, 1995).

[9] M. Broussard, *Artificial Unintelligence* (MIT Press, 2018) 1–39.

[10] E. Strickland, 'IBM Watson, heal thyself: how IBM overpromised and underdelivered on AI health care' (2019) 56(4) *IEEE Spectrum* 24–31; and Brooks, above n. 5.

and its presentation within our culture also tend to obscure the human endeavour and ingenuity behind it. As Fjelland put it,

> when it is argued that computers are able to duplicate a human activity, it often turns out that the claim presupposes an account of that activity that is seriously simplified and distorted. To put it simply: The overestimation of technology is closely connected with the underestimation of humans.[11]

The terminology itself contains a further layer of confusion. Defining AI as 'weak' or 'narrow' when these systems, although exhibiting no particular intelligence, can be extremely complex and powerful in application is further misleading, as it illustrates how central the gravitational pull of general/strong sci-fi sentient AI is to the field. They are only 'weak' when compared to an imagined sentient sci-fi strong general AI of the future and so we end up with the equally misleading 'weak' AI terminology covering both genuinely routine standard statistical programs and more complex and much less weak artificial neural networks that, for example, make life or death decisions in the medical arena.[12]

The Beauty of Maths

The tension between science and values has been continuous since the emergence of natural science as a field of enquiry centuries ago. From Bacon's development of scientific method,[13] to Galileo's condemnation by the Church for Copernican advocacy,[14] through Newton and Darwin and their internal dialogues about the tension between their scientific work and their religious beliefs,[15] to Nazi scientists pursuing horrific ideological science[16] and Soviet scientists working within a Marxist framework,[17] to Robert Oppenheimer, Albert Einstein and Norbert Wiener's deep and public concern about their

---

[11]   Fjelland, above n. 5 at 2–3.
[12]   N. Wirth, 'Hello marketing, what can artificial intelligence help you with?' (2018) 60(5) International Journal of Market Research 437.
[13]   C. Broad, 'Francis Bacon and scientific method' (1926) 118 Nature 523–524, https://doi.org/10.1038/118523a0.
[14]   M. Finocchiaro, Defending Copernicus and Galileo: Critical Reasoning in the Two Affairs (Springer, 2010).
[15]   I. Newton, Opera quae exstant omnia: Tomus primus, Volume 4 (Joannes Nichols, 1782) 436–437; S. Miles, 'Charles Darwin and Asa Gray discuss teleology and design' (2001) 53 Perspectives on Science and Christian Faith 196–201.
[16]   U. Deichmann, 'Science and political ideology: the example of Nazi Germany' (2020) 10 Mètode Science Studies Journal 129–137.
[17]   H. Sheehan, Marxism and the Philosophy of Science: A Critical History (Verso, 2018).

roles in the splitting of the atom and its weaponizing,[18] and more recently to fears of cancel culture in the scientific and particularly the AI community,[19] tension between science as reasoned empirical truth versus what are often perceived as less exact value-laden areas such as theological, political, philosophical, legal and ethical propositions has abounded.

This clash of cultures manifests itself particularly strongly within the AI community where a maths engineering culture of empirical truth rubs up against humanities and social science-led values cultures as commercial AI has emerged as an influence in society. The belief in technical terms that human intelligence (including culture, society, etc.) is machine like and can be replicated empirically or improved upon runs deep within AI engineering culture,[20] and is often accompanied by a strong rejection of human consciousness and values-based conscience in turn as nothing more than the sum of the empirical parts.[21] As Peters explains, '*technological determinism* is a battle cry of scholars against engineers, who are stereotypically hostile to the social sciences and humanities, who often regard human "factors" as obstacles, and whose native ideology is progress through bettering gadgets'.[22] As things have evolved, AI science has become dominated by those who come from subject areas that have no exposure to the humanities or social sciences and operate in technology companies' corporate bureaucracies where technical competency

---

[18] N. Wiener, 'Letters to the Editor: a scientist rebels', *Atlantic Monthly* (January 1947) 46.

[19] BBC, 'Science in the time of cancel culture' (2021), https://www.bbc.co.uk/sounds/play/m000xsvk.

[20] J. Kemeny, 'Man viewed as a machine' (1955) 192(4) *Scientific American* 58–67; C. Snow, *The Two Cultures* (Cambridge University Press, 1959); A. Turing, 'Computing machinery and intelligence' (1950) LIX(236) Mind 440, 443–460; and H. Simon, *Reason in Human Affairs* (Stanford University Press, 1983) 7–8. Cave describes this pursuit as 'Mastery over nature': S. Cave, 'AI: artificial immortality and narratives of mind-uploading', in S. Cave, K. Dihal and S. Dillon (eds), *AI Narratives: A History of Imaginative Thinking about Intelligent Machines* (Oxford University Press, 2020) Chapter 13, 311.

[21] See for example the interview with Professor Geoff Hinton J. Gill, 'Machines of many parts' *Times Higher* (19 August 2021) 5; F. Crick, *The Astonishing Hypothesis: The Scientific Search for the Soul* (Simon & Schuster, 1994); P. Winch, *Moral Integrity* (Blackwell, 1968); and J. Pitrat, *Artificial Beings: The Conscience of a Conscious Machine* (Wiley, 2009).

[22] J. Peters, '"You mean my whole fallacy is wrong": on technological determinism' (2017) 140(1) *Representations* 10–26 at 21.

and efficiency hold sway and awareness of the overall context of the AI project is often missing.[23] As O'Neil describes it,

> so many of the data scientists that are in work right now think of themselves as technicians and think that they can blithely follow textbook definitions of optimisation, without considering the wider consequences of their work. So, when they choose to optimise to some kind of ratio of false positives or false negatives, for example, they are not required by their bosses or their educational history to actually work out what that will mean to the people affected by the algorithms they're optimising. Which means that they don't really have any kind of direct connection to the worldly consequences of their work.[24]

The result of that, in the context of AI, is that if we are not careful, we risk moving away from governance through just laws developed over centuries in democratic rule of law societies to governance by numbers.[25] Beyond reasonable doubt becomes simply a high-level standard probability outcome.

Approaching the regulation of AI against this cultural background can be challenging as technological determinism is strongly linked to this broader empiricism versus values clash. Determinism argues that we accept that we as humans are simply subject to the technology.[26] As Natale et al. put it:

> The concept of technological determinism has not only been employed to criticize scholarly approaches to technological and media change, but also to describe popular narratives and myths that are used to support the interests and agendas of specific groups, assigning to technology a predominant role in shaping broad trans-

---

[23]   Understanding the context for the technical work being performed is essential for any moral context to emerge. Roszak uses the example of a psychiatrist doing excellent technical work in a concentration camp with little obvious improvement to the health of his patients because the context in which the patients live is so horrific. T. Roszak, *The Voice of the Earth: An Exploration of Ecopsychology* (Simon and Schuster, 1992).

[24]   T. Upchurch, 'To work for society, data scientists need a Hippocratic oath with teeth: interview with Cathy O'Neil', *Wired* (4 August 2018) https://www.wired.co.uk/article/data-ai-ethics-hippocratic-oath-cathy-o-neil-weapons-of-math-destruction.

[25]   A. Supiot, *La Gouvernance par les nombres* (Fayard, 2015); and P. Mirowski, *Machine Dreams* (Cambridge University Press, 2002). On the links between technological determinism and its potential to damage democratic institutions see W. Bijker, *Of Bicycles, Bakelites, and Bulbs: Toward a Theory of Sociotechnical Change* (MIT Press, 1995).

[26]   M. McLuhan, *Understanding Media: The Extensions of Man* (McGraw-Hill, 1964); R. Williams, *Television: Technology and Cultural Form* (Fontana, 1974); and B. Bimber, 'Karl Marx and the three faces of technological determinism' (1990) 20(2) *Social Studies of Science* 333–351.

formations and thereby presenting progressive and clear-cut visions about the future of technology and society.[27]

In this conception science as a neutral empirical truth orders the world without interference from messy human social construction. Regulation in a determinist model, should there be any, becomes a function of facilitating the technology. If, however, one recognizes the technology as just part of a broader human social construction potentially deployable by the humans who planned and developed it in their own interest, then regulation becomes about mitigating or guiding the human choices behind the technology and its operation in the real world, focused on the public democratic rule of law interest.[28] As Thompson noted,

> some vulgar practitioners of determinism apart, historians do not find that technology (or inventors), unaided, created industrialization or capitalist imperialism. Nor can technology creep, unaided, bring us to extermination. Historians find, rather, a collocation of mutually-supportive forces – political, ideological, institutional, economic – which give rise to process, or to the event. And each of these forces exists only within the medium of human agency.[29]

For regulatory purposes these are not just semantic debates but directly shape the way jurisdictions approach regulation. For very different ends the EU[30] (privacy) and China[31] (surveillance) recognize the human social construction behind technological development while the UK[32] and the US[33] have largely accepted an industry-led determinist deregulatory approach.

---

[27] S. Natale, P. Bory and G. Balbi, 'The rise of corporational determinism: digital media corporations and narratives of media change' (2019) 36(4) *Critical Studies in Media Communication* 323–338 at 327.

[28] F. de la Cruz Paragas and T. Lin, 'Organizing and reframing technological determinism' (2016) 18(8) *New Media & Society* 1528–1546.

[29] E. Thompson, 'Notes on extremism, the last stage of civilization', in *Beyond the Cold War* (Merlin Press, 1982) 43.

[30] High-Level Expert Group on Artificial Intelligence, 'Policy and Investment Recommendations for Trustworthy AI', 26 June 2019, B-1049 Brussels, 1–51.

[31] J. Zeng, 'Artificial intelligence and China's authoritarian governance' (2020) 96(6) *International Affairs* 1441–1459.

[32] HM Government Department for Business, Energy and Industrial Strategy, 'Industrial Strategy: Artificial Intelligence Sector Deal' (2018), 1–21.

[33] US National Artificial Intelligence Initiative 2021, https://www.ai.gov/.

Sci-Fi Libertarian Determinism and the Law

Within the past decade weak statistical artificial intelligence (AI) has reached
operational reality and is used within areas such as policing, marketing,
finance, medicine and even consumer goods such as fridges are sold as
artificially intelligent.[34] Within the academy, business and government, AI
conferences, reports and networks abound as the potential for even this limited
weak AI to change our societies has become apparent. However, what is
also apparent is that technological determinism in the context of AI has an
additional complex science fiction sentience veneer. Phrases like 'machine
learning', 'artificial neural networks' and 'training the AI' are used casually
and confusingly, implying human sentience and machine superiority, when
they generally refer to limited statistical models using mass computational
power to make decisions/predictions. As Brooks notes:

> When people hear that machine learning is making great strides in some new
> domain, they tend to use as a mental model the way in which a person would
> learn that new domain. However, machine learning is very brittle, and it requires
> lots of preparation by human researchers or engineers, special-purpose coding,
> special-purpose sets of training data, and a custom learning structure for each new
> problem domain. Today's machine learning is not at all the sponge-like learning
> that humans engage in, making rapid progress in a new domain without having to be
> surgically altered or purpose-built.[35]

Crucially, in general there is a widespread misunderstanding of the limits of
using AI statistical modelling to make decisions and its deeper societal and
particularly legal implications. In general, weak AI is misleadingly portrayed,
publicly interpreted as of an order of human intelligence and even when
problems are recognized, the background radiation is that tech and AI are
exceptional world-changing positive forces determining our future for good.[36]
It is all somewhat reminiscent of the treatment of the tobacco industry in the
1950s.[37]

In 2016, as part of a debate on conferring a form of legal personality on AI,
the European Parliament produced a report examining the issues. Legal personality forms the gateway to a legal system and the rights and obligations that

---

[34]   https://www.theverge.com/2020/1/2/21046822/samsung-lg-smart-fridge-family
-hub-instaview-thinq-ai-ces-2020.
[35]   Brooks, above n. 5.
[36]   Natale, Bory and Balbi, above n. 27.
[37]   S. Elliott, 'When doctors, and even Santa, endorsed tobacco', *New York Times* (6
October 2008) https://www.nytimes.com/2008/10/07/business/media/07adco.html.

confers.[38] Humans and important organizational forms such as companies and unions have historically claimed legal personality and, exceptionally, deities, rivers and certain higher-level mammals have been granted legal personality, but not machines or computer programs.[39] The report concluded:

> In reality, advocates of the legal personality option have a fanciful vision of the robot, inspired by science-fiction novels and cinema. They view the robot – particularly if it is classified as smart and is humanoid – as a genuine thinking artificial creation, humanity's alter ego. We believe it would be inappropriate and out-of-place not only to recognise the existence of an electronic person but to even create any such legal personality. Doing so risks not only assigning rights and obligations to what is just a tool, but also tearing down the boundaries between man and machine, blurring the lines between the living and the inert, the human and the inhuman.[40]

Ultimately the European Commission did not include AI legal personality in its legislative plans.[41]

The 2016 report is important in terms of the central danger of misunderstanding what AI is. Despite the excited sci-fi-inspired claims, AI is not human. It is a tool that can be used well or badly. In the end it is human decision-making as to its design and deployment that matters. It is not always easy to focus on this, as human agency is easily disregarded in the high-tech world, where human operators are often deliberately hidden behind technology platforms such as those used by Deliveroo,[42] Google/Facebook,[43] Amazon Mechanical Turk,[44] or IBM's AI Watson for Oncology.[45] Recognizing that technology is not a preordained deterministic force but part of a social construction produced by human decision-making, and comprehending who those humans are, is key in

---

[38]   A. Dignam and J. Lowry, *Company Law* (Oxford University Press, 2020) Chapter 2.

[39]   E. O'Donnell, and J. Talbot-Jones, 'Creating legal rights for rivers: lessons from Australia, New Zealand, and India' (2018) 23(1) *Ecology and Society* 7.

[40]   European Parliament's Committee on Legal Affairs study on European Civil Law Rules in Robotics, 2016 (PE 571.379) 15–16.

[41]   European Commission, 'Artificial intelligence: Commission outlines a European approach to boost investment and set ethical guidelines', Brussels, 2018, http://europa .eu.rapid/press-release_IP-18-3362_en.htm.

[42]   In this advertisement for Deliveroo the human delivery workers are literally invisible, https://www.youtube.com/watch?v=2f4u6HbH5xY.

[43]   A. Singh, 'Facebook moderators "develop PTSD"', *The Telegraph* (31 May 2017)   https://www.telegraph.co.uk/news/2017/05/31/facebookmoderators-develop -ptsd-exposed-worst-content-internet/.

[44]   https://www.mturk.com/.

[45]   See discussion below.

any democratic rule of law regulatory system to maximizing the public benefit while minimizing the dangers of AI.[46]

The science fiction base for AI, as alluded to in the 2016 report mentioned above, is particularly significant in fuelling a dangerous feedback loop for AI where those who attempt to build AI are inspired by it to achieve and surpass human intelligence and those end users subject to its rather more prosaic weak AI reality assume, based on sci-fi's cultural influence, enhanced intelligence in AI decision-making.[47] It seems odd to have to articulate it, but science fiction is fictional. The reality is that 1999 passed without a semi-autonomous main computer supporting a human colony on the moon,[48] *2000 AD* has come and gone without us discovering Verdus the robot planet,[49] 2001 passed and no HAL 9000 emerged,[50] while *Blade Runner* was set in 2019,[51] and there are still no androids by 2021.[52] Similarly, although the Marvel Universe is confusingly multidimensional, Vision the android is currently not flying around this version of Earth.[53] 2029 has not yet come, so Skynet[54] cannot be ruled out, but so far in 2021 robots, like the Daleks, are still not great at navigating stairs.

There is no doubt that science fiction can sometimes foreshadow and inspire real-world technology by imagining what might be possible and indeed, as Cave has noted, some of it is deliberately critical of misleading mainstream sci-fi.[55] However, sci-fi can also mislead in the AI context, both in its public presentation of fantastical sentient AI and in its deep relationship with AI scientists, who as a result pursue potentially unobtainable goals such as artificial general intelligence, driven by a form of science fiction-inspired 'cyber-theology'.[56] This may explain why AI seems to constantly defy Amara's Law that 'we tend

---

[46]   T. Pinch and W. Bijker, 'The social construction of facts and artefacts: or how the sociology of science and the sociology of technology might benefit each other' (1984) 14 *Social Studies of Science* 399–441; and S. Natale, 'Amazon can read your mind: a media archaeology of the algorithmic imaginary' in S. Natale and D. Pasulka (eds), *Believing in Bits: Digital Media and the Supernatural* (Oxford University Press, 2019) 19–36.

[47]   S. Cave, K. Dihal and S. Dillon, *AI Narratives: A History of Imaginative Thinking about Intelligent Machines* (Oxford University Press, 2020) 7–8.

[48]   *Space: 1999* was a popular UK science fiction TV series in the 1970s: https://en .wikipedia.org/wiki/Space:_1999#Other_media.

[49]   https://en.wikipedia.org/wiki/Robo-Hunter; also, still no hoverboards.

[50]   A. Clarke, *2001: A Space Odyssey* (New American Library, 1968).

[51]   *Blade Runner*, 25 June 1982, https://www.warnerbros.com/blade-runner.

[52]   Although we do have what seems like a dystopian sci-fi pandemic.

[53]   https://en.wikipedia.org/wiki/Vision_(Marvel_Comics).

[54]   https://en.wikipedia.org/wiki/The_Terminator.

[55]   Cave, above n. 20 at 322.

[56]   R. Geraci, *Apocalyptic AI: Visions of Heaven in Robotics, Artificial Intelligence, and Virtual Reality* (Oxford University Press, 2010).

to overestimate the effect of a technology in the short run and underestimate the effect in the long'.[57] With AI we seem to have constantly, over the past 70 years, overestimated its effect in the short term even though it has consistently failed to deliver in the short, medium and long term. In reality our best AI decision-making programs are probably better described as automated controls and are at heart statistical models with the usual human-influenced problems of poor design, data errors and data interpretation that statistical analysis involves.[58] The phrase 'Lies, damned lies and statistics', variously attributed to Twain, Disraeli or Balfour, has continual historical resonance because it recognizes that human judgement is at the heart of statistical integrity and not pure numerical scientific truth.[59] When presented behind a sci-fi veneer, AI has been enormously oversold in terms of its capabilities, while it also doesn't help that companies also regularly misrepresent products as AI.[60] That is not to say limited weak machine decision-making is not useful or that an AI product doesn't mimic or copy human intelligent behaviour – Apple's Siri and Amazon's Alexa are designed to do just that – but as Lipton, one of the world's leading AI scientists, has described cutting-edge AI,

> these are just statistical models, the same as those that Google uses to play board games or that your phone uses to make predictions about what word you're saying in order to transcribe your messages. They are no more sentient than a bowl of noodles, or your shoes.[61]

It is essential to understand this in designing regulatory safeguards for AI use because the humans designing, using or subject to the AI can similarly misunderstand the nature of the intelligence being observed and suffer as a consequence.

For marketing purposes the tech industry often merges general (sci-fi) and weak (real) AI, relying on the pre-existing appetite for science fiction in film, TV and literature to excite, reassure and sell to the public a determinist concept of the 'inevitability' of their technology.[62] That use of sci-fi is not

---

[57]   See above n. 5.
[58]   Broussard, above n. 9, Chapter 7.
[59]   P. Lee, 'Lies, damned lies and statistics', University of York (2017) https://www.york.ac.uk/depts/maths/histstat/lies.htm.
[60]   A. Ram, 'Europe's AI start-ups often do not use AI, study finds', *Financial Times* (5 March 2019) https://www.ft.com/content/21b19010-3c9f-11e9-b896-fe36ec32aece.
[61]   K. Quach, 'Facebook pulls plug on language-inventing chatbots?', *The Register* (1 August 2017) https://www.theregister.co.uk/2017/08/01/facebook_chatbots_did_not_invent_new_language/.
[62]   P. Leonardi and M. Jackson, 'Technological determinism and discursive closure in organizational mergers' (2004) 17(6) *Journal of Organizational Change Management* 615–631.

straightforward for the tech industry as it has an interesting duality: utopian visions of a leisure class served by intelligent robots simultaneously create fear of a dystopia, for most sci-fi is dystopian, where the humans are betrayed and enslaved.[63] The utopian vision within that duality creates a futuristic positive desire for making the world better,[64] while the dystopian vision reinforces an existential threat, which is resolved in the blurry (sci-fi = real) tech industry narrative of technology and technology companies playing a part in fighting the bad guys. Apple's famous Orwell-inspired 1984 Superbowl advert, for example, effectively defined the genre, as it has a heroic woman, representing Apple, fighting off a technologically enabled Big Brother figure who has sedated the population.[65] In this tech-centred world view we must trust the good heroic tech products and companies to protect liberty from the bad tech statist/autocratic future.[66] This narrative has continuing resonance in the perception of an AI arms race between democratic rule of law nations and China/Russia.[67] AI's ubiquity in general current public debate also allows additional mainstream association with film and media.[68] For example, Google Assistant advertising reworked the *Home Alone* film series around a utopian AI motif where Kevin McCallister is never threatened by intruders, because Google Assistant's control of the home keeps him safe from the bad humans.[69] Indeed, historically sci-fi writers for literature and film and AI scientists have had close links. Marvin Minsky, one of the key scientific figures in modern AI, both

---

[63]   K. Devlin and O. Belton, 'The measure of a woman: fembots fact and fiction' in S. Cave, K. Dihal and S. Dillon (eds), *AI Narratives: A History of Imaginative Thinking about Intelligent Machines* (Oxford University Press, 2020) Chapter 15, 360; and A. Jezard, 'Technophobia is so last century', *Financial Times* (2 March 2016) https://www.ft.com/content/a9ec6360-cf80-11e5-92a1-c5e23ef99c77.

[64]   F. Turner, *From Counterculture to Cyberculture: Stewart Brand, the Whole Earth Network, and the Rise of Digital Utopianism* (University of Chicago Press, 2008).

[65]   S. Stein, 'The "1984" Macintosh ad: cinematic icons and constitutive rhetoric in the launch of a new machine' (2002) 88(2) *Quarterly Journal of Speech* 169–192. Apple's 1984 Superbowl Advert can be viewed here https://youtu.be/2zfqw8nhUwA.

[66]   On tech companies' presentation of a determinist centrality in shaping society see A. Hoffmann, N. Proferes and M. Zimmer, '"Making the world more open and connected": Mark Zuckerberg and the discursive construction of Facebook and its users' (2018) 20(1) *New Media & Society* 199–218; and Natale, above n. 46, 19–36.

[67]   D. Sabbagh, 'MI6 needs tech sector's help to win AI race with China and Russia – spy chief', *The Guardian* (30 November 2021) https://www.theguardian.com/uk-news/2021/nov/30/mi6-will-need-to-be-more-open-to-stay-secret-spy-chief-to-say.

[68]   In February 2019, Microsoft AI sponsored coverage of the Oscars: https://youtu.be/RFUFwJMweCo.

[69]   Google's Advert can be viewed here: https://youtu.be/xKYABI-dGEA. Of course, in this AI version of *Home Alone* there is no threat and therefore no hilarious capers.

devoured and wrote science fiction, while also being a friend of Isaac Asimov and Arthur C. Clarke. He worked with Clarke and Kubrick on creating the vision of the menacing AI computer HAL 9000 that appears in *2001: A Space Odyssey*.[70] Indeed, many of the serious heuristic difficulties present in today's black box AI systems, discussed in Section II below, are foreshadowed in HAL's heuristic problem solving that results in the death of the crew.[71]

That sci-fi-inspired tech future has a further problematic layer in regulatory terms because it has also been accompanied by a strong industry belief that heroic, deterministic, new, empirically truthful technology and its development are free of law and regulation by their very nature. Those new technological frontiers are governed by mathematical calculations containing empirical truth and old outdated pre-existing value-laden laws cannot stand in the way.[72] In 1996, the publication of 'A Declaration of the Independence of Cyberspace' by John Perry Barlow captured what was to become the driving utopian determinist libertarian mindset of nascent internet tech companies and their founders – the root of the famous Facebook coder 'Move fast and break things' tech philosophy.[73] It begins:

> Governments of the Industrial World, you weary giants of flesh and steel, I come from Cyberspace, the new home of Mind. On behalf of the future, I ask you of the past to leave us alone. You are not welcome among us. You have no sovereignty where we gather.
>
>   We have no elected government, nor are we likely to have one, so I address you with no greater authority than that with which liberty itself always speaks. I declare the global social space we are building to be naturally independent of the tyrannies you seek to impose on us. You have no moral right to rule us nor do you possess any methods of enforcement we have true reason to fear.[74]

A key element in this tech determinist utopia is the emergence of the internet, which has allowed traditional and new businesses to deliver products and

---

[70]   Broussard, above n. 9 at 71–72.

[71]   See G. Matthews, 'A push-button type of thinking: automation, cybernetics, and AI in midcentury British literature' in S. Cave, K. Dihal and S. Dillon (eds), *AI Narratives: A History of Imaginative Thinking about Intelligent Machines* (Oxford University Press, 2020) Chapter 10, 253.

[72]   Natale, Bory and Balbi, above n. 27; B. Bimber, 'Karl Marx and the three faces of technological determinism' (1990) 20(2) *Social Studies of Science* 333–351; M. Smith and L. Marx, *Does Technology Drive History? The Dilemma of Technological Determinism* (MIT Press, 1994).

[73]   J. Taplin, *Move Fast and Break Things: How Facebook, Google, and Amazon Cornered Culture and Undermined Democracy* (Macmillan, 2017).

[74]   J. Barlow, 'A declaration of the independence of cyberspace', 8 February 1996, https://www.eff.org/cyberspace-independence.

services in radically new ways and to shelter behind the tech determinist libertarian view that this is all new and therefore existing laws do not apply. Tesla insists it is not a car company but a technology one, not subject to normal safety considerations.[75] Facebook, Apple and Google are not publishers or broadcasters so a range of laws to protect children or to pay artists should not apply,[76] while Amazon, Tesla and Uber have what would best be described as a distinctively antagonistic approach to compliance across a broad range of activities.[77] With its science versus values historical tension and a powerful sci-fi utopian veneer, AI represents the apotheosis of this tech world view and all of the companies above have become significant players in the AI field. They are the utopian technological future and to restrict their activities through existing laws is to strike at freedom itself. As Vance notes, commenting on tech leaders' futuristic world view, 'They were all geeks raised on science fiction and the vision of space we had in the 1960s and 70s. Now they have the money to make this a reality.'[78] US tech determinist libertarianism also has a particular business-focused flavour. Within the panoply of US libertarian

---

[75] T. Simonite, 'Tesla's dubious claims about autopilot's safety record', *MIT Technology Review* (6 July 2016) https://www.technologyreview.com/s/601849/teslas-dubious-claims-about-autopilots-safety-record/.

[76] Metropolitan International Schools Ltd v (1) Designtechnica Corporation (2) Google UK Ltd & (3) Google Inc. [2009] EWHC 1765 (QB); S. Levin, 'Is Facebook a publisher?', *The Guardian* (3 July 2018) https://www.theguardian.com/technology/2018/jul/02/facebook-mark-zuckerberg-platform-publisher-lawsuit; 'What is the Google Books settlement?', *Daily Telegraph* (5 February 2010) https://www.telegraph.co.uk/technology/google/7164237/What-is-the-Google-Books-Settlement.html; and R. Williams, 'NSPCC: make tech firm directors legally and personally responsible for child safety', *iNews* (12 February 2019) https://inews.co.uk/news/technology/nspcc-make-tech-firm-directors-legally-and-personally-responsible-for-child-safety/.

[77] G. Hall, 'Elon Musk disputes union claims', *Silicon Valley Business Journal* (27 February 2017) https://www.bizjournals.com/sanjose/news/2017/02/27/elon-musk-tesla-fremont-factory-uaw-tsla.html; and I. Johnson, 'Amazon: devastating expose accuses internet retailer of oppressive and callous attitude to staff', *The Independent* (17 August 2015) https://www.independent.co.uk/news/business/news/amazon-devastating-expose-accuses-internet-retailer-of-oppressive-and-callous-attitude-to-staff-10458159.html; M. Isaac, 'How Uber deceives the authorities worldwide', *New York Times* (3 March 2017) https://www.nytimes.com/2017/03/03/technology/uber-greyball-program-evade-authorities.html; S. Cao, 'Tesla has lost over 40 execs in a year', *The Observer* (20 February 2019) https://observer.com/2019/02/elon-musk-dane-butswinkas-tesla-general-counsel-resigns/; and D. Shepardson, 'Amazon.com goes for jugular in FCC spat with SpaceX's Musk', Reuters (8 September 2021) https://www.reuters.com/technology/amazoncom-goes-jugular-fcc-spat-with-spacexs-musk-2021-09-08/.

[78] D. Tynan, 'Rocket men: why tech's biggest billionaires want their place in space', *The Guardian* (5 December 2016) https://www.theguardian.com/science/2016/dec/05/tech-billionaires-space-exploration-musk-bezos-branson.

political philosophy, this comes closest to the autarchist libertarian school. As its inceptor Robert LeFevre described that distinction in 1965:

> If one believes in freedom, one must believe in economic freedom – full latitude of choice in any and all economic areas, for each person. This can never be accomplished by any procedure, organized or otherwise, which uses violence (even the violence implicit in taxation) to take from an owner anything which is rightfully his.[79]

As such, the drive by tech billionaires such as Tesla's Elon Musk and Amazon's Jeff Bezos to explore space is not just seeking adventure or a place to use up their billions. The ability to operate off-planet carries both an exciting sci-fi premise and the autarchic libertarian utopian determinist promise of tech companies being able to operate off-planet in a genuinely law-free zone.[80] Tech billionaires generally also appear to have a very specific admiration of Ayn Rand's individualist libertarian work.[81] This background radiation of determinist libertarian push back has an effect as governments, particularly the UK and US governments, have facilitated a deregulated libertarian tech-exceptional view, and industry self-regulation, as will be observed later, is accepted. As Natale et al. note:

> Representing corporations as forces shaping the past, present and future of technology and society, corporational determinism informs perceptions and behaviors of consumers, stakeholders and policy makers, supporting the agendas of those corporations that have engaged in consistent efforts to create and disseminate these narratives ... [C]orporational determinism presents these companies' dominance as inevitable, disregarding the fact that their power is also the fruit of political, economic, and social choices taken by different groups including governments, organizations, and users.[82]

---

[79] R. LeFevre, 'Autarchy vs Anarchy' (1965) 1(4) *Rampart Journal of Individualist Thought* 30–49 at 49.

[80] C. Graham, 'Factories in space: Amazon founder Jeff Bezos unveils vision for the future', *The Telegraph* (2 June 2016) https://www.telegraph.co.uk/technology/2016/06/01/factories-in-space-amazon-founder-jeff-bezos-unveils-vision-for/.

[81] J. Freedland, 'The new age of Ayn Rand: how she won over Trump and Silicon Valley', *The Guardian* (10 April 2017) https://www.theguardian.com/books/2017/apr/10/new-age-ayn-rand-conquered-trump-white-house-silicon-valley; and T. Streeter, 'The deep romantic chasm: libertarianism, neoliberalism, and the computer culture' in J. Lewis and T. Miller (eds), *Critical Cultural Policy Studies: A Reader* (Basil Blackwell, 2003) 161–171.

[82] S. Natale, P. Bory and G. Balbi, 'The rise of corporational determinism: digital media corporations and narratives of media change' (2019) 36(4) *Critical Studies in Media Communication* 323–338 at 334.

In the AI context, pushing an illusion of general AI as if it were real, or blurring general and weak AI is extremely important to creating these determinist regulatory push backs.

Why does this matter? It matters for the regulatory push back as mentioned, but it matters also because it can facilitate, as will be observed, unlawful hiring practices, racial and sexual discrimination, unnecessary financial hardship and, in the case of self-driving cars or Watson for Oncology, place lives at risk. As Waters notes, 'Strip away the gee-whizz research that hogs many of the headlines (a computer that can beat humans at Go!) and the technology is at a rudimentary stage.'[83]

Hiding that AI is simply comprised of statistical models can also hide that it is not new or techy and so not logically part of our deregulated tech utopian future. Statistical models were first used in the 17th century and have a long and problematic history when used badly or when their predictive power is misunderstood.[84] Unfortunately, the tech industry seems to have hidden its statistical models so well behind the AI sci-fi facade that they have produced narrow/weak AI statistical and probability decision models that ignore three centuries of experience working with these models and their dangers. Poorly designed statistical and predictive models will fail; bias and dirty data are a big problem; and lawful human design, interpretation and continual audit of the results are essential. Additionally, software and hardware can be buggy and unreliable and the tech industry in general has a long and painful record of failing to evaluate the risks of its products and being delusional as to their capabilities.[85] As Charette considered,

> software failures tend to resemble the worst conceivable airplane crash, where the pilot was inexperienced but exceedingly rash, flew into an ice storm in an untested aircraft, and worked for an airline that gave lip service to safety while cutting back on training and maintenance.[86]

Developing high-quality AI is a highly skilled endeavour that is both expensive and time-consuming. Mass computational power, while it allows greater statistical scale, does not move the needle at all with regard to basic statistical integrity. Highly skilled human design, operation and oversight are still essential even if you've got access to a 442-petaflop computer. Facebook's

---

[83] R. Waters, 'Everything still to play for with AI in its infancy', *Financial Times* (14 February 2019) https://www.ft.com/content/bf3d708c-3077-11e9-8744-e7016697f225.

[84] W. Willcox, 'The founder of statistics' (1938) 5(4) *Review of the International Statistical Institute* 321–328.

[85] R. Charette, 'Why software fails' (2005) 42(9) IEEE Spectrum 42–49.

[86] Ibid., 48.

historical 'Move fast and break things' philosophy is dangerous for users and those subject to its AI outcomes when combined with Facebook's determinist belief that it is shaping the future for good.[87] Eventually, though, there are significant consequences for the company itself and its clients, when the thing they break is the law.

In the US state of Idaho, for example, in 2012, despite widespread knowledge of high-level corrupt data and enormously problematic outcomes in testing, a statistical decision-making algorithm was put into operation by public officials, resulting in Medicaid cuts to 4000 disabled people. The widespread hardship this caused resulted in the American Civil Liberties Union (ACLU) bringing a successful court case to reinstate the payments.[88] As the ACLU noted afterwards,

> the unfortunate part, as we learned in this case, is that it costs a lot of money to actually test these things and make sure they're working right. It cost us probably $50,000, and I don't think that a state Medicaid program is going to be motivated to spend the money that it takes to make sure these things are working right. Or even these private companies that are running credit predictions, housing predictions, recidivism predictions – unless the cost is internalized on them through litigation, and it's understood that 'hey, eventually somebody's going to have the money to test this, so it better be working.'[89]

However, poor design and testing of AI is an industry choice. It doesn't have to be so bad. If it's developed and used properly, recognizing the dangers, AI can be a useful tool for societal progress. That is, after all, AI's attraction. Freeing humans from dangerous or labour-intensive tasks, improving health and enhancing human ability to analyse the world is a positive goal.[90] A tool like a telescope allows humans to enhance their observational ability and ultimately send a probe outside the solar system, and a clock allows humans to gauge time more accurately, which in turn allows us to run a rail network. Well-designed

---

[87]   Ibid.; Natale, above n. 46.

[88]   *Toby Schultz v Richard Armstrong* Case No. 3:12-CV-58-BLW.

[89]   J. Stanley, 'Pitfalls of artificial intelligence decisionmaking', ACLU blog (2 June 2017)   https://www.aclu.org/blog/privacy-technology/pitfalls-artificial-intelligence -decisionmaking-highlighted-idaho-aclu-case.

[90]   Bernard Marr, '3 daunting ways artificial intelligence will transform the world of work', *Forbes* (7 August 2020) https://www.forbes.com/sites/bernardmarr/ 2020/08/07/3-daunting-ways-ai-will-transform-the-world-of-work/?sh=7bb855ee1dcb and McKinsey Global Institute, 'Notes from the AI frontier: applying AI for social good', Discussion Paper, McKinsey (December 2018) https://www.mckinsey.com/~/ media/mckinsey/featured%20insights/artificial%20intelligence/applying%20artificial %20intelligence%20for%20social%20good/mgi-applying-ai-for-social-good -discussion-paper-dec-2018.pdf.

weak AI can analyse huge data sets a human simply could not do and can produce counterintuitive data analysis outcomes that would be impossible for a human to discover on their own. Used badly, as will be observed, AI has the potential to send innocent people to jail, discriminate against women and minorities, unfairly exclude people from the financial system and public services, injure and kill road users, and misdiagnose patients.

II   FLAWED AND DANGEROUS AI

Commercial AI Version 0.1 – Lessons Learned?

AI products currently abound, ranging from domestic appliances, such as smart dishwashers, to smart medical devices, AI phones and computers, AI lending, AI smart speakers, AI human resources and AI quasi-judicial decision-making models. All are powered by versions of statistical/predictive models within the weak/narrow AI category. This section focuses on the major problematic aspects of the first wave of commercial weak AI (human bias, the 'black box' explainability problem, self-interested AI outcomes, trust issues and the undermining of legal norms) and argues for regulatory intervention to protect citizens in democratic rule of law jurisdictions.

The humans in the machine
While AI is the tool that can produce both positive and problematic outcomes, behind the AI facade are preliminary human decisions that cumulatively led to that AI outcome. Humans set the budget, design the AI project, decide on the data, write and debug the code, calibrate it against real human decisions, decide when to put it into operation and use it in the real world. If those humans, particularly those designing the project, are not representative of society, and have explicit and/or unconscious world views, this can strongly bias the outcomes. Within AI they are mostly men (see Figure 4.1), particularly in the technical AI roles that matter, and mostly white men.[91] As Devlin and Belton consider when examining the dominant cultural narrative that frames tech decision-making,

> in the current tech world, the narrative is predominantly from the point of view of the white, heterosexual male. Man is the default user and woman is the used. The most recent Global Gender Gap Report from the World Economic Forum (2018) found that only twenty-two percent of AI professionals globally are female.

---

[91]   White men predominate, with the largest minority being Asian males. M. Garcia, 'Racist in the machine: the disturbing implications of algorithmic bias' (2016) 33(4) *World Policy Journal* 111–117 at 114.

An investigation by WIRED and Element AI reported that only twelve percent of leading machine learning specialists were women (Simonite 2018). Given an industry so notorious for bias in recruitment, data, and product development, it is perhaps more understandable why such gendered tech narratives exist. Disrupting the narrative means disrupting the industry; disrupting the industry means disrupting the narrative.[92]

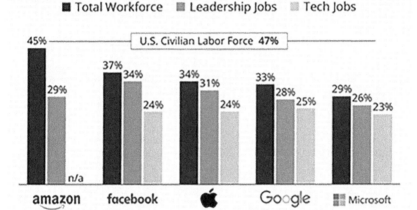

Women's Representation in Big Tech

Percentage of female employees in the workforce of major tech companies*

■ Total Workforce ■ Leadership Jobs ▥ Tech Jobs

U.S. Civilian Labor Force 47%

45% 29% n/a

37% 34% 24%

34% 31% 24%

33% 28% 25%

29% 26% 23%

 amazon   facebook   🍎   Google    Microsoft

* latest available data as of June 2021
Source: Company reports

statista

Figure 4.1   Women in the major technology companies

For example, if the data for testing an AI model is chosen by men who have unconscious bias, they may choose samples that are representative of their

---

[92]   Devlin and Belton, above n. 63, 376–377.

world experience but unrepresentative generally. Even men in minor roles reviewing data sets may not recognize a data deficiency because of their bias, which in turn can reinforce the original bias, while women in minor roles may not have the power to overturn the deficiencies. This has happened already where AI image recognition systems have been calibrated/trained unthinkingly with dominant images of white men.[93] Similarly with word-embedding AI techniques necessary for understanding written language or the spoken word, traditional gender roles have been attributed by historically male coders to women and men. In this attribution system women are homemakers and men are scientists.[94] Predominantly white men are responsible for designing AI systems so the AI systems reflect those designers' conscious and unconscious world view. At a practical level the AI systems can, as a result, have operational problems. Facial recognition systems are very good at recognizing white men but poor at recognizing black women.[95] Google's voice recognition system was designed and tested on men and has significant problems recognizing women's voices.[96]

Even within the world of popular culture, the fictional tech start-up nerds in film and literature are unfailingly male and their often-overt sexism is somehow portrayed as loveably socially dysfunctional. In the sci-fi AI world that has been so influential in AI development we also find a particularly strong gender bias in women's' roles. As Fung notes:

> AI is subject to gender stereotypes in science fiction. From the first sci-fi film 'Metropolis' to the more recent 'Ex-Machina', to popular TV series such as *Humans* and *Westworld*, we see female androids created by men in a sexualized form, starting in submissive servitude or becoming rebellious femme fatales.
> We are used to heroes and villains with physical power in sci-fi being male – the Terminator, Nero in Matrix, Ultron, etc. But there have been few attempts at creating female robots with physical power, such as T-X in the Terminator.[97]

---

[93] J. Buolamwini and T. Gebru, 'Gender shades' (2018) 81 *Proceedings of Machine Learning Research* 1–15.

[94] T. Bolukbasi, K. Chang, J. Zou, V. Saligrama and A. Kalai, 'Man is to computer programmer as woman is to homemaker?' in D. Lee, M. Sugiyama, U. Luxburg, I. Guyon and R. Garnett (eds), *Advances in Neural Information Processing Systems 29* (Curran Associates, Inc., 2016) 4349–4357.

[95] Buolamwini and Gebru, above n. 93.

[96] R. Tatman, 'Google's speech recognition has a gender bias', Making Noise and Hearing Things (12 July 2016) https://makingnoiseandhearingthings.com/2016/07/12/googles-speech-recognition-has-a-gender-bias/; and H. Devlin and A. Hern, 'Why are there so few women in tech', *The Guardian* (8 August 2016) https://www.theguardian.com/lifeandstyle/2017/aug/08/why-are-there-so-few-women-in-tech-the-truth-behind-the-google-memo.

[97] Devlin and Hern, above n. 96.

Within the tech industry these gender biases seem to go even deeper than technical roles and pervade what AI start-ups get funded by venture capital funds, with women-led AI start-ups far less likely to be funded than male ones.[98]

The problem of AI bias is much broader than just gender bias, as underrepresentation and misrepresentation of a wide range of groups and views within AI data sets abounds. Siri, for example, Apple's virtual assistant, initially refused to provide information on abortion services.[99] California's Criminal Justice COMPAS algorithm, used to assess risk of reoffending, was found to be racially biased, as was a US federal agency-backed lending algorithm.[100] Google's facial recognition system was so poorly calibrated on non-white faces that it misidentified black people as gorillas, while Microsoft's chat bot Tay quickly became a sex-crazed racist when trained to learn from other Twitter users' views, and Amazon's Alexa, trained on data drawn from internet users, set children potentially deadly challenges.[101] These outcomes are all the product of human behaviour, not determinist technological autonomy that produces a perfect world. If our experience of this first wave of commercial AI shows one thing, it is, ironically, the excellence of this commercial AI in revealing the bias of those humans who developed it.

Probably one of the greatest examples of tech AI bias has occurred in attempts to create AI hiring processes. In those cases, the calibrating 'training' of the AI is based around specific definitive known human data decision outcomes that were deemed successful – the CVs of those who were hired previously. In such an AI system new CVs are analysed to see if they have the characteristics of those who were successfully hired in the past. If the AI detects a pattern that matches the known outcomes of those previously hired by humans to about 90% accuracy, then an operational model exists that could work with the CVs of new applicants.

---

[98] P. Fung, 'This is why AI has a gender problem', World Economic Forum (30 June 2019) https://www.weforum.org/agenda/2019/06/this-is-why-ai-has-a-gender -problem/.

[99] D. Rushe, 'Siri's abortion bias embarrasses Apple', *The Guardian* (1 December 2011) https://www.theguardian.com/technology/2011/dec/01/siri-abortion-apple -unintenional-omissions.

[100] Broussard, above n. 9 at 154–156; A. Chouldechova, 'Fair prediction with disparate impact: a study of bias in recidivism prediction instruments' (2017) 2 *Big Data* 5; and E. Martinez and L. Kirchner, 'The secret bias hidden in mortgage-approval algorithms', *The Markup* (25 August 2021) https://themarkup.org/denied/2021/08/25/the -secret-bias-hidden-in-mortgage-approval-algorithms.

[101] C. Dougherty, 'Google Photos mistakenly labels black people "gorillas"', *New York Times* (1 July 2015) https://bits.blogs.nytimes.com/2015/07/01/google-photos -mistakenly-labels-black-people-gorillas/; and Garcia, above n. 91 at 112.

In August 2018, Amazon abandoned its AI hiring program when it discovered that it was eliminating women from consideration.[102] Based on ten years' previous hiring data, the AI excluded women and sometimes hired unqualified workers. On investigation, Amazon was able to identify key aspects of the AI decision-making that led to those outcomes. The AI was 'trained' as normal against a decade of CVs of successful candidates. The elements the AI favoured in reaching its decisions turned out to have significant flaws. Words in the CV indicating membership of 'women's' clubs or graduates from all-women colleges eliminated or downgraded candidates as they were not usually found in past CV data, which was dominated by men. More subtle eliminations occurred with the AI favouring applicants who used male engineer-type verbs such as 'executed' or 'captured' that were not found in female CVs. In other words, the heuristic AI had found that the way to get a 90% accurate score in training on past data outcomes was to favour characteristics that were male, which unfortunately in turn discriminated against women. In a tech industry dominated by men, it had simply reflected and revealed the bias and limited choices of past decision-makers and used those same features to determine present outcomes.[103]

While this made headlines around the world, what perhaps should have made headlines was that this has been happening with employment-based computer programs since the 1980s.[104] The most famous example occurred at St George's Medical School in London, where a computer hiring program excluded women and those with non-European names from consideration. The issue was the same as the Amazon AI example: the program was based on previous successful candidates' CVs and had embedded the previous bias of past human decision-makers, which had gone unnoticed by male designers and users with similar world views. In 1987, an investigation by the Commission for Racial Equality found that the hospital had engaged in racial and sexual discrimination.[105] Amazon abandoned its hiring AI system shortly after its problems came to light, but other major companies, such as Unilever and

---

[102] J. Dastin, 'Amazon scraps secret AI recruiting tool', Reuters (10 October 2018)   https://www.reuters.com/article/us-amazon-com-jobs-automation-insight/amazon-scraps-secret-ai-recruiting-tool-that-showed-bias-against-women-idUSKCN1MK08G.

[103] Dastin, above n. 102.

[104] O. Schwartz, 'Untold history of AI: algorithmic bias was born in the 1980s', IEEE Spectrum (2019) https://spectrum.ieee.org/untold-history-of-ai-the-birth-of-machine-bias#toggle-gdpr.

[105] S. Lowry and G. MacPherson, 'A blot on the profession' (1988) 296(6623) *The British Medical Journal* 657–658; and Garcia, above n. 91.

Microsoft's LinkedIn, use a similar system or are seeking to implement one.[106] Other Amazon AI decision-making systems with similar problematic outcomes are in use in the public sector within the policing and quasi-judicial systems of the UK and US, where the outcomes of their decisions have similarly shown bias; in particular racial bias.[107] A bias-generating AI system such as Amazon's hiring AI, it seems, is unacceptable when operating within Amazon itself but exporting it to other organizations to be inflicted on the wider public is acceptable. In a broader sense the Amazon example illustrates that the unconstrained control of AI development within the tech industry risks exporting that industry's particularly problematic gender, racial and technical bias (see the discussion of the black box proposition below) outside the tech sphere to companies where those specific biases have not been present or at least not present to the extent they are within a narrow, male, science-dominated and sci-fi-influenced tech industry. This tech bias contagion within AI has the potential to do enormous harm.

In a high-quality AI model the design, operation and outcomes should always have a wide range of human oversight from humans with different backgrounds because, as discussed above, bias is seriously problematic. In short, weak AI is not a neutral, intelligent, technological agent shaping human society but rather one designed, made and implemented by a particularly narrow and problematic group of humans. This is widely misunderstood even by the AI tech industry, as the Amazon example illustrates.

Black boxes and explainability

However, not all AI is based on basic machine learning. Some tasks, such as image recognition and speech recognition/translation, contain nuance and subtleties that basic weak AI statistical systems will not capture. As such, more complex, deep-learning AI models, such as artificial neural networks, have been developed to operate slightly differently, combining various

---

[106] B. Marr, 'The amazing ways how [*sic*] Unilever uses artificial intelligence', *Forbes* (12 December 2018) https://www.forbes.com/sites/bernardmarr/2018/12/14/the-amazing-ways-how-unilever-uses-artificial-intelligence-to-recruit-train-thousands-of-employees/#3e7b38436274; and J. Burn-Murdoch, 'The problem with algorithms: magnifying misbehaviour', *The Guardian* (14 August 2013) https://www.theguardian.com/news/datablog/2013/aug/14/problem-with-algorithms-magnifying-misbehaviour.

[107] New Statesman/IBM, 'AI in the public sector', *New Statesman* (22 June 2018) https://www.newstatesman.com/wp-content/uploads/sites/2/files/ns_ibm_supplement_june_2018_1_.pdf; J. Angwin, J. Larson, S. Mattu and L. Kirchner, 'Machine bias', ProPublica (23 May 2016) https://www.propublica.org/article/machine-bias-risk-assessments-in-criminal-sentencing; and M. Burgess, 'UK police are using AI to inform custodial decisions', *Wired* (1 March 2018) https://www.wired.co.uk/article/police-ai-uk-durham-hart-checkpoint-algorithm-edit.

machine-learning statistical algorithms into a framework originally designed to mimic how the neural networks in the human brain operate.[108] As Jones describes it:

> In the 1980s, one better way seemed to be deep learning in neural networks. These systems promised to learn their own rules from scratch and offered the pleasing symmetry of using brain-inspired mechanics to achieve brain-like function. The strategy called for simulated neurons to be organized into several layers. Give such a system a picture and the first layer of learning will simply notice all the dark and light pixels. The next layer might realize that some of these pixels form edges; the next might distinguish between horizontal and vertical lines. Eventually, a layer might recognize eyes, and might realize that two eyes are usually present in a human face…[109]

Artificial neural networks are particularly good at locating patterns within data sets. So, from examples of cat images, an artificial neural network can work with new images and eventually identify, with hopefully 90%-plus accuracy, a cat or maybe even a particular type of cat. In all, its success in real-world applications has been its ability to automate and speed up pattern recognition across a wide range of uses, such as speech recognition, internet searches or mapping the brain. However, this complexity can come with a significant flaw; explaining the basis for the program's decisions can be difficult, and this is the root of the black box proposition.[110]

The black box proposition is that the decision-making inside the AI system is so complex that it is not possible to know why a particular outcome arose. This does not occur because inside the AI black box is an inscrutable deep thinker – it is still a statistical model – but because the AI has been put into use when only half-built; it is missing a key diagnostic component that would explain the outcomes. The black box proposition is in essence an AI industry defensive response. For the same reason that bias has historically been a problem with AI and computer programs generally, so too have these systems been deployed: because a narrow group of mostly male designers from a maths/engineering culture have not been concerned to know the basis of the decision, just that it works within certain technical parameters. In effect a technical echo of the line in *Jurassic Park* about the scientific preoccupation

---

[108] W. Sarle, 'Neural networks and statistical models' in *Proceedings of the Nineteenth Annual SAS Users Group International Conference* (SAS Publishing, 1994) 1538–1550.

[109] N. Jones, 'Computer science: the learning machines' (2014) 505 *Nature* 146–148 at 147.

[110] P. Voosen, 'How AI detectives are cracking open the black box of deep learning', *Science* (6 July 2017) https://www.sciencemag.org/news/2017/07/how-ai-detectives-are-cracking-open-black-box-deep-learning.

with whether it 'could' be done rather than if it 'should' be done.[111] In some situations, such as image analysis, where someone is searching for cat pictures on the internet, this technical development bias might be fine, as explaining why a cat image was or wasn't chosen won't usually be important; but where explainability is important, for example in the legal or medical arena, it is seriously problematic, as the hidden reason for the decision may be dangerous or unlawful.[112] Unfortunately, explainability has not until recently begun to pervade that engineering culture.[113]

These systems have been deployed because the designers have not been concerned about the basis of the AI's decision, but with its operational 'beauty', even if they have no idea how it works, and this strongly exhibits a form of narrow maths/engineering mindset bias.[114] As Lanier has expressed it, a belief in scientific truth and the search for sentient AI takes on the hallmarks of religious fervour when it takes hold within a narrow engineering culture.[115] For computer scientists and engineers, the key may be that the AI produces seemingly high percentage outcomes, but for lawyers, medical staff and citizens subject to its outcomes, and ultimately for these systems to be lawful, safe or useful in operation, the key is the basis upon which those operational decisions are made. Medical staff need to know why dosages are to be increased and lawyers need to know why a custodial decision or deportation has been ordered, otherwise their clients are at risk of physical harm or unlawful imprisonment or both. As Shah has noted: 'How to ensure that the algorithm is fair, how to make sure the algorithm is really interpretable and explainable – that's still quite far off.'[116]

This lack of explainability raises a significant legal red flag with the application of heuristic deep-learning AI black box systems in democratic rule of law jurisdictions where citizens can challenge state decisions based on flawed decision-making, or in situations where recourse to the courts or

---

[111] G. Recchia, 'The fall and rise of AI: investigating AI narratives with computational methods' in S. Cave, K. Dihal and S. Dillon (eds), *AI Narratives: A History of Imaginative Thinking about Intelligent Machines* (Oxford University Press, 2020) Chapter 16, 402. See https://www.quotes.net/movies/jurassic_park_6097.

[112] J. Zerilli, A. Knott, J. Maclaurin and C. Gavaghan, 'Transparency in algorithmic and human decision-making: is there a double standard?' (2018) *Philosophy & Technology* 1–23, https://doi.org/10.1007/s13347-018-0330-6.

[113] Zerilli et al., above n. 112.

[114] S. Hossenfelder, *Lost in Math: How Beauty Leads Physics Astray* (Civitas, 2018).

[115] J. Lanier, *Who Owns the Future?* (Allen Lane, 2013) 186.

[116] Dastin, above n. 102.

appeal from the courts depends on knowing the reasons for a decision.[117] In short, the absence of due process in AI decision-making is a serious threat to the rule of law even though often it is branches of the justice system that are utilizing these black box systems.[118] Similarly, as observed below, knowing the reason for a medical diagnosis or why a self-driving car crashed is crucial. Indeed, even knowing why a particular image was chosen can be important. As Fjelland considers:

> In a traditional computer program all the parameters are explicit. This guarantees full transparency. In a neural network this transparency is lost. One often does not know what parameters are used. Some years ago, a team at University of Washington developed a system that was trained to distinguish between huskies and wolves. This is a task that requires considerable skill, because there is not much difference between them. In spite of this the system had an astonishing 90% accuracy. However, the team discovered that the system recognized wolves because there was snow on most of the wolf pictures. The team had invented a snow detector![119]

In the health sphere, similar heuristic 'snow detector' issues have occurred where, for example, an AI working on pneumonia X-ray image scans, rather than identifying signs of pneumonia on the scans, as the researchers planned, focused on identifying the X-ray machines that took the scans, as certain machines were used when patients were particularly ill with pneumonia and therefore had a higher correlation with pneumonia than other factors. They had invented an X-ray machine identifier and not a pneumonia identifier.[120] These types of systems operate on identifying patterns and not necessarily patterns of huskies or pneumonia; just patterns that achieve a high level of statistical success. In no way is it looking for huskies or pneumonia, nor does it know what it has found; it is simply finding patterns associated with a defined outcome, no matter what that pattern is. If the pattern associated with success is snow or a particular X-ray machine then that will be the heuristic and often procrustean focus of the AI.[121] If that inherent heuristic element isn't under-

---

[117] See for example *Council of Civil Service Unions v Minister for the Civil Service* [1984] UKHL 9.

[118] Durham police have been using a black box AI system with opaque outcomes to make custodial decisions since 2017. See Burgess, above n. 107.

[119] Fjelland, above n. 5 at 4.

[120] J. Zech, M. Badgeley, M. Liu, A. Costa, J. Titano and E. Oermann, 'Variable generalization performance of a deep learning model to detect pneumonia in chest radiographs: a cross-sectional study' (2018) *PLoS Med.* Nov 6;15(11):e1002683; doi: 10.1371/journal.pmed.1002683; PMID: 30399157; PMCID: PMC6219764.

[121] For a list of amazing heuristic examples see https://docs.google.com/spreadsheets/d/e/2PACX-1vRPiprOaC3HsCf5Tuum8bRfzYUiKLRqJmbOoC-32JorNdfyTiR RsR7Ea5eWtvsWzuxo8bjOxCG84dAg/pubhtml.

stood by those designing, producing and using the AI, then serious harm can occur.

Both Google and IBM have been developing AI health applications based around their general AI programs. IBM's Watson for Oncology offers a salutary lesson in the limits of the black box. As with Google's AlphaGo game-playing AI, IBM developed Watson to play a popular US TV game called Jeopardy, in which the contestants are given the answer to a question, and they must provide the question. Six years and enormous resources went into the project, with Watson eventually triumphing over a Jeopardy grand master in 2011. Finding a business outlet for Watson's very specific skill set proved challenging, but eventually Watson for Oncology was the outcome. The only problem was that the skill set for Jeopardy was not easily transferable to real-world cancer treatment. The answer was to apply a Great and Powerful Oz[122] solution and have outcomes provided by doctors in one hospital in the US for Watson to draw on. As Ross and Swetlitz found in 2017, in an investigation into the problems being reported about Watson for Oncology:

> The system is essentially Memorial Sloan Kettering in a portable box. Its treatment recommendations are based entirely on the training provided by doctors, who determine what information Watson needs to devise its guidance as well as what those recommendations should be.[123]

In some ways IBM became a victim of the general AI misunderstanding and its own marketing claims that Watson would cure cancer, when really Watson is no different from other types of machine learning where tags such as 'cat' or 'not a cat' are used to identify images to train the AI. In this case, it was doctors at one US hospital that did the tagging as to symptoms and treatment plans.

In the context of medical care, Watson for Oncology revealed certain key problems. First, in a complex field such as cancer care, a narrow data set of cancer diagnoses based in one hospital in a middle-class US setting is unlikely to be easily scalable for treatment all over the world, where very different medical and nutritional circumstances are present. Second, those using Watson found it difficult to understand why it was recommending a particular course of treatment, when it was counterintuitive or possibly wrong. Watson could provide literature to read that might be relevant but could not explain why it was relevant or the key reasons for the recommendation. The concern of medical staff using Watson being that the black box might be focused on

---

[122] Baum, above n. 3.
[123] C. Ross and I. Swetlitz, 'IBM pitched its Watson supercomputer as a revolution in cancer care', STAT (5 September 2017) https://www.statnews.com/2017/09/05/watson-ibm-cancer/.

'snow' rather than 'huskies' and in life-or-death situations, the possibility that it is 'snow' is too dangerous. Responding to this demand, IBM now sells an AI product that it claims helps understand the black box outcomes of its other AI products.[124] Things might have been different had IBM set out to design an AI application to cure cancer, starting with an understanding of the complexity of real-world cancer treatment, rather than setting out to design an AI to play Jeopardy and attempting to adapt it.

In March 2018, an autonomous Uber car crashed into and killed a woman wheeling a bicycle across a road during testing. Problems with the maintenance of the car and the failure of the human safety backup driver in the car combined with its AI decision-making to cause the death.[125] Tesla similarly had a fatality linked to the failure of its Autopilot driving system. While the accidents dented public confidence in autonomous vehicles, the implication for AI more generally was that the investigators found it difficult to determine the decision-making of the AI, particularly in the Tesla fatality.[126] Decisions inside the AI black box were so complex, it seemed, that they struggled to fully discover their role in the fatality.

This marks a significant change to the regulatory challenge, where knowing what happened is essential for a range of regulators, from road/air safety to medical and financial. The proposition from the manufacturers, at least at first, was that where AI is involved, it is an autonomous intelligent black box and not a statistical/probability model designed and implemented at too early a stage by the company. If the AI made the decision autonomously then the proposition seems to be that it was not Uber, Tesla, IBM or Google's fault. With this approach even weak AI would have to be accommodated in an autonomous legal liability process.[127] As Stilgoe considered in response to the black box autonomy proposition of self driving cars:

> The terms 'self-driving cars', 'autonomous vehicles' and 'driverless cars' have been used almost interchangeably in public discourse ... The differences in nuance implied by these terms should not distract us from a larger concern, which is with

---

[124]   IBM Openscale, https://www.ibm.com/cloud/watson-openscale.

[125]   National Transportation Safety Board, 'Preliminary Report HWY18MH010' (NTSB, 2018).

[126]   J. Stilgoe and A. Winfield, 'Self-driving car companies should not be allowed to investigate their own crashes', *The Guardian* (13 April 2018) https://www.theguardian.com/science/political-science/2018/apr/13/self-driving-car-companies-should-not-be-allowed-to-investigate-their-own-crashes and https://www.nytimes.com/2021/03/23/business/teslas-autopilot-safety-investigations.html.

[127]   C. Reed, E. Kennedy and S. Silva, 'Responsibility, autonomy and accountability: legal liability for machine learning' (2016) Queen Mary School of Law Legal Studies Research Paper No. 243/2016.

the rhetoric of autonomous technology. Technology, however, is never self-driving ... Claims that technology has a will of its own ... typically disguise a political agenda that is libertarian and deregulatory.[128]

The autonomous black box is an illusion. A black box is a half-finished, poorly designed, admittedly complex heuristic statistical model, that has been deployed too early in its development because of a narrow, self-reflective, maths/engineering culture that focused on 'could' rather than 'should'.

Self-interest AI design
Some AI designers, however, understand that because AI is a product of human design, the potential exists for AI to shape the world to their own private ends in novel AI circumstances. This presents particular public interest regulatory concerns. In the 1970s fears arose in the AI literature that in the trolley problem,[129] or lose/lose scenarios, the autonomous car AI would be programmed to save the car passengers over those outside it.[130] Indeed, as autonomous vehicles reached more realistic end-stage development, Mercedes executives appeared to confirm that Mercedes AI systems were programmed to save the driver and passengers over those outside the car.[131] Important legal concerns arise here. AI does genuinely present novel possibilities for better decision-making that lie outside the realm of human ability, but only if it is well designed and the normative public interest aspects of the human AI design decisions are recognized and implemented. An autonomous car may make better decisions because its sensors and AI decision-making can potentially react quicker than a human can. For example, if something appears suddenly in front of a human driver, their reaction is to break suddenly or swerve to avoid the object. The reaction will be the same whether the object is a plastic bag or a human. In each case, the driver chooses to place themselves, the passengers and potentially other road users at risk over an unknown external object because the human cannot determine what the object is in time to make the best decision. In the plastic bag example, breaking or swerving is not likely to be the best choice. The AI can potentially make a better choice if programmed to place the lives

---

[128] J. Stilgoe, 'Machine learning, social learning and the governance of self-driving cars' (2018) 48(1) *Social Studies of Science* 25–56 at 35.
[129] In a classic trolley test a human has an option to switch a trolley (tram/train) car that will kill a group of people to another track where it will kill only one. See P. Foot, *Virtues and Vices* (Oxford University Press, 1978) Chapter 2.
[130] B. Casey, 'Amoral machines, or: how roboticists can learn to stop worrying and love the law' (2017) 111(5) *Northwestern University Law Review* 231–250.
[131] M. Taylor, 'Self driving Mercedes will prioritise occupant safety over pedestrians', *Car and Driver* (7 October 2016) https://www.caranddriver.com/news/a15344706/self-driving-mercedes-will-prioritize-occupant-safety-over-pedestrians/.

of those in the car and other road users in priority to the bag. However, in the trolley test situation, where it is a choice between saving the driver and passengers or someone stepping onto the street in front of the car, choices are already being made by the car manufacturer to favour the driver and the passengers. After all, the industry logic goes, they paid for the product.[132]

Similarly, Facebook's AI algorithms are deliberately used to shape people's perception of events and can facilitate discriminatory behaviour.[133] China's development of AI is primarily driven by its recognition of AI's design potential to achieve Xi Jinping's personal authoritarian ends. Designed bias was exposed in the financial sector when in 2010 the bank Capital One used its understanding of algorithmic bias to deliberately channel ethnic minority customers to higher interest credit cards.[134] Online retailers, including Amazon, use or have used differential pricing based on algorithm bias.[135] In 2010 and 2015 flash crashes in the financial markets were blamed on algorithmic trading. This was correct, but what was little understood was that these were not rogue trading algorithms; these were algorithms that were deliberately designed by traders to manipulate the market and cause the crash.[136] Novel 'designed' AI decision-making such as this has important public interest regulatory implications. It should not be left to the AI designers to decide, in their own interests, the financial market prices, interest rates, general price fixing, who to vote for, or who lives and dies.

---

[132] J. Bonnefon, A. Shariff and I. Rahwan, 'Autonomous vehicles need experimental ethics: are we ready for utilitarian cars?' (2015) 352 Science 1573–1576; P. König and P. Gordon. 'Using virtual reality to assess ethical decisions in road traffic scenarios' (2017) 11 Frontiers in Behavioral Neuroscience 122.

[133] W. Knight, 'Forget killer robots, bias is the real AI danger', *MIT Technology Review* (3 October 2017) https://www.technologyreview.com/s/608986/forget-killer -robotsbias-is-the-real-ai-danger/; A. Madrigal, 'What Facebook did to America', *The Atlantic* (12 October 2017) https://www.theatlantic.com/technology/archive/2017/10/ what-facebook-did/542502/; and Department of Housing and Urban Development, 'HUD charges Facebook with housing discrimination', Press Release No. 19-035 (28 March 2019).

[134] Garcia, above n. 91 at 114.

[135] V. Heffernan, 'Amazon's Prime Suspect', *New York Times* (6 August 2010) https://www.nytimes.com/2010/08/08/magazine/08FOB-medium-t.html.

[136] S. Brush, T. Schoenberg and S. Ring, 'How a mystery trader with an algorithm may have caused the flash crash', Bloomberg News (22 April 2015) https://www .bloomberg.com/news/articles/2015-04-22/mystery-trader-armed-with-algorithms -rewrites-flash-crash-story; and A. Weinberg, 'Should you fear the ETF? ETFs are scaring regulators and investors: Here are the dangers – real and perceived', Wall Street Journal (6 December 2015) https://www.wsj.com/articles/should-you-fear-the -etf-1449457201.

Trusting the AI

An additional exacerbating factor that drives potential AI harm is the general misunderstanding, linked to the sci-fi veneer, that AI has superior intelligence to humans and therefore that the human user and humans subject to the AI should defer to its outcomes even when an outcome is manifestly problematic and unexplained. In the medical profession there is a long and painful history of deference to computer outcomes in complex diagnosis situations such as radiology dosages, where experienced professionals have simply accepted clearly mistaken dosages produced by an assumed superior computer. As a *New York Times* investigation found in 2010, in the context of computerized radiology dosages,

> while this new technology allows doctors to more accurately attack tumors and reduce certain mistakes, its complexity has created new avenues for error – through software flaws, faulty programming, poor safety procedures or inadequate staffing and training. [H]ospitals … are often too trusting of the new computer systems and software, relying on them as if they had been tested over time, when in fact they have not.[137]

In 2018 and 2019 two crashes within a few months of each other, involving Boeing's new 737 Max 8 quasi-autonomous fly-by-wire system, have thrown up further issues of complexity atrophy and AI complexity. Pilots cushioned by years of fly-by-wire autonomous flying may have been unable to deal with suddenly having to fly a plane in difficult circumstances, when that plane has been aerodynamically designed to be primarily piloted or assisted by AI, or may have been fighting to correct a fly-by-wire decision made by the computer system but not understood by the pilots.[138] The assumed superior ability of the computer to make the right decision impacted strongly at the design stage and exacerbated the secondary complexity issues experienced by the pilots.

These combinations may also have greater impact where AI is being used by non-experts, such as in an employment or public sector situation. Richard Eppink, the legal director of the ACLU Idaho, who has been at the forefront

---

[137] W. Bogdanich, 'Radiation offers new cures, and ways to do harm', *New York Times* (23 January 2010) https://www.nytimes.com/2010/01/24/health/24radiation.html.

[138] G. Topham, 'Ethiopian flight 302: second new Boeing 737 to crash in four months', *The Guardian* (10 March 2019) https://www.theguardian.com/world/2019/mar/10/ethiopian-flight-302-second-new-boeing-737-max-8-to-crash-in-four-months; and Stilgoe, above n. 128 at 34.

of litigation challenging problematic AI decision-making in the public sector, considered:

> My hunch is that this kind of thing is happening a lot across the United States and across the world as people move to these computerized systems. Nobody understands them, they think that somebody else does – but in the end we trust them. Even the people in charge of these programs have this trust that these things are working.[139]

In the AI context, complexity/superiority atrophy adds to the already problematic issues identified earlier, making it difficult for users to tell the difference between a counterintuitive and potentially life-saving AI outcome and a mistake.

Undermining legal norms – ten in a hundred
Even the highest quality AI decision-making models present challenges for the user and those subject to its decision-making. AI decision-making is not 100% accurate relative to the human decisions it has been trained against. A really high-quality system might get to 90% but many systems are in use at lower accuracy rates. Accuracy of 90% plus in the calibrating/training process is also not what it seems. Most large AI data sets are incomplete and have been statistically enhanced to complete them. This means that, in reality, their accuracy may well be below 90% in application, as some of the data is deliberately incorrect in order to make it operational.[140] Poorly designed software, and bugs in the software, and problems with hardware can also affect AI accuracy. Indeed, large-scale human facial recognition AI systems deployed by the Metropolitan Police and South Wales Police have been revealed to have accuracy rates outside the lab of only 2% and 10% respectively, generating thousands of false positive criminal identifications of innocent citizens.[141] Uncertain environments that do not conform to the training environment can also be problematic. For example, currency-trading AI used to trade UK currency was suspended when the unpredictability of fluctuations due to Brexit

---

[139] J. Stanley, 'Pitfalls of artificial intelligence decision making highlighted in Idaho ACLU case', ACLU (2 June 2017) https://www.aclu.org/blog/privacy-technology/pitfalls-artificial-intelligence-decisionmaking-highlighted-idaho-aclu-case.

[140] Broussard, above n. 9, Chapter 7.

[141] J. Sharman, 'Metropolitan Police's facial recognition technology 98% inaccurate', *The Independent* (13 May 2018) https://www.independent.co.uk/news/uk/home-news/met-police-facial-recognition-success-south-wales-trial-home-office-false-positive-a8345036.html.

made it useless, as it was trained on historical data.[142] An ahistorical event, i.e. something that has not happened before, is impossible to train an AI for. Similarly, AI judicial and medical decision-making models become unreliable as new variables appear that depart from the training data.[143] In essence, when the present is not like the past AI struggles, and if this is not recognized and the AI is not shut down, it locks in a future based on the past.

All this is acceptable and still useful if decisions relate to whether an image is a dog or a cat or predictive text outcomes, but 90% accuracy is much less acceptable in other contexts. In a judicial criminal process, for example, where ostensibly no innocent person should go to jail, a high-quality 90% accurate AI decision system implemented in a judicial context would result in ten in a hundred innocent citizens (or higher if from a minority group) going to jail, who would not have if humans made the decisions. A 90% lab-based accuracy in effect becomes the deeply flawed empiricization of the test of beyond reasonable doubt. As noted above, in operation that same system will have much lower accuracy as new variables in uncertain and unpredictable environments, such as courts and hospitals, are encountered that depart from its training data. As mentioned previously, certain types of black box AI would present additional insurmountable challenges in both the criminal context and in judicial review, as the reason for the decision would remain unknown and its heuristic outcomes deeply untrustworthy. In 2019 Partnership on AI produced a report stimulated by the widespread use and planned mandatory use of AI decision-making in the US judicial criminal system. In recommending that such systems should not be used to solely determine questions of individual liberty it stated:

> Using risk assessment tools to make fair decisions about human liberty would require solving deep ethical, technical, and statistical challenges, including ensuring that the tools are designed and built to mitigate bias at both the model and data layers, and that proper protocols are in place to promote transparency and accountability. The tools currently available and under consideration for widespread use suffer from several of these failures…[144]

---

[142] E. Szalay, 'The pound's "breathless marathon" tests traders' nerves', *Financial Times* (12 April 2019) https://www.ft.com/content/5ce4ae6a-5d0d-11e9-939a-341f5ada9d40.

[143] S. Levmore and F. Fagan, 'The impact of artificial intelligence on rules, standards, and judicial discretion' (2019) 93(1) *Southern California Law Review* 1, https://ssrn.com/abstract=3362563; and Fjelland, above n. 5 at 3–4.

[144] Partnership on AI, 'Report on algorithmic risk assessment tools in the US Criminal Justice System' (2019) 3, https://www.partnershiponai.org/report-on-machine-learning-in-risk-assessment-tools-in-the-u-s-criminal-justice-system/.

In the medical context similar failures might mean ten in a hundred dying who would not have otherwise died, or more if they did not match the training data set in an unpredictable environment. In the employment context a 90% accurate system would mean ten in a hundred not hired who would have been hired in a human decision-making process. Those ten will likely be statistical outliers who do not fit the norm for the organization, most likely women, ethnic minorities or those with different educational qualifications or backgrounds. Potential organizational innovators would be excluded to the detriment of the organization. As O'Neil points out, tech companies generally build systems for others to use which can shelter them from the effect of their AI. As she notes:

> Companies that build the algorithm to decide who to hire, do not care and don't have to respond to public outcry. There really probably isn't even an outcry because the effects are happening silently and the people that suffer from these algorithms are poorer, less powerful people.[145]

Despite the limits of AI decision-making, the potential for bias, the black box issues, the private versus public interest clash and the potential for complexity/ superiority atrophy, a huge driver of AI decision-making development for the public sector, private sector companies, and their clients, is cost. Cost savings of AI over human decision-making are enormous.[146] Unilever estimates a saving of 70,000 person hours using its HR AI system instead of interviewing and assessing candidates using humans.[147] Weighed against the long-term diversity and innovation of the organization in terms of candidates' sex, race, ethnicity and educational background, the balance is likely to fall in favour of cost saving. Indeed, even where diversity and innovation are valued by an organization, the AI exclusion of diverse innovators may not be recognized or quantifiable in the cost evaluation of AI implementation. While the flaws are problematic and often unlawful, they are also complex to understand and shrouded in an exciting sci-fi utopian veneer. If it is good enough and the cost savings are huge, then it will get implemented, flaws and all.[148]

---

[145] Upchurch, above n. 24.

[146] McKinsey, 'Disruptive technologies' (2013) 43, https://www.mckinsey.com/ ~/media/McKinsey/Business%20Functions/McKinsey%20Digital/Our%20Insights/ Disruptive%20technologies/MGI_Disruptive_technologies_Full_report_May2013 .ashx.

[147] Marr, above n. 106.

[148] McKinsey, 'How bots, algorithms, and artificial intelligence are reshaping the future of corporate support functions' (2018) https://www.mckinsey.com/business-functions/mckinsey-digital/our-insights/how -bots-algorithms-and-artificial-intelligence-are-reshaping-the-future-of-corporate

While in the Mercedes (passengers over pedestrians) and Capital One (charge minorities more) examples the companies recognized the normative possibilities of coding the AI to achieve an outcome that favoured their private interests over the general public, amazingly, in the Amazon employment AI example, with all its resources in AI development, Amazon seemingly gave no thought to the basic statistical integrity problem of data bias or that the AI outcomes in an employment context had to be legal. The narrowness of technical design focus, utopian sci-fi assumptions that the tech is good or the notion that this is a new determinist unregulated frontier have left a troubling absence of basic normative legal design planning at the heart of AI decision-making systems and allow the possibility of both designing against the public interest or freezing historical bias forever, locking out and locking up minorities and outliers from participation in society. As Yampolskiy puts it:

> Spam filters block important emails, GPS provides faulty directions, machine translation corrupts meaning of phrases, autocorrect replaces desired word with a wrong one, biometric systems misrecognize people, transcription software fails to capture what is being said; overall, it is harder to find examples of AIs that don't fail.[149]

As such, AI novel sentient superintelligence beings enslaving the humans is far from being our problem; rather it is mostly the consequences of poorly designed and understood weak AI applications that cause harm rather than some evolutionary superior development in thinking machines.[150] It is the mundane applications of AI that are dangerous as it has expanded into a wide range of sectors and with it the potential for AI to facilitate, among other things, illegal practices and discrimination in housing, employment, education, social welfare, insurance, finance, differential pricing, liberty, privacy and dignity, as well as undermining democratic institutions.[151] The possibility

---

-support-functions?cid=eml-web   and   https://techpricecrunch.com/blog/artificial -intelligence-statistics/.

[149] R. Yampolskiy and M. Spellchecker, 'Artificial intelligence safety and cybersecurity: a timeline of AI failures', ArXiv (25 October 2016) abs/1610.07997, 5. See also Recchia, above n. 111 at 404.

[150] For a list of AI examples where the AI correctly following its programming leads to failure, see https://docs.google.com/spreadsheets/d/e/2PACX-1vRPiprOaC3HsCf5Tu um8bRfzYUiKLRqJmbOoC-32JorNdfyTiRRsR7Ea5eWtvsWzuxo8bjOxCG84dAg/ pubhtml.

[151] See D. Kelnar, *The State of AI 2019: Divergence* (MMC Ventures, 2019) Chapter 8, https://www.stateofai2019.com/ and James X. Dempsey, 'Artificial intelligence: an introduction to the legal, policy and ethical issues', Berkeley Center for Law & Technology (10 August 2020) 1–46, https://www.law.berkeley.edu/wp -content/uploads/2020/08/Artificial-Intelligence-An-Introduction-to-the-Legal-Policy -and-Ethical-Issues_JXD.pdf.

of AI as both a designed and an unthinking driver of inequality is of huge concern. That regulatory space needs to be filled rapidly as poorly designed and potentially strongly private interest-serving AI is increasingly rolled out across the public and private sectors.

CONCLUSION

In essence we have two regulatory challenges, one philosophical (should it be a deterministic enabling deregulatory approach or a human construction approach) and one technical (how do we use regulation to fix the problems we have already identified). For the philosophical challenge the scientific versus values proposition isn't quite as black and white as it is often viewed by the AI community. The core Copernican/Galileo and Nazi observations about negative values-based state approaches to regulating science are entirely valid observations about the historical negative role of some forms of state in scientific endeavour. However, while those approaches are present in China, where for example algorithms must conform with the Chinese Communist Party's increasingly autocratic values,[152] they are not present in democratic rule of law jurisdictions. In democratic rule of law jurisdictions there is no equivalent of forcing scientists to advocate that the Sun revolves around the Earth or that we experiment on prisoners as a way of addressing AI's pre-existing problems. The AI problems identified in this chapter are neither in the realm of historical extreme values or indeed blurry ethical or moral dilemmas, but cut at core legal pre-existing protections necessary for the functioning of a democratic rule of law jurisdiction. If there is a values-led danger in democratic rule of law states, it is of a tech determinist corporatocracy. However, despite tech companies treating AI problems as simply ethical issues,[153] discrimination based on gender, race, disability and other characteristics, misuse of data, distorting elections, financial fraud, employment law breaches, car and aeroplane crash investigations and issues such as explainability plus criminal tests of beyond reasonable doubt are not matters that can be turned into ethical choices but core protective aspects of law in democratic rule of law jurisdictions that protect us from the very theocracy and autocracy that in turn could lead to distorted

---

[152] J. Kynge and S. Yu, 'China and Big Tech: Xi's blueprint for a digital dictatorship', *Financial Times* (7 September 2021) https://www.ft.com/content/9ef38be2-9b4d-49a4-a812-97ad6d70ea6f.

[153] Some companies are better than others, with Google in particular a significant negative outlier. However, whether they respond negatively or positively to these issues, all treat engagement as possibly good ethical practice rather than compliance with the law. M. Branscombe, 'Google grapples with ethical AI', *The New Stack* (3 March 2021) https://thenewstack.io/google-grapples-with-ethical-ai/.

values suppressing scientific endeavour. These issues are already regulated by law because of centuries of legal development designed to protect citizens. So while there are genuine issues to discuss around blurry ethical constraints being imposed on AI scientists at early stages of development,[154] attempts by the tech industry to carve out deterministic ethical responses to the problems of first-wave commercial AI are self-servingly deregulatory and strike at key aspects of our democratic rule of law systems.[155] Democratic rule of law compliant regulation rather than determinist deregulation is essential given the existing track record of commercial AI, a dysfunctional tech industry culture and the potential to cause widespread harm within our society.

And so to how we might tackle the technical regulatory problem. Although the problems we have identified are already regulated in law, they are happening in somewhat novel ways, invisibly interconnected into many areas of our lives and are developed by technology companies that come from a traditionally unregulated sector. As we have already noted, there are broadly three differing strategic approaches to regulation emerging across leading AI nations. In China AI development occurs either through direct state development of AI or through a concessionary private sector AI development whereby companies, although technically legally separate from the state, are simply creatures of the state to control at will.[156] In essence this is a model that understands the human social construction potential of AI as surveillance technology but does not considers privacy from the state or state accountability to be concerns and so does not sit easily with democratic rule of law systems.[157] It does, however, exert influence within other jurisdictions as perceptions of the Chinese model as superior or as 'winning' because of its perceived advantages with data

---

[154] T. Sopher, 'Retired UW computer science professor embroiled in Twitter spat over AI ethics and "cancel culture"', *Geekwire* (16 December 2020) https://www.geekwire.com/2020/retired-uw-computer-science-professor-embroiled-twitter-spat-ai-ethics-cancel-culture/.

[155] GlobalData Thematic Research, 'Why Google's AI ethics blunders are a PR nightmare', *The Verdict* (25 February 2021) https://www.verdict.co.uk/google-ai-ethics-ethical/; and J. Desmond, 'Unethical use of AI being mainstreamed by some business execs, survey finds', *AI Trends* (2 September 2021) https://www.aitrends.com/ethics-and-social-issues/unethical-use-of-ai-being-mainstreamed-by-some-business-execs-survey-finds/.

[156] C. Che and J. Goldkorn, 'China's "Big Tech crackdown": A guide', *SupChina* (2 August 2021) https://supchina.com/2021/08/02/chinas-big-tech-crackdown-a-guide/; and A. Dignam and M. Galanis, *The Globalization of Corporate Governance* (Ashgate, 2009) 9–10.

[157] B. Marr, 'China poised to dominate the artificial intelligence (AI) market', *Forbes* (15 March 2021) https://www.forbes.com/sites/bernardmarr/2021/03/15/china-poised-to-dominate-the-artificial-intelligence-ai-market/?sh=301bf4b01b38.

control[158] and limited accountability are often used to push back the privacy and accountability basis of those other models.[159]

The second strategic approach to AI regulation has been pioneered by the European Union and is focused again on having a role in the human construction potential of the technology, but in this model protecting the citizen through high levels of privacy and accountability built into the AI, focused around the protective data use mechanisms in the General Data Protection Regulation (GDPR).[160] The overall intention is to use protective regulation to guide a high-trust technical AI model for use within the EU.[161] The third approach has been pioneered by the US and the UK; while sharing some of the data protection and governance concerns of the European Union, it focuses more on either abstaining from regulating or enabling, often through deregulatory legislation, to create safe harbours, the private sector development of AI.[162]

In terms of operational regulation China is the most developed of the leading AI jurisdictions. In the Chinese model, state regulatory control is already operational and used to serve the authoritarian ends of Xi Jinping, who shapes the development of the AI citizenship apparatus through his control of the Cyberspace Administration of China.[163] As the *Financial Times* described it:

> Such moves comprise a crucial part of the vision of Xi Jinping, China's leader, to build what some analysts call a 'techno-authoritarian superpower' in which

---

[158] Data taken from a highly surveilled society may not be the AI advantage it is often perceived to be. See Z. Kallenborn, 'The race is on: assessing the US–China artificial intelligence competition', Modern War Institute (16 April 2019) https://mwi.usma .edu/race-assessing-us-china-artificial-intelligence-competition/.

[159] G. Allison and E. Schmidt, 'Is China beating the U.S. to AI supremacy?', Avoiding Great Power War Project, Belfer Center for Science and International Affairs, Harvard Kennedy School (August 2020) 1–24.

[160] M. Iglesias, J. Van Gyseghem, C. Holder and J. Triaille, *Legal and Regulatory Implications of Artificial Intelligence. The Case of Autonomous Vehicles, M-Health and Data Mining* (Publications Office of the European Union, 2019).

[161] European Commission, 'White Paper on Artificial Intelligence – A European approach to excellence and trust' (February 2020) Brussels COM/2020/65 final, 1–26.

[162] Department for Digital, Culture, Media & Sport and Department for Business, Energy & Industrial Strategy, 'Growing the Artificial Intelligence Industry in the UK' (2017); UK AI Council, 'AI Roadmap' (January 2021) 1–22, https://assets.publishing .service.gov.uk/government/uploads/system/uploads/attachment_data/file/949539/AI _Council_AI_Roadmap.pdf; A. Bundy, 'Preparing for the future of artificial intelligence' (2017) 32 *AI & Society* 285–287. The Biden administration has put in place a National Artificial Intelligence Initiative to advise it on AI strategy. See https://www .ai.gov/about/.

[163] X. Qiang, 'The road to digital unfreedom: President Xi's surveillance state' (2019) 30(1) *Journal of Democracy* 53–67.

people are monitored and directed to an unprecedented degree through the agency of government-controlled cyber networks, surveillance systems and algorithms.[164]

Given that one of the core propositions of this chapter is that regulatory intervention is justified given the reality of the existing failures of commercial AI and the potential for continued failure to cause significant damage to core aspects of democratic rule of law jurisdictions, the Chinese model has little to offer those jurisdictions except further erosion. In regulatory terms, among the democratic rule of law systems, the EU has more detailed regulatory proposals based around a risk assessment approach. In the EU model, AI that poses an unacceptable risk to safety, livelihood and the rights of people will be banned. The EU model also includes an AI education programme. High-risk AI that could be used, for example, in education and the judicial system will be subject to strict evaluation to ensure high data integrity, operation and oversight before it can be sold on the market. Limited risk AI, such as chatbots, will be required to have warnings for the user, and minimal risk AI, such as spam filters, will be allowed without restriction.[165] It is intended that a two-year transition period from 2022 would allow the development of technical and governance standards and that from the second part of 2024 the standards would be applied. The UK, perhaps predictably given Brexit, sees the EU standards as an opportunity. Despite widespread recognition in the UK of the dangers of AI,[166] the regulatory direction is the opposite of the EU's, with the UK government planning to remove the GDPR, remove the right to human review of algorithmic decisions and move to more 'flexible' post-Brexit data integrity standards while continuing its pre-existing deregulatory AI enabling plan.[167] In the United States the Biden administration, while making anti-tech noises during the election, has pushed its regulatory policy on AI down the road by setting up the National Artificial Intelligence Initiative to advise it. It is not yet clear if this will lead to a change in regulatory approach to AI as its advisory report will only arrive

---

[164] Kynge and Yu, above n. 152.

[165] EU Commission, Regulatory Framework Proposal on Artificial Intelligence (2021), https://digital-strategy.ec.europa.eu/en/policies/regulatory-framework-ai.

[166] The Committee on Standards in Public Life, 'Artificial Intelligence and Public Standards: A Review by the Committee on Standards in Public Life' (February 2020) 1–77; and UK AI Council, above n. 162.

[167] P. Foster, M. Murgia and J. Espinoza, 'UK suggests removing human review of AI decisions in data protection law', *Financial Times* (9 September 2021) https://www.ft.com/content/519832b6-e22d-40bf-9971-1af3d3745821; and R. Cellan-Jones, 'Data protection "shake-up" takes aim at cookie pop-ups', BBC News (26 August 2021) https://www.bbc.co.uk/news/technology-58340333.

in November 2022.[168] In a world where even IBM, Google and Microsoft[169] are advocating some sort of lead from government on AI, the approach of the UK and US seems odd, fixated as it is on the challenge of China's AI (the US)[170] or being as competitive as possible and viewing deregulation as offering an advantage (the UK).[171] In reality, AI leadership on high-quality AI development that avoids a problematic determinist approach for democratic rule of law states through regulatory standards is solely present in the EU regulatory framework. Although it is not clear yet what the exact form of the EU's AI standards will be, education, design, data integrity, transparency and human oversight seem central to the proposed framework and aim to address many of the concerns with first-wave commercial AI identified in this chapter.[172] In an ideal world, given concerns about China's autocratic AI development, the leading democratic rule of law nations would converge around a set of high trust standards for AI.[173] Unfortunately, currently there is a divide that needs bridging between the deterministic deregulatory instincts of the US and UK and the EU's high-trust social construction approach. As B.F. Skinner, the American psychologist, once stated, 'the real problem is not whether machines think but whether [people] do'.[174]

---

[168]   The White House, 'The Biden Administration Launches the National Artificial Intelligence Research Resource Task Force' (10 June 2021) https://www.whitehouse .gov/ostp/news-updates/2021/06/10/the-biden-administration-launches-the-national -artificial-intelligence-research-resource-task-force/.

[169]   R. Torres, 'At Davos, tech leaders call for AI regulation', CIODive (22 January 2020)   https://www.ciodive.com/news/at-davos-tech-leaders-call-for-ai-regulation/ 570768/.

[170]   Allison and Schmidt, above n. 159.

[171]   Department for Business, Energy & Industrial Strategy (DBEIS), 'Made Smarter. Review 2017' (2017) 9, https://assets.publishing.service.gov.uk/government/uploads/ system/uploads/attachment_data/file/655570/20171027_MadeSmarter_FINAL _DIGITAL.pdf.

[172]   European Commission, Proposal for a Regulation of the European Parliament and of the Council Laying Down Harmonised Rules on Artificial Intelligence (Artificial Intelligence Act) and Amending Certain Union Legislative Acts, COM/2021/206 final (2021)   https://eur-lex.europa.eu/legal-content/EN/TXT/?qid=1623335154975&uri= CELEX%3A52021PC0206.

[173]   This may already be emerging through EU Trade agreements. Japan, for example, intends explicitly to build on the same principles and link its AI framework to the EU's: Japan, Bureau of Science, Technology and Innovation Policy, Cabinet Office, 'Social Principles for Human-Centric AI' (April 2019) 1–10.

[174]   B. Skinner, *Contingencies of Reinforcement: A Theoretical Analysis* (Appleton, 1969).

5. Newer technologies, older attitudes, and retrograde regulation

David R. Lawrence and John Harris

INTRODUCTION

> The concept of altering the human germline in embryos for clinical purposes has been debated over many years from many different perspectives, and has been viewed almost universally as a line that should not be crossed ... Advances in technology have given us an elegant new way of carrying out genome editing, but the strong arguments against engaging in this activity remain.[1]

In 2015, Francis Collins, the then-director of the US National Institutes of Health, issued this statement as part of a wider reaction to developments in heritable genome-editing research. We, the authors of this chapter, found his statement misleading and short-sighted at best, and potentially harmful at worst. In a chapter we wrote at the time,[2] we advocated a more rational approach in evaluating controversial emerging biotechnologies, in the face of calls for wholesale bans on the use of CRISPR/Cas9 to edit genes in non-viable IVF zygotes, and on mitochondrial replacement therapy (MRT). Seven years later, after a range of startling biotechnological news stories and with the advent of novel beings becoming increasingly likely, we have seen a singular failure to adjust approaches to biotechnology regulation and a continuation of the same illogical leaps and the same subsequent harms. Our prior focus was around genome editing in and of itself, but the technologies we discussed are the very ones that will likely contribute to these new forms of sentient or

---

[1] Francis Collins, 'Statement on NIH Funding of Research Using Gene-editing Technologies in Human Embryos', National Institutes of Health (29 April 2015) <http://www.nih.gov/about/director/04292015_statement_gene_editing_technologies .htm> accessed 27 April 2022.

[2] And which was not available in print until 2017: John Harris and David R. Lawrence, 'New Technologies, Old Attitudes, and Legislative Rigidity' in Roger Brownsword, Eloise Scotford and Karen Yeung (eds), *Oxford Handbook on the Law and Regulation of Technology* (Oxford University Press 2017) 915.

sapient life. New and future technologies that build upon them are likely to be subject to similar hostility in certain quarters. They will also be similarly permissible under the range of differing moralities exemplified by international biolaw regimes. This chapter will focus on technologies with which we are familiar; but we must make no mistake – the proceedings around them and the attitudes displayed towards them are precisely those which will be levelled towards novel beings.

When considering the kinds of technology of concern to this volume, i.e. bio- and artificial intelligence (AI)-related technologies, which may themselves raise issues of moral interest or which might lead to the creation of entities qualifying for moral status equivalent to (or even surpassing) our own, our concerns of seven years ago are given a new urgency and weight. There is an increasingly insistent need to alter our deliberative regulatory process in order to avoid the deleterious effects of allowing regressive attitudes to emerging technologies to prevail, and to evolve our thinking about the most effective ways to manage both those things we can predict, and those we can only speculate on. We have always acted in arrears and suffered the consequences when science and technology outpace and outreach our regulatory capacities. Now, we risk not only harming ourselves, but causing suffering to those things we may create. There is thus a moral imperative that we evolve our approach, and no longer stick to the old ways of dealing with new technologies.

NEWER TECHNOLOGIES

The above quotation from Collins came, as we noted at the time, in the wake of the commotion in the popular media[3] that arose after the publication of research conducted in China[4] by Liang *et al.*, in which the genome of a human embryo was edited to correct mutations which are the basis of potentially severe β thalassemia-type blood disorders. This was likely the first instance of a heritable genome-editing story entering the mainstream consciousness outside science fiction and speculation, and the scientific establishment were quick to react; holding an international summit and calling for – as does Collins – 'a call for a moratorium on the clinical use of gene editing that involves alterations in the genomes of human germline cells'.[5] It should perhaps be noted here that

---

[3]   E.g. Tim Stanley, 'Three Parent Babies: Unethical, Scary and Wrong', *The Telegraph* (3 February 2015) <http://www.telegraph.co.uk/news/health/11380784/Three-parent-babies-unethical-scary-and-wrong.html> accessed 2 May 2022.

[4]   Puping Liang *et al.*, 'CRISPR/Cas9-Mediated Gene Editing in Human Tripronuclear Zygotes' (2015) 6 *Protein & Cell* 1.

[5]   Michael McCarthy, 'Scientists Call for Moratorium on Clinical Use of Human Germline Editing' (2015) *BMJ* 351.

in Liang's research, as well as that proposed by other laboratories who were at the time applying for licences in the UK to conduct similar research using the CRISPr/Cas9 process,[6] the embryos were or would have been destroyed once the procedure had been carried out and verified. No embryo involved in the research was ever used, or considered for use, in implantation or any other mode that might result in a living and viable being. The line between research and 'clinical use' is often vague, but it cannot be suggested that the latter took place here – a moratorium was being called pre-emptively, on something that had not yet happened – and that was not even being proposed.

To relate this to the theme of this volume, we might at face value think of this as a kind of extreme proactive (self-)regulation on the part of the scientific community. A full cessation of research such as this is, inarguably, acting ahead of the actual development of the technology and any contingent challenges it brings, to prevent what were seen as potential serious harms to what is sometimes referred to as the 'common heritage of humanity'.[7] However, it is also true that this is a classic example of knee-jerk reactivity to a perceived threat – 'we don't like the sound of this, so let's make it go away and not deal with it'. Old attitudes such as this tend not – and here we speak more generally than specifically regarding the call from the 2015 summit – to lend themselves to great depth of subtle analysis. As such, we are comfortable classifying calls for wholesale bans or moratoria as commonly being something other than the kind of considered, proactive approaches explored elsewhere in this volume. They may not fall into the same category as the 'reactive' regulatory approaches discussed – acting purely after the fact – but they do share in the lack of will to employ pragmatic, educated foresight as a means of steering technological development to desirable ends. We will return to this idea later.

Despite the appeals for a moratorium, research connected to heritable germline interventions continued apace. Around the time of the call, the UK Parliament approved, in principle, the use of MRTs;[8] and the technique has been tacitly approved,[9] or even legalised, in a number of countries since – including most recently Australia.[10] Several children have been born, includ-

---

[6]   'Niakan Lab Human Embryo Genome Editing Licence', The Francis Crick Institute (2016) <https://www.crick.ac.uk/research/labs/kathy-niakan/human-embryo-genome-editing-licence> accessed 2 May 2022.

[7]   Universal Declaration on the Human Genome and Human Rights (adopted 11 November 1997) BR/2001/PI/H/1.

[8]   The Human Fertilisation and Embryology (Mitochondrial Donation) Regulations 2015.

[9]   Sara Reardon, 'Reports of "Three-Parent Babies" Multiply', *Nature* (19 October 2016)   <https://www.nature.com/news/reports-of-three-parent-babies-multiply-1.20849/> accessed 2 May 2022.

[10]   Mitochondrial Donation Law Reform (Maeve's Law) Bill 2021.

ing to Greek parents in 2019,[11] and at least ten in Ukraine – likely more, but up-to-date figures are difficult to come by, not least since the murderous, illegal and entirely unprovoked invasion of that country by its neighbour Russia.[12] In the UK, at least 14 licences were granted by the Human Fertilisation and Embryology Authority (HFEA) within the first 18 months of availability,[13] although it is not clear, due to privacy requests from possible parents, whether any babies have been born from the treatment.[14] Even in countries where it was not strictly legal, children were born through mitochondrial donation – perhaps most notably in Mexico, in the case that brought most attention to the technique.[15] As we noted in our 2015 paper, Collins' claim 'regarding germline modification being "universally" shunned'[16] seems less than accurate.

More recently, in 2018, the infamous 'CRISPR babies' affair came to light – where the aims of the earlier suggested moratorium on heritable genome editing were completely upended. At the Second International Summit on Human Gene Editing,[17] He Jiankui formally presented the creation of the first gene-edited human babies, known to the world as Lulu and Nana.[18] A third child (and second birth) is reported to have followed in 2019.[19] This

---

[11]   James Gallagher, '"Three-Person" Baby Boy Born in Greece', *BBC News* (11 April 2019) <https://www.bbc.co.uk/news/health-47889387> accessed 28 April 2022.
[12]   Hitika Sharma *et al.*, 'Development of Mitochondrial Replacement Therapy: A Review' (2020) 6 *Heliyon* e04643; Dorothy Walas, 'Three Parent Baby – Pronucleus Transfer', EggDonationFriends (2019) <https://www.eggdonationfriends.com/3-parent -baby-groundbreaking-pronucleus-transfer-interview-with-nadiya-clinic> accessed 16 April 2022. As we go to press the situation in Ukraine continues to worsen, putting into acute perspective our concerns in this chapter.
[13]   Per Jackie Doyle-Price MP, in a written answer to a Parliamentary question, HC UIN 241389, tabled 5 April 2019. Available from <https://questions-statements .parliament.uk/written-questions/detail/2019-04-05/241389#> accessed 2 May 2022.
[14]   Tim Elliot, 'How Far Should Genetic Engineering go to Allow this Couple to have a Healthy Baby?', *The Sydney Morning Herald* (21 March 2020) <https://www .smh.com.au/national/how-far-should-genetic-engineering-go-to-allow-this-couple-to -have-a-healthy-baby-20191231-p53nx2.html> accessed 18 April 2022.
[15]   César Palacios-González and María de Jesús Medina-Arellano, 'Mitochondrial Replacement Techniques and Mexico's Rule of Law: On the Legality of the First Maternal Spindle Transfer Case' (2017) 4(2) *Journal of Law and the Biosciences* 384–390.
[16]   Collins (n. 1).
[17]   'Second International Summit on Human Gene Editing', National Academies (27 November 2018) <https://www.nationalacademies.org/event/11-27-2018/second -international-summit-on-human-gene-editing> accessed 2 May 2022.
[18]   Henry T. Greely, 'CRISPR'D Babies: Human Germline Genome Editing in the "He Jiankui Affair"' (2019) 6 *Journal of Law and the Biosciences* 111.
[19]   Jon Cohen, 'Inside the Circle of Trust' (2019) 365 *Science* 430.

caused uproar among the scientific community,[20] which roundly criticised He Jiankui.[21] It inspired fresh calls from scientists and ethicists for a halt on the use of CRISPR on human embryos,[22] but it also inspired copycats – most publicised was the intent of a Russian lab led by Denis Rebrikov, though it is not clear that the work was ever carried out.[23]

Much of the outcry from the media focussed on the idea that heritable germline editing – particularly when it was no longer theoretical – is in some way inherently morally wrong.[24] These are arguments that have long been made and which are, perhaps, not of particular interest here. However, the criticism among the scientific and bioethical community – whilst not devoid of this view – heavily featured a more technical bent to its ethical condemnation, focussing on recklessness and flaws in the procedure.[25] Further commentary concentrated on the fact that, in the judgement of the scientific community, the 'genome-editing technology itself is, in most people's opinion, not yet ready for use'.[26]

The Chinese establishment was quick to condemn He's work and declare it illegal,[27] and commentators made the point that, despite outside perceptions,

[20] David Cyranoski, 'The CRISPR-Baby Scandal: What's Next for Human Gene-Editing', *Nature* (26 February 2019) <https://www.nature.com/articles/d41586 -019-00673-1> accessed 2 May 2022.

[21] Joyce Harper, 'World's First Gene-Edited Babies? Premature, Dangerous and Irresponsible', *The Conversation* (26 November 2018) <https://theconversation.com/ worlds-first-gene-edited-babies-premature-dangerous-and-irresponsible-107642> accessed 2 May 2022.

[22] Eric S. Lander *et al.*, 'Adopt a Moratorium on Heritable Genome Editing', *Nature* (13 March 2019) <https://www.nature.com/articles/d41586-019-00726-5> accessed 15 April 2022.

[23] David Cyranoski, 'Russian Biologist Plans More CRISPR-Edited Babies', *Nature* (10 June 2019) <https://www.nature.com/articles/d41586-019-01770-x> accessed 2 May 2022.

[24] Recounted in, amongst many, Suzanne Sataline, '"Of Course It's Not Ethical": Shock At Gene-Edited Baby Claims', *The Guardian* (27 November 2018) <https:// www.theguardian.com/science/2018/nov/27/he-jiankui-chinese-gene-edited-baby -claims-scientists-shocked-global-outcry> accessed 2 May 2022.

[25] Henry T. Greely, 'He Jiankui, Embryo Editing, CCR5, the London Patient, and Jumping to Conclusions', STAT (15 April 2019) <https://www.statnews.com/2019/04/ 15/jiankui-embryo-editing-ccr5/> accessed 2 May 2022.

[26] Robin Lovell-Badge, 'CRISPR Babies: A View from the Centre of the Storm' (2019) 146(3) *Development* dev175778.

[27] Lily Kuo, 'Work on Gene-Edited Babies Blatant Violation of the Law, Says China', *The Guardian* (29 November 2018) <https://www.theguardian.com/science/ 2018/nov/29/work-on-gene-edited-babies-blatant-violation-of-the-law-says-china> accessed 2 May 2022.

Chinese science is far from unregulated.[28] It should be noted that He's research activity was subsequently suspended as an 'abomination' and a violation of Chinese law[29] – ultimately, he was convicted of breaking regulations pertaining to reproductive use of 'manipulated' embryos, and received three years' imprisonment alongside lesser sentences for two of his collaborators.[30] Yet the fact remains that He was able to conduct the work unimpeded, heedless of the (supposed) international consensus against doing so. Indeed, there is evidence that He conducted his work in close correspondence with leading Western scientists.[31]

Despite the evidence – in our view – that the He Jiankui case demonstrates that illegality is not any kind of guarantee against morally significant technology development or use in the immediate aftermath of the births there were fears of 'a knee-jerk reaction that might cause countries still working on regulations to make it unnecessarily hard to do this research'.[32] Had that been the case (and conceivably it still could come to pass – there have been strong calls for a further moratorium and for strict regulations to be put in place[33]), it seems likely that we would only have seen further 'undercover' research performed. Potentially this would come with even greater risks taken, less regard for ethical standards, and rather less happy outcomes than Lulu and Nana have enjoyed so far. It may not be too much to suggest that the 2015 (and earlier) calls for moratoria and bans directly contributed to the undercover nature of

---

[28] Sarah Zhang, 'Chinese Scientists Are Outraged by Reports of Gene-Edited Babies', *The Atlantic* (28 November 2018) <https://www.theatlantic.com/science/archive/2018/11/china-crispr-babies/576784/> accessed 2 May 2022.

[29] Steven Jiang, Helen Regan and Joshua Berlinger, 'China Suspends Scientists Who Claim to Have Produced Gene-Edited Babies', CNN (28 November 2018) <https://edition.cnn.com/2018/11/29/health/china-gene-editing-he-jiankui-intl/index.html> accessed 2 May 2022.

[30] David Cyranoski, 'What CRISPR-Baby Prison Sentences Mean for Research', *Nature* (3 January 2020) <https://www.nature.com/articles/d41586-020-00001-y> accessed 2 May 2022. At the time of writing, He Jiankui had recently been released: Antonio Regalado, 'The Creator of the CRISPR Babies Has Been Released from a Chinese Prison', *MIT Technology Review* (4 April 2022) <https://www.technologyreview.com/2022/04/04/1048829/he-jiankui-prison-free-crispr-babies/> accessed 5 April 2022.

[31] Sandy LaMotte, 'Rice Professor Under Investigation for Role in "World's First Gene-Edited Babies"', CNN (28 November 2018) <https://edition.cnn.com/2018/11/27/health/gene-edited-babies-rice-investigates-professor/index.html> accessed 2 May 2022.

[32] David Cyranoski and Heidi Ledford, 'How the Genome-Edited Babies Revelation Will Affect Research', *Nature* (27 November 2018) <https://www.nature.com/articles/d41586-018-07559-8> accessed 2 May 2022.

[33] Lander *et al.* (n. 22).

the He-led research; if there was reason to think any suggestion of the work being done would draw ire and opprobrium, it would have made sense to keep it secret until a success could be presented as a fait accompli.

The implication of the scientific community's focus on the key moral problem as stemming from broadly technical rather than substantive issues is instructive. It is undoubted that there is significant interest in using processes similar to He's in order to prevent and treat diseases – He's own stated purpose – and we might speculate that some geneticists may be secretly pleased that someone took this step to test the technique. Rightly or wrongly, we will now see what the consequences might be – and if they are not negative, it could set a precedent. We could think of it as a crack in the dam; even if no one dares widen it quite yet, it will likely lead to the dam breaking in future. Indeed, some high-profile commentators have offered cautious support for He's work. At the time, George Church suggested that if the children were healthy, as appears to be the case, then the situation might be viewed in future like that of Louise Brown, the first IVF baby – rather than a Jesse Gelsinger, who died in a 1999 gene therapy trial – the backlash for which delayed the further deployment of gene therapies by some time.[34] Among other voices, Arthur Caplan suggested that – whilst He was wrong not to wait until there was proof of safety and efficacy in human embryo editing – 'genetic engineering of human beings is inevitable', and that '[t]his idea that we're not going to do gene editing when it gets close to enhancement or improvement, I find it silly and head-in-the-sand kind of stuff.'[35] Clearly, there is no real expectation that any moratorium or knee-jerk ban would hold fast.

He Jiankui's work was hardly the first such crack in the dam of consensus against heritable genome editing. As we noted in our earlier work,

> The consensus against germline interventions *per se* – a consensus that one of us long ago argued was ill-conceived[36] – is now crumbling. The recent vote in the UK Parliament[37] to change the law concerning germline interventions (along with

---

[34] Jon Cohen, '"I Feel an Obligation to be Balanced." Noted Biologist Comes to Defense of Gene Editing Babies', *Science* (28 November 2018) <https://www.science.org/content/article/i-feel-obligation-be-balanced-noted-biologist-comes-defense-gene-editing-babies> accessed 2 May 2022.

[35] Anna Almendrala, 'World's First Gene-Edited Babies Could Set Genetic Science Backward, Experts Fear', *Huffington Post* (27 November 2018) <https://www.huffingtonpost.co.uk/entry/gene-edited-babies-hiv-scientists_n_5bfd80eae4b0771fb6bed214> accessed 2 May 2022.

[36] John Harris, *Wonderwoman and Superman: The Ethics of Human Biotechnology* (Oxford University Press 1992) Chapter 8.

[37] Gretchen Vogel and Erik Stokstad, 'U.K. Parliament Approves Controversial Three-Parent Mitochondrial Gene Therapy', *Science Magazine* (3 February 2015)

the previously mentioned recent application to conduct such research in human embryos) and the willingness of the United States Institute of Medicine of the National Academies to make a serious and objective re-assessment of these issues,[38] are just two examples.[39]

The examples we deployed were quite new at the time of writing. Since then, that crumbling has continued – notably with the 'Jiankui affair'. In 2016, Kathy Niakan at the Crick Institute led the first laboratory to be licensed to undertake CRISPR/Cas9 embryo editing research in the UK.[40] Any embryos had to be destroyed after 14 days, and certainly could never have been implanted or brought to term as were Lulu and Nana – although, as noted above, their 'creation' was illegal in China as well. In the wake of this, various actors have produced guidance to try and influence policy development around genome editing. Internationally, a commission run jointly by the US National Academies of Medicine and Sciences and the UK Royal Society published a report in 2020 setting out a list of recommendations for a responsible translational pathway to deploy the technology.[41] In 2021, the World Health Organization published reports[42] providing proposals for governance in order that human genome editing be established 'as a tool for public health, with an emphasis on safety, effectiveness and ethics'.[43] The existence of these reports could be interpreted as evidence of a recognition that germline editing technology is here to stay, and must therefore be engaged with. Their existence is also mildly encouraging; they are not themselves regulatory instruments, so we cannot say they represent a change in legislative attitude to emerging technology, and nor do they truly come before the impact of the science has been

---

<http://news.sciencemag.org/biology/2015/02/u-k-parliament-approves-controversial-three-parent-mitochondrial-gene-therapy> accessed 2 May 2022.

[38] National Academies of Sciences, Engineering, and Medicine, *Mitochondrial Replacement Techniques: Ethical, Social, and Policy Considerations* (The National Academies Press 2016) <https://doi.org/10.17226/21871> accessed 2 May 2022.

[39] Harris and Lawrence (n. 2).

[40] Crick Institute (n. 6).

[41] National Academy of Medicine, National Academy of Sciences, and the Royal Society, *Heritable Human Genome Editing* (The National Academies Press 2020). <https://doi.org/10.17226/25665> accessed 1 May 2022.

[42] WHO Expert Advisory Committee on Developing Global Standards for Governance and Oversight of Human Genome Editing, *Human Genome Editing: Recommendations* (World Health Organization 2021) <https://www.who.int/publications/i/item/9789240030381> accessed 2 May 2022.

[43] 'WHO Issues New Recommendations on Human Genome Editing for the Advancement of Public Health', WHO (12 July 2021) <https://www.who.int/news/item/12-07-2021-who-issues-new-recommendations-on-human-genome-editing-for-the-advancement-of-public-health> accessed 2 May 2022.

felt. They are simultaneously proactive and reactive – coming after the fact of heritable genome editing was demonstrated, but attempting a form of foresight into the developments that may yet come. They come too late to prevent the Jiankui affair, but perhaps have an opportunity to influence governance of the science in future; they are aided in this, perhaps, by the recoil from any further human embryo editing experimentation in the wake of the twins' birth slowing matters.

However, this undercover research, this lawbreaking, could all have been avoided. This eventuality was entirely predictable; we should not have been surprised that someone would try to bring to term an edited embryo. The recommendations, reports, and other attempts to influence the future of development ought to have been in place already, able to facilitate and manage attempts to do so. It is one thing to conduct controversial research under dark of night, and quite another to be able to do it in daylight, legitimised and scrutinised alternately as part of a broader scientific community. We will return to our proposed approach later.

LEGISLATIVE RIGIDITY

We have established that moratoria and the like are ineffective. Recent examples such as MRT use and the CRISPR twins demonstrate that the work will happen regardless. In part, we put this down to our contention in our original chapter that 'we may assume that differing global moralities are free to exist unimpeded under international biolaw regimes, and they do not in any way represent unified opinion against a technology such as germline modification'.[44] In other words, it does not seem reasonable to call for an international ban on something where it is almost certain that not all will agree that such a ban is either needed or morally required. Just as this is true of genome editing, it is true of the prospect of novel beings, or any morally inflected technology – novel beings perhaps most of all, given their potential to upset the social balance or 'frighten the horses'.

In our prior piece, we described at some length the ways in which the international biotechnological legal landscape – with particular focus on the Council of Europe's Convention on Human Rights and Biomedicine (ECHRB) – fails to demonstrate the 'universal consensus' invoked by Collins. Examining again the example of the ECHRB, it seems important to note that we are no closer to such a consensus – and the issues of concern to that document are likely to be less controversial than the emergence of new morally valuable entities.

---

[44] Harris and Lawrence (n. 2).

The ECHRB was intended to constitute a binding reference for patient rights and general human rights in the context of advancements in biotechnology and medical science. It has, numerically speaking, been quite successful in its uptake. The official listings at the time of our original publication indicated that out of 47 member states, 35 were signatories, and of these, 29 have ratified the Convention. Since that time, only one further state – Andorra – has signed, in 2021.[45] Notably, they have not ratified the Convention, and it seems unlikely at this stage that any further nations will do so unless there are major new additions to the Council of Europe.

It is also worth noting once more that several of the leading member states in biotechnological research, for example the United Kingdom, Germany, and Belgium, made clear their disagreement with the Convention by choosing not to sign at all. It was indicated in the UK that these disagreements were to do with the restrictiveness of the Convention chiefly over Article 18, regarding cloning human embryos for research, amongst other 'significant articles that conflict with [UK] legislation'.[46] On the other hand, the German position was that the document was too permissive.[47] We think that this paints the issue rather starkly; if two nations with similar cultural backgrounds and advanced techno-regulatory regimes can have entirely opposed reactions, what hope can there be for unity?

With technologies likely to contribute to the birth of the novel being developing so quickly, there is the further problem that many nations will not have had the time or expertise to cultivate a comprehensive stance. As a result, it seems likely that we won't be able to avoid a divided world for this kind of research. Nations with developed regulation of biotechnology will be able to adapt more easily to the latest advances and put measures in place; although as discussed, this is no guarantee of useful or effective action or indeed international cooperation. Other states will scramble to keep up, leaving scientists to proceed potentially without appropriate oversight of the ethical or social implications of their work. This, of course, assumes that all governments will want to restrict this kind of research, which they may not. Some may see value in being a home of scientific freedom, or of biotechnological advancement in a new field.

---

[45] Convention for the Protection of Human Rights and Dignity of the Human Being with Regard to the Application of Biology and Medicine (Council of Europe's Convention on Human Rights and Biomedicine) (ECHRB).

[46] Science and Technology Committee, 'Fifth Report' (HC 2004-5, 7–11) para. 17.

[47] Roberto Andorno, 'The Oviedo Convention: A European Legal Framework at the Intersection of Human Rights and Health Law' (2005) 2 *Journal of International Biotechnology Law* 133.

There has been the suggestion that many of the original signatories and ratifiers of the ECHRB, to continue the example, did so 'with no indication of engagement by parliamentary deputies, specialist committees, professional bodies, or the wider public'.[48] We must ask, then, whether what might be termed 'mimetic' uptake of legislation without proper and mature consideration in this manner can be truly considered to represent consensus. We must consider that for the most part, the newly sovereign states (largely post-Soviet Bloc) that signed quickly lacked specialist bioethical and patient rights legislation,[49] having had to construct and legislate for a recently democratised state; and may have signed partly in pursuit of legitimisation. There is strong support for this view in that in many cases their human rights policy was formed on the basis of Council of Europe guidelines, and we note that most of the constitutions of these nations hold that the norms of ratified international treaties are directly applicable in the national legislation.[50] These states were presented with ready-made legislation covering gaps in their own, which was fully and legally applicable with no further domestic law-making required. None of the states engaged in meaningful debate over any part of the Convention, if at all, and so ratifications came quickly and without dissent. This example perhaps demonstrates how inappropriate regulatory policy can be perpetuated, and given the pace of geopolitics, once law is in place matters tend not to be seriously re-evaluated until the situation is desperate. By that time, reactive regulatory changes are likely to be rather too late to be of much impact – or, as with the CRISPR births, to put the genie back into the bottle. Knee-jerk reactions used just to do something, anything, in the face of a controversial or 'undesirable' development, such as pre-emptive bans, have a similar problem in as much as once they are in place it is likely to require significant efforts to have such a thing repealed, reduced, or opened up. The longer the precedent exists for decisions made relying on such a ban, the more this is compounded. A lack of forethought now is liable to make remedy more difficult later.

RETROGRADE ATTITUDES

A further consideration is that emerging bio- and AI-based technologies, especially ones with the potential to create morally valuable entities – whether those be genetically modified *Homo sapiens* like Lulu and Nana, intelligent

---

[48]   Frances Millard, 'Rights Transmission by Mimesis: The Biomedicine Convention in Central Europe' (2010) 9 *Journal of Human Rights* 427.

[49]   Toma Birmontiene, 'Health Legislation in Eastern European Countries: The Baltic States' (2004) 11 *European Journal of Health Law* 77.

[50]   Tom Goffin *et al.*, 'Why Eight EU Member States Signed, But Not Yet Ratified the Convention for Human Rights and Biomedicine' (2008) 86 *Health Policy* 222.

synthetic bioroids, or some other novel being – are not likely to be prevented by knee-jerk regulatory reactions. Going from no regulation, or low-level regulation of subsidiary technologies, to immediate action in the wake of some major technological development does not lend itself to particularly well-considered choices. It is often, to coin a phrase, a case of closing the stable door after the horse has bolted, and very likely, any response in such circumstances will be to slam the door hard. As we have endeavoured to point out at length, it's also likely that the horse will just leave through a side door in any case.

As we have also seen, overly restrictive regulation is also not likely to be effective for the simple reason that it won't be taken up by all parties. It may be the case that it solves the issue to the satisfaction of an individual country, but novel beings, and moral technologies more broadly, are in our view a question that cannot be constrained by national borders. This is of course a problem for both proactive and reactive approaches to regulation; either can be circumnavigated, and in some cases this can result in 'brain drain' as scientists move abroad to continue their work, as famously occurred in the US over stem-cell research during the Bush era.[51] We are familiar with examples, from both kinds of regulation discussed in this volume, that have resulted from international disconnects on regulatory strategy. 'Medical tourism' has become a boom sector[52] within the health-care industry, with people travelling from all over the world to private clinics that provide – or claim to provide[53] – stem-cell, reproductive, and transplant therapies unavailable in their home countries. As mentioned above, there have been high-profile cases of people travelling from the US to Mexico[54] in order to skirt national laws and access mitochondrial replacement therapy. It is probably reasonable to assume that those with the means to do so might try to access gene editing abroad when it is not legally available in their own countries, perhaps to avoid passing on a known heritable condition they carry. Home DNA-testing kits have become widespread (although not necessarily accurate[55]), and so the number of people

---

[51]   Nicholas Watt, 'US Faces Science Brain Drain after Europe Backs Stem Cell Funding', *The Guardian* (25 July 2006) <https://www.theguardian.com/world/2006/jul/25/eu.genetics> accessed 2 May 2022.

[52]   James E. Dalen and Joseph S. Alpert, 'Medical Tourists: Incoming and Outgoing' (2019) 132 *American Journal of Medicine* 9.

[53]   Gina Kolata, 'A Cautionary Tale of "Stem Cell Tourism"', *New York Times* (23 June 2016) <https://www.nytimes.com/2016/06/23/health/a-cautionary-tale-of-stem -cell-tourism.html> accessed 2 May 2022.

[54]   César Palacios-Gonzalez, 'Mitochondrial Replacement Techniques, The Mexican Case', *The Niche* (30 September 2016) <https://ipscell.com/2016/09/mitochondrial -replacement-techniques-mexican-case/> accessed 2 May 2022.

[55]   Adam Rutherford, 'How Accurate Are Online DNA Tests?', *Scientific American* (15 October 2018) <https://www.scientificamerican.com/article/how-accurate-are -online-dna-tests/> accessed 2 May 2022.

wanting to edit the genome of any potential child is likely to increase simply through availability of knowledge. A lack of or loose medical regulations also tends to produce predatory clinics that charge huge amounts for what sound like wonder cures but might be, at best, a sugar pill or, at worst, something actively harmful.[56] Novel beings themselves may not be the subject of medical tourism, but it is a damning blind spot for piecemeal regulatory responses to biotechnologies.

Perhaps the most damaging potentiality of all is that poorly thought-through regulation might contribute to destroying the reputation of promising developing technologies; and that in turn will cause both unnecessary but also unethical delay in bringing valuable technologies into the clinic and the marketplace. Retrograde approaches such as bans and calls for moratoria, in particular, risk creating or reinforcing moral panics,[57] partly due to the notion that bans are quite drastic measures, to be used when something has no redeeming qualities, and partly because they discourage learning further about the subject of that ban – after all, if it is banned, what's the point? We are perhaps rightly fearful of things that will harm us collectively, and rarely do we stop to ascertain the truth of such a harm; rather, we seek to stave it off.[58] This has been borne out throughout history, from Socrates' wariness of writing,[59] to newspaper crosswords being feared to cause illiteracy,[60] to videogame violence;[61] and in the sciences, such as the headlines around the aforementioned Louise Brown or Dolly the sheep. We read headlines about AI technologies sensationalised as figures of fear – 'terminator tech'[62] being a common refrain alongside calls

---

[56]   Gerhard Bauer, Magdi Elsallab and Mohamed Abou-El-Enein, 'Concise Review: A Comprehensive Analysis of Reported Adverse Events in Patients Receiving Unproven Stem Cell-Based Interventions' (2018) 7 *Stem Cells Translational Medicine* 676.

[57]   Nicholas Bowman, 'Banning Smartphones for Kids Is Just Another Technology-Fearing Moral Panic', *The Conversation* (11 July 2017) <https://theconversation.com/banning-smartphones-for-kids-is-just-another-technology-fearing-moral-panic-74485> accessed 2 May 2022.

[58]   As Lawrence discusses in Chapter 2 of this volume: 'Repugnance, denial, and fear: societal challenges for regulation of novel beings'.

[59]   Matt Bluemink, 'Socrates, Memory & The Internet', *Philosophy Now* (October/November 2017) <https://philosophynow.org/issues/122/Socrates_Memory_and_The_Internet> accessed 2 May 2022.

[60]   Alan Connor, 'Crosswords: The Meow of the 1920s', *The Guardian* (15 December 2011) <https://www.theguardian.com/crosswords/crossword-blog/2011/dec/15/crosswords-meow-meow-1920s> accessed 2 May 2022.

[61]   Karen E. Dill and Jody C. Dill, 'Video Game Violence: A Review of the Empirical Literature' (1998) 3–4 *Aggression and Violent Behavior* 407.

[62]   Paul Rodgers, 'Elon Musk Warns of Terminator Tech', *Forbes* (5 August 2014) <http://www.forbes.com/sites/paulrodgers/2014/08/05/elon-musk-warns-ais-could-exterminate-humanity/> accessed 18 April 2022.

to ban or prevent development of certain types of robotics. We have also seen something similar with the mixed global regulatory responses to the public's reluctance to try genetically modified foods. Despite the scientific consensus that 'there is no evidence that GMOs present unique safety risks',[63] various jurisdictions continue to ban or very tightly control them. This in turn has fuelled the fire of activists destroying experimental crops such as Golden Rice,[64] conspiracy theories,[65] and more.

CONCLUSION: WHITHER LIES CAUTION?

All the above lends itself to the idea that the world is rapidly moving towards a two-tier system of cutting-edge biomedical research, broadly divided between countries with minimal regulation and those that refuse to allow anything but the earliest stages of this work.

Unfortunately, the obvious solution – internationally agreed standards and regulations – may be a pipedream. We have consistently failed to find global consensus on biotechnological issues, as discussed above. Even if it is possible to reach common ground, developing and implementing mutually acceptable terms that are flexible enough to address the developments that spur such regulatory attempts, as well as handle the inevitable further technological progress, will take many years. It seems likely that in the meantime, more and more controversial practices will take place in a variety of regulated and unregulated circumstances, unless there is a serious reckoning regarding our attitudes to the regulation of emerging technologies.

In our previous work, we stopped short of offering a comprehensive suggestion for quite what should constitute this new approach – and we will do so again here, partly because to do so satisfactorily would require a dense book of its own and partly because the other contributions to this volume do an excellent job of exploring crucial aspects of this by themselves. But we would reiterate ourselves in calling for a recognition of reality, and in advocating proactive pragmatism. This is not pragmatism in the sense of expediency – no longer can we afford to rely on approaches that are the most efficient in the moment, the most convenient, or the least effort. We hope we have demonstrated why this

---

[63]   'Restrictions on Genetically Modified Organisms: United States. Public and Scholarly Opinion', Library of Congress (30 June 2015) <http://www.loc.gov/law/help/restrictions-on-gmos/usa.php#Opinion> accessed 10 April 2022.

[64]   Marcel Kuntz, 'Destruction of Public and Governmental Experiments of GMO in Europe' (2012) 3 *GM Crops & Food* 258.

[65]   Giuseppe A. Veltri and Ahmet K. Suerdem, 'Worldviews and Discursive Construction of GMO-Related Risk Perceptions in Turkey' (2011) 22 *Public Understanding of Science* 137.

does not suffice, and only opens up new problems. We consider reactive regulatory approaches, as well as retrograde attitudes such as pre-emptive bans, to be ineffective at best – being easily circumvented – or damaging, at worst, halting the progress of research and harming those who might benefit.

Rather, we ask for pragmatism in the sense of realism. We may not know the precise shape of forthcoming technologies or indeed novel beings, and we may not know exactly what issues may arise; but we know that these things are coming, whatever we do. We can make highly educated predictions as to how they may look, and we know we must address them to avoid harms. We also know what values we wish to uphold, what traits and moral statuses we wish to protect. It seems incumbent on us to try and do so, even if we are not in total possession of the facts. Working towards forms of proactive regulation, whilst requiring painstaking analysis and international agreement of a type that will be far from easy to establish, is the only way to accomplish this without allowing these harms to happen once, twice, and then scrambling to keep up. Inevitably, we could not do so. Harms would be compounded, and we risk either abandoning control or being led back, once more, to knee-jerk reactions that solve nothing.

Proactive regulation, too, would fall victim to rogue actors such as He Jiankui. There is little that could be done to prevent such actors without stifling levels of oversight; and even then the increasing sophistication of at-home 'DIY Bio' laboratories may prove too much for the watchmen. It is already possible to use CRISPR at home – commercial kits are easily available.[66] However, this is part of our call for realism in a new approach – we know that this is likely to factor, we know that we cannot, truly, control a determined laboratory. So we must embrace this fact, and strive instead to set guidelines, regulation that seeks to permit rather than ban, and which suggests means to conduct the inevitable research whilst ensuring that ethics and values are upheld. Some commentators may say that the easy way to do this is to let it all just happen and then crack down after, but we don't think that this is a satisfactory approach, and will only lead to greater problems, as we have tried to elucidate. Rather, we should make the concerted effort now, to work out what we want to protect and how to steer emerging technological development; and to follow up as science progresses to ensure those desires continue to be fulfilled. We are on the edge of the era of the novel being, and we ought to make best use of our foresight.

---

[66] Lisa McDonnell *et al.*, 'CRISPR in Your Kitchen: An At-Home CRISPR Kit to Edit Genes in Saccharomyces Cerevisiae Used during a Remote Lab Course' (2022) 23 *Journal of Microbiology & Biology Education* 321.

PART II

Reactive regulation

6. Being novel? Regulating emerging technologies under conditions of uncertainty[1]

Joseph T.F. Roberts and Muireann Quigley

1   INTRODUCTION

If we accept that at some point novel beings – be they synthetic, biological, or biohybrid in nature – will be brought into existence, then we need to consider how the law should take account of (the emergence of) such beings. This is a sticky problem, because any attempt to engage in preparatory regulation with respect to novel beings is mired in uncertainty. Principally this uncertainty relates to the fact that there is a large – perhaps insurmountable – epistemic gap when it comes to all manner of (legally and morally) significant facts about novel beings. Put simply, we do not know what type of beings they will be, either in terms of their physical nature/embodiment, mental/cognitive characteristics, or how these will influence their preferences and values.[2] Essentially this means that, as these beings do not yet exist, we do not have access to the relevant context-dependent information needed to propose a detailed regulatory regime.

In light of these epistemic difficulties and uncertainties, in this chapter we do not propose a fine-grained account of law and regulation for novel beings. Instead, we outline some tentative normative principles which could help guide the regulation and governance of both novel beings, once they come into existence, and precursor technologies. By precursor technologies, we mean those technologies which exist now, but which are likely to serve as important stepping-stones to the eventual emergence of particular novel beings.

[1]   Our thanks to the Editors, Laura Downey, and the anonymous reviewer for their comments on this piece. Any errors or omissions remain our own. Work on this was generously supported by a Wellcome Trust Investigator Award in Humanities and Social Sciences 2019–2024 (Grant No: 212507/Z/18/Z).
[2]   Alex McKeown, 'What Do We Owe Novel Synthetic Beings and How Can We Be Sure?' (2021) 30 *Camb Q Healthc Ethics* 479.

In this chapter we will focus primarily on one type of precursor technology: digital-based, task-specific expert systems. These are computer programs consisting of a knowledge base and a set of rules for applying this knowledge (known as an inference engine), which are designed to perform specific tasks.[3] As such, they represent potential precursors to the kinds of advanced artificial general intelligences (AGIs) which would qualify as novel beings possessing moral status. Although we focus primarily on AGIs to illustrate how the principles can be applied to both precursor technologies and novel beings, the principles outlined are intended to apply to other forms of precursor technologies (and their associated novel beings) as well. It may be that, upon further examination, some of the principles may require modification or reinterpretation to govern the development of other forms of precursor technologies and their associated novel beings. Given space constraints, however, we cannot explore the specific application of the principles outlined to other forms of novel being.

In order to think about what principles might be useful and appropriate, we first set out why the emergence of novel beings might be a problem for the law. Given the multiple levels of uncertainty we identify, we then move on to discuss different potential options in 'regulating for uncertainty'.[4] Our intermediate conclusion is that, although some form of anticipatory regulation is required, at least initially the epistemic uncertainty is such that a principles-based approach may be the most fruitful for both regulators and regulatees. And, from this, more specific and granular law, regulation, and governance may develop once some of the uncertainties regarding these (potential) novel beings have been resolved. Principles-based approaches, we argue, allow us to engage in anticipatory regulation and governance of precursor technologies without hampering our future ability to regulate the existence of novel beings (should they emerge). However, in so doing, we note some (not insignificant) drawbacks of such an approach. In the last substantive section of the chapter, we suggest and outline four principles which could help to guide law and regulation regarding (the emergence of) novel beings. These are the principles of non-domination, responsibility, explicability, and non-harm. We end the chapter by outlining some drawbacks of our suggested approach, noting that, in the longer term, it is likely that a multilayered (and

---

[3]   David Lawrence and Sarah Morley, 'Regulating the Tyrell Corporation: The Emergence of Novel Beings' (2021) 30 *Camb Q Healthc Ethics* 421, 423.

[4]   Nayha Sethi, 'Regulating for Uncertainty: Bridging Blurred Boundaries in Medical Innovation, Research and Treatment' (2019) 11 *LIT* 112. For a general overview of some of the issues and potentials regarding the regulation of (emerging) technologies see Lyria Bennett Moses, 'Regulating in the Face of Sociotechnical Change' in Roger Brownsword, Eloise Scotford, and Karen Yeung (eds) *The Oxford Handbook of Law, Regulation, and Technology* (Oxford University Press 2018).

somewhat hierarchical) approach encompassing different sorts of regulatory and governance strategies and tools may be necessary.

2 THE EMERGENCE OF NOVEL BEINGS?

Despite the claim inherent in the name, the creation of 'novel beings' is not entirely new. Humans have been cross-breeding both plants and animals to create new varieties and species for a very long time.[5] Humans also have a long history of selectively breeding individuals within species to select for desired characteristics (e.g. different breeds of dog) and breeding between species to create hybrids (e.g. mules and hinnies). Having said that, the types of novel beings at issue in this book, and of interest in this chapter, are arguably of a different ilk. Whereas new species of plants and animals that humans have bred in the past might be viewed as simply tweaks on the existing system over millennia,[6] the forms of novel being we will be discussing in this chapter are distinctive in two ways.

First, they are novel in a stronger sense of the word. Whereas premodern forms of plant and animal breeding were different in some regards to their predecessors, they can be understood as variations on a theme which are continuous with what came before. The novel beings we are talking about in this chapter, however, are likely to be entirely 'new' (in the not-existing-before sense) types of beings with new forms of consciousness, capable of having their own motivations, goals, and values. The creation of novel beings with the 'capacity for consciousness at the same level as, or surpassing ours, and perhaps meeting the philosophical criteria for philosophical personhood',[7] therefore, involves a qualitative jump not present in the cross-breeding of plants and animals.

Second, prior to the widespread acceptance of genetics in the last 100 years,[8] the creation of new varieties of crops and breeds of animal through selective breeding was a slow and haphazard process.[9] Although humans had a role in selecting for desired traits in the plants and animals they bred, they had little control over the process. In this sense, we could say new types of beings 'emerged' from the process of selective cross-breeding, as opposed to

---

[5] Noel Kingsbury, *Hybrid: The History & Science of Plant Breeding* (University of Chicago Press 2009).

[6] Dominic Berry, 'Plants Are Technologies' in Jon Agar and Jacob Ward (eds) *Histories of Technology, the Environment, and Modern Britain* (UCL Press 2019). ₁

[7] David Lawrence and Margaret Brazier, 'Legally Human? "Novel Beings" and English Law' (2018) 26 *Med L Rev* 309.

[8] Kingsbury (n. 5) 40.

[9] Kingsbury (n. 5) 47.

them being 'created'. The difference between creation and emergence is that creation implies a greater role for agency and control than emergence does. Whereas describing something as emerging implies that the thing in question is appearing (or recently appeared), the term creation implies the contribution of a creator.[10] The types of novel beings we will be considering may soon come into existence through advances in artificial intelligence (AI), synthetic genomics, gene printing, and/or cognitive enhancement.[11] There are, thus, a variety of different types of novel beings that could emerge and inhabit the Earth with us. These could include: AGIs,[12] genetically modified animals,[13] cognitively enhanced humans,[14] or synthetic biological constructs.[15] It is not completely clear yet *whether* we will be able to create the types of beings we will be considering in this chapter. Neither is it completely clear *when* they will come into existence if their creation proves to be technically feasible. In debates regarding AI, for example, it is a contentious issue whether the creation of an AGI is physically possible; that is, whether an AI which could think and learn like us is compatible with the laws of nature.[16] And even if it is physically possible, there are still enormous challenges to be overcome before

---

[10]   Given that control is a matter of degree, there is a spectrum between completely random emergence (where novelty appears without agency) and fully intentional and deliberate creation (where agency directs the process entirely). What is distinctive about the kinds of novel beings we consider is the greater extent to which we have control over the process of bringing them into existence, even if the process is not complete. They are thus closer to the 'creation' side of the spectrum than pre-genetic plant breeding and animal husbandry practices. However, as we intend our discussion to be applicable to scenarios in which novel beings are brought into existence in the absence of full control over the process, we use the term 'emergence' to describe the appearance of novel beings, as opposed to the term 'creation'.

[11]   David Lawrence, 'Commentary: On Understanding Novel Minds' (2019) 28 *Camb Q Healthc Ethics* 599; David Lawrence, 'Advanced Bioscience and AI: Debugging the Future of Life' (2019) 3 *Emerging Top Life Sci* 747; David Lawrence and Sarah Morley, 'Novel Beings: Moral Status and Regulation' (2021) 30 *Camb Q Healthc Ethics* 415; Lawrence and Morley (n. 3) 421.

[12]   Lawrence and Brazier (n. 7) 314; Lawrence and Morley (n. 3) 423.

[13]   Gardar Arnason, 'The Moral Status of Cognitively Enhanced Monkeys and Other Novel Beings' (2021) 30 *Camb Q Healthc Ethics* 492.

[14]   Lawrence and Brazier (n. 7) 312; Lawrence and Morley (n. 3) 422.

[15]   Lawrence and Brazier (n. 7) 316.

[16]   Paul Churchland and Patricia Smith Churchland, 'Could a Machine Think?' (1990) 262 *Sci Am* 32; Kevin Warwick, *Artificial Intelligence: The Basics* (Routledge 2012) 65; Joanna Bryson, Mihailis Diamantis, and Thomas Grant, 'Of, for, and by the People: The Legal Lacuna of Synthetic Persons' (2017) 25 *A.I.& L* 283; Margaret Boden, *Artificial Intelligence: A Very Short Introduction* (Oxford University Press 2018) 130.

an AGI is technologically possible.[17] These challenges include, amongst others, the improved ability to recognise visual inputs[18] and the ability to accurately model language, creativity, and human emotion.[19] Part of the difficulty in doing these things is that we do not yet fully understand how these processes work in humans,[20] making modelling them in an artificial environment extremely difficult.

Despite these difficulties, for the purpose of this chapter, we are going to presume that at some point these kinds of novel beings could be brought into existence. This includes both presuming that their creation might be technically feasible and that doing so would not be explicitly legally prohibited (neither of which might turn out to be the case at some point in the future). If we accept this possibility, then we need to consider how the law could and should take account of such beings. Broadly, their potential future existence raises two types of questions for the law. On the one hand, we have questions of how to regulate the *emergence* of such beings. On the other hand, we have questions about how these beings should be regulated *once they have come into existence*. Each of these limbs of the dilemma raises its own distinct set of questions.

In relation to the *emergence* of novel beings, for example, questions arise about whether we should allow the creation of novel beings at all. Further questions stem from answering this either in the negative or positive. For instance, if we ought not to allow them to come into existence, how can we prevent this from occurring? Would legal prohibition be effective? Or, if we ought to allow them to be created, then how should we regulate their creation? These are difficult questions with no immediately obvious answers. Similarly, those in relation to regulating novel beings once they come into existence seem no easier to resolve. For instance, there will be questions about how they ought to be treated, morally and legally speaking, as well as ones about the legal rules needed to govern their behaviour and actions. In setting out some of these, we also note that novel beings will not emerge in a vacuum. They will be preceded, as noted earlier, by precursor technologies. As such, to add to the challenge, there are further questions regarding how we could and should regulate precursor technologies to achieve the goal of either preventing (or facilitating) the development/emergence of novel beings.

For the sceptics out there (and to some degree that includes the authors of this chapter), it is worth noting that even though there are doubts about whether

---

[17] Boden (n. 16) 130; Lawrence and Morley (n. 3) 423.
[18] Boden (n. 16) 37.
[19] Ibid. 50.
[20] Ibid. 59.

novel beings will arise (and if so, when), there is still value in thinking about how we ought to govern their emergence. The first reason it is important is that, so long as there is a possibility that novel beings will exist, we ought to consider how to respond in order to be prepared for their emergence if it does happen. Of course, in hindsight, we may come to realise that this turned out to be wasted effort if novel beings deserving of moral status are never created; either because we opt to legally prohibit their creation or because they are impossible in principle, for a reason we do not yet understand. That, however, does not necessarily mean that we ought not to devote intellectual resources to considering the problem now. The second reason is that considering these questions before they are actual problems can influence the *development* of the precursor technologies that might give rise to the creation of novel beings.[21] Considering these questions prior to the emergence of the novel beings is valuable even if novel beings are never brought into existence, because of the fact that it can help us consider and mitigate problems with the technology we have in the present.

So having briefly made the case for why we ought to consider the legal, regulatory, and governance implications of (the emergence of) novel beings, we freely admit that we could not even begin to answer the questions set out above in this chapter. Such a task would be incredibly complex and daunting. Instead, below, we identify uncertainty as being one of the principal challenges in this area and outline the layered and multilevel nature of this uncertainty. We then examine some ways in which we could approach the regulation and governance of novel beings, focusing on the example of digital-based, task-specific expert systems as potential precursors to AGIs.

3   REGULATING FOR UNCERTAINTY?[22]

As noted earlier, regulating (the development and emergence of) novel beings is a sticky problem for the law, because all attempts at engaging in preparatory regulation inescapably involve high levels of uncertainty. Put simply, we are ignorant of many of the legally (and morally) relevant facts that we would need to know to answer the kinds of questions set out in the previous section. The epistemic gaps in relation to novel beings are multilayered and encompass

---

    [21]   Deborah G. Johnson, 'Software Agents, Anticipatory Ethics, and Accountability' in Gary E. Marchant, Braden R. Allenby, and Joseph R. Herkert (eds) *The Growing Gap Between Emerging Technologies and Legal Ethical Oversight: The Pacing Problem* (Springer 2011) 66; Virginia Dignum, 'Responsibility and Artificial Intelligence' in Markus D. Dubber, Frank Pasquale, and Sunit Das (eds) *Oxford Handbook of Ethics of AI* (Oxford University Press 2020) 221.
    [22]   Sethi (n. 4) 112.

different levels of uncertainty. These uncertainties include at least four aspects. First, as noted earlier, we do not yet know *whether* such novel beings will come to exist, precisely *how* their existence could be brought about, or *when* they will be brought into existence. Second, we do not know, beyond informed speculation, which forms of the precursor technologies we are currently developing (if any) will ultimately be the successful springboards for the emergence of a novel being. Third, we have little knowledge regarding what the impacts of bringing these beings into existence will be.[23] Fourth, and potentially most importantly, we do not yet have a clear idea of what these novel beings will be *like*. We cannot anticipate what their physical make-up will be, what kinds of cognitive abilities they will have, what their mental lives will be like phenomenologically (i.e. from the inside) or, as McKeown has put it, 'how their corporeality shapes their options, preferences, values, and is constitutive of their moral universe'.[24] The corollary to all of this is that novel beings represent what Giddens terms 'manufactured risk'.

> Manufactured risk is risk created by the very progression of human development, especially by the progression of science and technology. Manufactured risk refers to new risk environments for which history provides us with very little previous experience. We often don't really know what the risks are, let alone how to calculate them accurately in terms of risk.[25]

In short, as these beings do not yet exist, we do not yet have access to the relevant context-dependent information needed to propose a detailed regulatory and/or governance regime to govern their existence.

Given this level of epistemic uncertainty, what is to be done? We could take a 'wait and see' approach.[26] And in some ways this might appear to be a better route, as at least some of the uncertainties would resolve themselves if we simply waited. Indeed, this is frequently the approach of the law when it comes to new and emerging technologies.[27] We often do not know what the full implications of a new form of technology will be before or even while it is in development. As a consequence, the law can be reactive.[28] As Brownsword notes, in the main, 'regulators do not try to anticipate the development of a new

---

[23] Our thanks to the anonymous reviewer for prompting us to include this.
[24] McKeown (n. 2) 479.
[25] Anthony Giddens, 'Risk and Responsibility' (1999) 62 *MLR* 1, 4.
[26] For a good discussion of the 'wait and see' approach generally (as well as specifically in the context of blockchain technologies) see Michèle Finck, *Blockchain Regulation and Governance in Europe* (Cambridge University Press 2018) 154–155.
[27] Ibid.
[28] Roger Brownsword, 'Legal Regulation of Technology: Supporting Innovation, Managing Risk, & Respecting Values' in T. L. Pittinsky (ed.), *Science, Technology,*

technology; rather, they address new technologies only when they must'.[29] They do not take a pre-emptory approach and tend, at least in the early stages (until they get a better sense of the risks and benefits), to draw on existing legal and regulatory regimes/elements and adapt them to the new technologies.[30] An example of such an approach discussed by Finck is the current approach to smart contracts.[31] Regarding these, the Law Commission recently concluded that:

> Current legal principles can apply to smart legal contracts in much the same way as they do to traditional contracts, albeit with an incremental and principled development of the common law in specific contexts. In general, difficulties associated with applying the existing law to smart legal contracts are not unique to them, and could equally arise in the context of traditional contracts.[32]

Arguably only time will tell whether this conclusion will hold regarding this particular technology.

In the case of novel beings, this 'wait and see' approach would seem, at least on the face of it, not to be satisfactory. This is because the consequences of not acting/pre-empting/preparing could be substantial. The problem is neatly encapsulated by the so-called 'Collingridge Dilemma' (also known as the dilemma of control)[33] which, as articulated by Bennett Moses, holds that 'attempts to control a technology early in its development suffer from the difficulty of not knowing its final form and ultimate effects, while attempts to control a technology after it has become entrenched are virtually impossible'.[34] We have already set out the epistemic uncertainties with regard to novel beings, but the message here is that if we wait until they emerge or are near emergence, it will almost certainly be too late to prevent this (if that is what is decided) or to do much to influence the shape and trajectory of these beings'

& *Society: New Perspectives & Directions* (Cambridge University Press 2019) 109; Lawrence and Morley (n. 11) 415.

[29]   Brownsword (n. 28) 109.

[30]   Ibid. 110.

[31]   Finck (n. 26) 154.

[32]   Law Commission, 'Smart Legal Contracts: Summary' (LC 401, 2021) <https://www.lawcom.gov.uk/project/smart-contracts/> accessed 7 April 2022.

[33]   David Collingridge, *The Social Control of Technology* (Frances Pinter 1980) 19.

[34]   Lyria Bennett Moses, '*Sui Generis* Rules' in Marchant, Allenby, and Herkert (n. 21) 89. See also Graeme Laurie, Shawn H.E. Harmon, and Fabiana Arzuaga, 'Foresighting Futures: Law, New Technologies, and the Challenges of Regulating for Uncertainty' (2012) 4 *LIT* 1, 5–6. For a recent analysis of neglected aspects of Collingridge's work in the context of responsible research innovation, see Audley Genusa and Andy Stirling, 'Collingridge and the Dilemma of Control: Towards Responsible and Accountable Innovation' (2018) 47 *Res Policy* 61.

lives (if they ought to be permitted to come into existence in the first place). As such, despite the fact that the uncertainties in relation to novel beings seem deeper than those surrounding other emerging technologies, engaging in some form of anticipatory governance and/or preparatory regulation is likely to be necessary.[35] We may find in the future that our attempts at pre-empting the technologies focused on possibilities that failed to materialise, but nevertheless such attempts are still valuable, if only because they can help to guide the regulation of precursor technologies.

So does this mean that we ought to go ahead and devise a detailed new legal regime? Well, this is also not the solution in this case. Bennett Moses notes four things about technological change and the law: first, that it can bring about 'pressure to enact new laws'; second, there is often 'a need to resolve uncertainties in the application of law in new contexts'; third, existing 'legal rules … apply poorly in [these] new contexts'; and fourth, existing law can become obsolete in the face of new developments.[36] The consequence of this, she maintains, can be a tendency to create *sui generis* legal rules – that is a set of particularised rules – to deal with new technologies or technological change. Yet this may not always be the best route. Laurie and colleagues give the example of the ban on cloning in the Human Fertilisation and Embryology Act 1990 as one of 'legislating too early' in the face of uncertainty.[37] As originally enacted, section 3(3)(d) prohibited the granting of a licence for 'replacing a nucleus of a cell of *an embryo* with a nucleus taken from a cell of any person, embryo or subsequent development of an embryo'.[38] However, as time went on it became clear that this wording only captured one form of 'cloning'. At the time of drafting, scientific advances relating to stem cell production from so-called therapeutic cloning via cell nuclear replacement (whereby the nucleus of an oocyte is replaced with that of another cell) had not been anticipated.[39]

---

[35]   For some work on anticipatory governance generally, as well as in relation to emerging technologies broadly, see Laurie et al. (n. 34); Leon S. Fuerth, 'Foresight and Anticipatory Governance' (2009) 11 *Foresight* 14; David H. Guston, 'Understanding "Anticipatory Governance"' (2014) 44 *Soc Stud Sci* 218; David Sarewitz, 'Anticipatory Governance of Emerging Technologies' in Marchant, Allenby, and Herkert (n. 21).

[36]   Bennett Moses (n. 34) 77.

[37]   Laurie et al. (n. 34) 6, note 23.

[38]   Emphasis added.

[39]   There is not the space to go into it here, but the result of this was the controversial *R (on the application of Quintavalle) v Secretary of State for Health* [2003] 2 WLR 692, in which the ProLife Alliance (PLA) argued that the Human Fertilisation and Embryology Authority could not grant a licence for cell nuclear replacement (CNR) under its remit as CNR fell outside the scope of the 1990 Act. Although the High Court found for the claimant at first instance, this was overturned on appeal and the Court of Appeal judgment was affirmed in the House of Lords.

In the case of novel beings which we are considering here, acting too early could result in law that is quickly outpaced by technological developments or in advances that were simply never envisaged at the time of drafting of the relevant statutes or regulations. The reason is that the epistemic uncertainties *right now* are so great that we do not have enough context-specific information to apply existing legal rules, let alone create any kind of new *sui generis* regime. This is quite apart from the fact that acting too early to create a *sui generis* regime for each and every potential new novel being and its technologies would be costly, time-consuming, and impractical.

Given this, if we ought not to simply 'wait and see' and we are not in a position to either apply existing law or create bespoke legal frameworks, what is to be done?

4   A PRINCIPLES-BASED APPROACH

Our suggestion is that, in light of the epistemic difficulties we face trying to understand *what* novel beings will be like and *how* they will emerge, a principles-based approach might prove useful *at the moment*. As we get closer to making novel beings a reality, our ignorance in these respects will likely diminish, enabling us to move beyond guiding principles. However, until this occurs, a principles-based approach would be a feasible and practical one. So what do we mean by a principles-based approach (PBA)? And what are the potential benefits and drawbacks of such an approach?

4.1   Principles, Rules, Regulation, and Governance

PBAs take their cue from the narrower principles-based regulation (PBR).[40] As outlined by Black, Hopper, and Band, 'Principles-based regulation means moving away from reliance on detailed, prescriptive rules and relying more on high-level, broadly stated rules or Principles to set the standards by which regulated firms must conduct business.'[41] PBR is an approach which has found favour in the United Kingdom in a number of areas, these include stem

---

[40]   As will be explained below, we follow Laurie and Sethi in talking about 'principles-based approaches' rather than just principles-based regulation. See Graeme Laurie and Nayha Sethi, 'Towards Principles-Based Approaches to Governance of Health-Related Research Using Personal Data' (2013) 1 *EJRR* 43, Nayha Sethi and Graeme Laurie, 'Delivering Proportionate Governance in the Era of eHealth: Making Linkage and Privacy Work Together' (2013) 13 *Med Law Int* 168.

[41]   J. Black, M. Hopper, and C. Band, 'Making a Success of Principles-Based Regulation' (2007) 1 *LFMR* 191.

cell research, finance, and the legal profession.[42] One of the most successful examples of its use, and outlined in detail by Devaney,[43] is the approach of the Human Fertilisation and Embryology Authority (HFEA), which is responsible for the regulation of fertility clinics and the use of human embryos for research.[44] Whilst the HFEA derives its regulatory mandate directly from the Human Fertilisation and Embryology Act 1990 (as amended), the Act itself does not contain all the details of the regulatory regime. Instead, the Authority is required by virtue of section 8(1)(ca) to set out a statement of general operating principles which are to guide both the work of the HFEA itself and any activities governed by the Act.[45] In practice this has been achieved by integrating these general principles into the HFEA's Codes of Conduct.[46]

Currently, the Code of Conduct contains a set of 13 'regulatory principles' which those carrying out activities licensed under the Act must adhere to.[47] As noted by Devaney, 'They are intended to be high-level, broadly stated and self-contained provisions containing qualitative terms as opposed to prescriptive rules.'[48] Principle 1, for instance, states that licensed centres must 'treat prospective and current patients and donors fairly, and ensure that all licensed activities are conducted in a non-discriminatory way';[49] while Principle 2 requires that centres must 'have respect for the privacy, confidentiality, dignity, comfort and well-being of prospective and current patients and donors'.[50] Such an approach could, on the face of it, be contrasted with more rigid rules-based regulation, which 'relies on compliance with specific rules'.[51] We say 'on the face of it', because, as we will see, attempting to identify a clear

---

[42] Although note the criticisms regarding its use in the financial sector, with some noting that weaknesses with this approach contributed to the 2007–2008 financial crisis. See, for example: Julia Black, 'Forms and Paradoxes of Principles-Based Regulation' (2008) 3 *CMLJ* 425; Julia Black, 'The Rise, Fall, and Fate of Principles Based Regulation' in Kern Alexander and Niamh Moloney (eds) *Law Reform and Financial Markets* (Edward Elgar Publishing 2011); Sarah Devaney, 'Regulate to Innovate: Principles-Based Regulation of Stem Cell Research' (2011) 11 *Med L Int* 53.

[43] Devaney (n. 42); Sarah Devaney, *Stem Cell Research and Collaborative Regulation of Innovation* (Routledge 2014) Chapter 2.

[44] Human Fertilisation and Embryology Authority, 'How we Regulate' <https://www.hfea.gov.uk/about-us/how-we-regulate/> accessed 23 February 2021.

[45] For more on this see: Devaney (n. 43) 38–40.

[46] Ibid. 39–40.

[47] Human Fertilisation and Embryology Authority, *Code of Practice* (9th edn, HFEA 2021) 12–13, <https://portal.hfea.gov.uk/media/1756/2021-10-26-code-of-practice-2021.pdf> accessed 7 April 2022.

[48] Devaney (n. 43) 40.

[49] HFEA (n. 47) 12.

[50] Ibid.

[51] Laurie and Sethi (n. 40) 45.

distinction between rules-based and principles-based approaches may not prove particularly straightforward or illuminating.[52]

Indeed, as Laurie and Sethi argue, there are numerous instances 'whereby so-called "principles" in legislation are, in fact, operating as rules or in a rule-like manner'.[53] They draw on data protection legislation to aptly illustrate this. Whilst the old Data Protection Directive explicitly contained eight 'principles', these did not function as such in practice, because 'derogation from any of the principles represent[ed] a clear breach of law'.[54] As anticipated by Laurie and Sethi at the time they were writing, the current EU General Data Protection Regulation (GDPR) (Regulation (EU) 2016/679) is also constructed around 'principles'.[55] These seven principles are also to be found in the Data Protection Act 2018 (and the post-Brexit UK GDPR).[56] Yet the move from Directive to Regulation actually reduces any leeway in interpretation and application of the 'principles' which EU countries, for instance, may have had in the past.[57] By the same token, the example HFEA principles given above are in reality a mixture of more or less rule-like features, with each Guidance Note within the Code of Practice outlining the mandatory requirements as set out in the HFE Act and the HFEA's interpretation of these requirements, along with other less rule-like aspects of the guidance. Given all of this, we agree with Sethi, who favours 'talk of "rule and principle-type features"' rather than attempting any definitive delineation between rules and principles.[58]

---

[52] Nayha Sethi, 'Rules, Principles, and the Added Value of Best Practice in Health Research Regulation' in Graeme Laurie, Edward Dove, Agomoni Ganguli-Mitra, et al. (eds) *The Cambridge Handbook of Health Research Regulation* (Cambridge University Press 2021) 169.

[53] Laurie and Sethi (n. 40) 46.

[54] Ibid., 50.

[55] Ibid., 51. At the time their article was written and published, the EU Data Protection Regulation was still in draft form and had yet to be passed and implemented.

[56] In the EU GDPR these are: Article 5 – Principles relating to processing of personal data; Article 6 – Lawfulness of processing; Article 7 – Conditions for consent; Article 8 – Conditions applicable to child's consent in relation to information society services; Article 9 – Processing of special categories of personal data; Article 10 – Processing of personal data relating to criminal convictions and offences; and Article 11 – Processing which does not require identification. These are mirrored in the 2018 Act and thus the UK GDPR.

[57] Ibid.

[58] Ibid. There is, of course, a large literature on rules and principles, including within legal theory (where the distinction featured prominently in the Dworkin–Hart debate). We do not have the space to delve into this in this chapter, which in any case has been dealt with extensively and competently by others elsewhere. See, for example, Nayha Sethi, 'Reimagining Regulatory Approaches: On the Essential Role of Principles in Health Research Regulation' (2015) 12 *Scripted* 91; Ronald Dworkin, 'The Model of Rules' (1967) 35 *U Chi L Rev* 25; H.L.A. Hart, *The Concept of Law* (2nd

In a similar vein, attempting to draw a distinction between approaches which could be classified as regulation-based and those which are governance-based may not always be straightforward; and again, potentially not all that helpful. Broadly speaking, regulation has a narrower focus than governance,[59] with some viewing the former as a subset of the latter.[60] For our purposes, we take the lead again from Laurie and Sethi, who distinguish between the two as follows:

> ...while *regulation* will tend to be a state-driven, vertically-orientated, top-down, command-and-control deployment of formal (hard law) instruments, *governance* is often a far more horizontally-orientated enterprise, more likely driven by local actors, and more reliant on soft law options such as guidance or professional codes.[61]

What is interesting about the example HFEA principles set out above (and indeed other HFEA principles) is that they ought not to be viewed strictly – or necessarily – as pure 'regulatory' principles (albeit they are labelled as such within the HFEA's Code of Practice[62]). In practice they are, to varying degrees, principles which encapsulate a mixture of regulation and governance features. They can be viewed as regulatory to the extent that they are top-down principles put in place via the state-backed regulator. Whilst they are not command and control instruments in and of themselves, the mandate does derive from hard law. However, they can be viewed as tending more towards a governance approach in implementation. This is because how some aspects of these high-level principles are cashed out and implemented is dependent on the specifics of local guidance and practice.

For Laurie and Sethi, therefore, 'it is preferable to talk of a principles-based *approach*'.[63] Doing so recognises that (1) distinctions between rules and principles, as well as between regulation and governance, are not always clear-cut and (2) a mix of approaches may be necessary depending on the context. For them, the purpose of principles is to initiate and drive suitably reflective and

---

edn, Oxford University Press 1994) 259; Michael Bayles, 'Hart vs. Dworkin' 10 *L & Phil* 351.

[59]   See generally Julia Black, 'Critical Reflections on Regulation' (2002) 27 *Aust J Leg Philos* 1.

[60]   John Braithwaite, Cary Coglianese, and David Levi-Faur, 'Can Regulation and Governance Make a Difference?' (2007) 1 *Reg Gov* 1, 3.

[61]   Laurie and Sethi (n. 40) 47.

[62]   HFEA (n. 47) 13–14.

[63]   Laurie and Sethi (n. 40) 44; Sethi (n. 52) 167.

nuanced conversations about the target behaviours or technologies. Thus, regardless of terminology, the important takeaway is this:

> Principles should be seen as fundamental starting points to guide deliberation and action. Thus, their purpose is to point actors or decision-makers in the direction of the relevant values and considerations to be taken into consideration when a particular decision or course of action is being contemplated ... Principles require reflection and justification for actions which, in themselves, are signals of 'good governance'.[64]

In this spirit, in section 5, we outline four potential starting principles for the regulation and governance of (the emergence of) novel beings. These are the principles of non-domination, responsibility, explicability, and non-harm. For each of these principles we will outline the higher order proposition which they represent, why we think they might be helpful, and some potential drawbacks. However, before we do this, it is worth taking a closer look at some of the general benefits and disadvantages of a principles-based approach.

4.2   Weighing Up Principles-Based Approaches

It seems that there are a number of epistemic and pragmatic benefits to using a principles-based approach when regulating under conditions of uncertainty. As we have already noted, we do not know enough to do anything more concrete/particularised at this point in time (the first horn of the Collingridge Dilemma). Yet we do need to do *something*, otherwise by the time novel beings exist – or are on the brink of existence – it will likely be too late to do anything substantive to alter the direction of the technologies (the second horn of the dilemma).

Given this, first and foremost, a principles-based approach offers a way to do *something*. But importantly, it gives us a way to do something which can be *action-guiding*. Whilst general principles do not give us the content of what must be done, they at least lay out the contours to help us decide on the content. We can see this in the principles set out in the HFEA Code of Conduct. The two examples of the HFEA principles given earlier (fair treatment/non-discrimination and respect for privacy, confidentiality, etc.) do not prescribe or give detail about *how* they ought to be enacted or achieved, but they do contain the normative target to aim for. We accept that there might be reasonable disagreement, especially in difficult boundary cases, about whether or how a given principle applies to a particular situation. However, not all

---

[64]   Laurie and Sethi (n. 40) 46.

cases involve grey areas. In more clear-cut cases, having a general statement of the normative goal is sufficient to guide conduct.

Second, and relatedly, in setting out the normative contours rather than detailed content, a principles-based approach offers a degree of flexibility.[65] There could be multiple ways in which the principles could be enacted and implemented, allowing us to correct course or tweak details as we go along. As such, we obviate the need to specify too early the exact shape of the regulatory and governance space which will flow from the principles, allowing it to develop organically from the application and reinterpretation of the general principles. As Laurie and Sethi note, it negates the need for 'detailed anticipatory drafting for every perceivable situation';[66] something which in any case would be nigh on practically impossible.

This is not to say that a principles-based approach is a panacea. Indeed, some of the purported strengths of this bring their own challenges. For instance, a significant problem with generality and flexibility as strengths is that – depending on how they are implemented in practice – they can become weaknesses. To wit, if principles are too general, they may not be substantively action-guiding. Alternatively (or indeed in addition), the principles could be open to interpretations which are simply too wide; in which case they may be action-guiding, but permit any number of actions which were not intended at the outset or which actually run counter to the original underlying regulatory aims. The challenge is to ensure that regulation is flexible enough to be adequately responsive, without losing too much transparency or specificity. Moreover, as Brownsword notes, 'Flexibility comes at the price of predictability.'[67] A lack of predictability is problematic under any particular regulatory regime, because regulatees need to know what their obligations are and what they must do to fulfil those obligations.

We will come back to these potential difficulties after we have discussed our potential principles for the regulation and/or governance of (the emergence of) novel beings. But for now, we simply want to note that there are ways to mitigate, or perhaps avoid entirely, the sorts of negative sequelae that can attend a principles-based approach. The first is that each principle could be accompanied by a fuller explanation of the purpose and normative aim of that principle. That way, when it comes to filling in the detail at a later date, regulators (and regulatees) have a meaningful reference point to help with appropriate interpretation.

---

[65] Black, Hopper, and Band (n. 41) 193.
[66] Laurie and Sethi (n. 40) 45.
[67] Brownsword (n. 28) 127.

Second, and relatedly, an account, not just of the purpose of each individual principle, but of the principles as a collective, could be given. This could help to reduce ambiguity over the normative direction of travel intended. For instance, the HFEA Code of Practice states that 'The Code of Practice contains regulatory principles for licensed centres, and guidance notes which provides guidance to help clinics deliver *safe, effective and legally compliant treatment and research.*'[68] This thus seems to be a statement of intent regarding the normative purposes of the principles in the Code of Practice; that is, the normative goal is the delivery of 'safe, effective, and legally compliant treatment and research'.

Third, as noted by Devaney, principles-based approaches can be used in conjunction with more prescriptive rules.[69] These rules can be used to set boundaries which must not be crossed or to set out immoveable lines. For example, whilst the HFEA Code of Practice contains the overarching principles and states that 'The regulatory principles inform every part of this Code of Practice,'[70] the Code is also very clear on which elements constitute mandatory requirements as laid down either in the HFE Act (as amended) or some other aspect of law. For instance, Principle 1 requires that patients and donors are treated fairly and in a non-discriminatory way.[71] But this is then detailed in terms of obligations under, amongst other things, the Equality Act 2010; noting that a fertility centre's policies and guidance must comply with the Act's requirements. Another example of principles being used in conjunction with more prescriptive elements can be found in the General Medical Council's *Good Medical Practice*. Here the guidance often contains sub-principles which make the guidance more specific. For instance, para. 14 says 'you must recognize and work within the limits of your competence'.[72] Then, as a specification, 14.1 says 'you must have the necessary knowledge of the English language to provide a good standard of practice and care in the UK'.[73] This makes clear that speaking English is a part of what makes a practitioner working in the UK competent to practise medicine. These more prescriptive elements help practitioners to interpret the principles with a view to increasing compliance.[74] Importantly, however, and related to Laurie and

---

[68]   HFEA (n. 47) 11, emphasis added.

[69]   Devaney (n. 42) 60.

[70]   HFEA (n. 47) 13.

[71]   Ibid.

[72]   General Medical Council, 'Good Medical Practice' (GMC 2013) 7 <https://www.gmc-uk.org/ethical-guidance/ethical-guidance-for-doctors/good-medical-practice> accessed 6 April 2022.

[73]   Ibid.

[74]   Devaney (n. 42) 60.

Sethi's position that principles should be 'starting points to guide deliberation and action',[75] the HFEA very explicitly states that it does not purport to offer the definitive interpretation of the law, and thus application of the principles, within its guidance notes.[76]

Fourth, as recently proposed by Sethi in the context of global health emergencies, principles and any attendant guidance could be complemented by a set of best practice examples. These would function as 'a mid-level translational mechanism, serving as a bridge from *text* to *context*, more specific than principle-like guidelines, yet not as specific as rule-like guidelines'.[77] Whilst accepting that 'best practice' need not (and is unlikely to) mean ideal practice, Sethi locates the utility of such an approach in its ground-up nature.[78] Best practice examples will come from a range of actors and stakeholders on the ground and will 'genuinely reflect the experiences of those involved'.[79] Examples of best practice case studies can be found, for instance, on the GMC website, where there are a number of structured vignettes to accompany 'Good Medical Practice' and other GMC guidance. These involve reading through a clinical interaction and choosing the appropriate next step. There is then an explanation of what the doctor did (i.e. what the GMC views as 'best practice'). Thus the GMC's scenarios involve not only setting out an example of best practice, but are structured to encourage reflection and learning on the part of the doctors using the resource.[80]

We do not purport that the above suggestions are the only (or even the best) ways to mitigate some of the challenges and increase the utility of a principles-based approach. However, they offer at least a partial solution to some of the drawbacks of this type of regulation. Having set out our stall in this respect, let us now move on to look at four principles which might be helpful in the regulation and governance of (the emergence of) novel beings.

---

[75]   Laurie and Sethi (n. 40) 46.

[76]   HFEA (n. 47) 11.

[77]   Nayha Sethi, 'Research and Global Heath Emergencies: On the Essential Role of Best Practice' (2018) 11 *Public Health Ethics* 237, 242.

[78]   Ibid. 245.

[79]   Ibid. Sethi's discussion in this respect focused on those involved in dealing with the global health emergencies such as the H5N1, Zika, and Ebola outbreaks. For a discussion of the use of principles and best practice in the context of the linkage of health data in Scotland, see Sethi and Laurie (n. 40).

[80]   General Medical Council, 'Good Medical Practice in Action' <https://www.gmc -uk.org/gmpinaction/> accessed 6 April 2022.

5   TENTATIVE PRINCIPLES FOR THE
        REGULATION OF NOVEL BEINGS

In this section we propose four tentative principles that could guide the
regulation of both precursor technologies and novel beings (if and when
they emerge). These are the principles of non-domination, responsibility,
explicability, and non-harm. The principles of responsibility, explicability,
and non-harm will be familiar to readers interested in the regulation and governance of AI. The originality of our approach lies in extending this framework
by adding a principle of non-domination, and in proposing that these principles
should be applied, not just to the regulation of current and future AI, but also to
the regulation of other precursor technologies and the novel beings with moral
status they might give rise to.

Given the epistemic uncertainties we have outlined, the goal is not to
provide a detailed regulatory regime. Instead, the goal of this section is to
illustrate how the use of principles could help us guide the regulation of
precursor technologies without hampering our ability to regulate novel beings
in the future. For each proposed principle we outline what is meant by the
principle, how it could be applied to both pre- and post-emergence scenarios,
and some of the uncertainties that need to be resolved in each case before the
principles could be translated into a detailed regulatory regime to govern (the
emergence of) novel beings. The section concludes by arguing that, although
there are uncertainties to be resolved before the principles outlined can be
applied, a principles-based approach offers us the normative guidance necessary to implement the principles as and when the knowledge required to do so
becomes available.

5.1   Non-Domination

The first proposed principle is the principle of non-domination. Domination
is a relationship that exists between an 'agent' of domination and a 'subject'
of domination in which the agent of domination has the power to arbitrarily
interfere with the life of the subject of domination.[81] Following Lovett we
understand arbitrariness as being a matter of 'the absence of established and
commonly known rules, law or conventions effectively governing the use
of power in a social relationship'.[82] In other words, domination 'consists in
a state of subordination or subjugation, whereby somebody's latitude-to-Φ is

---

[81]   Frank Lovett, 'Domination: A Preliminary Analysis' (2001) 84 *Monist* 98.
[82]   Ibid. 103.

dependent on the tolerance or leniency of someone else'[83] (where Φ denotes some action or other).

The principle of non-domination holds that no moral agent ought to be dominated by any other moral agent. Ensuring non-domination is important because not being subject to the arbitrary will of another is an important part of being free. Freedom as non-domination is not focused on minimising interference with any given agent's activities; it is primarily about ensuring that certain agents do not have *arbitrary* power over others. Ensuring non-domination for all requires constraining the power of *all* agents to ensure *no* agent can interfere arbitrarily with *any other* agent. It follows that enforcing the principle of non-domination (and the other principles outlined below) will sometimes require interference with some agents' pursuit of their plans. Importantly, however, this does not constitute domination if the interference is constrained through commonly known rules (such as those enforced by publicly legitimised principles-based regulation).

The use of precursor technologies – such as task-specific expert systems described in the introduction – have the potential for domination. Currently this type of AI is largely being developed and deployed by profit-seeking corporations to a variety of business and industry ends. Moreover, as Lawrence and Morley point out, they are doing so in a largely unregulated fashion as these activities are not effectively constrained by existing (UK) company law.[84] If we allow corporations to continue to self-regulate without any form of public control, the ways in which this technology is deployed will not be subject to commonly known rules that effectively constrain the power of these corporations. Under a pure self-regulation model, corporations are essentially a law unto themselves.[85]

This is a problem even if we grant, for the sake of argument, that we ought to trust that the commercial goals of these corporations are in line with the wider societal interests (which is a big concession). From a domination perspective, the objection to a solely self-regulation regime is not simply that many corporations will prioritise profit over any negative impacts on wider stakeholders or society (although this is likely to be the case). It is also that people's freedom is limited by corporations under a self-regulatory regime. Even if corporations could be trusted to self-regulate appropriately (which is doubtful), without public control over the regulatory regime, consumers of products which rely on AI are potential subjects of domination.

---

[83] Matthew Kramer, 'Liberty and Domination' in Cecile Laborde and John Maynor (eds) *Republicanism and Political Theory* (Blackwell 2008) 32.

[84] Lawrence and Morley (n. 3) 427.

[85] Ibid. 422.

Applied to the pre-emergence scenario, the principle of non-domination thus implies that we need to have some form of public oversight over the way in which expert systems (and other precursor technologies) are deployed if we are to make the rules which govern their use non-arbitrary. Constraining the power of developers of precursor technology will require moving away from regimes of self-regulation and towards regulation by publicly backed regulators. Implementing a publicly backed regulatory regime might prove to be a challenge, as it might conflict with the commercial interests of developers. However, the challenge of imposing regulation on a recalcitrant industry is not necessarily insurmountable.

More difficult problems arise when we try to apply the principle of non-domination to a post-emergence scenario. The first difference is the number of potential domination relationships to consider. Whereas in the case of precursor technologies the agent of domination is the corporation, if novel beings with moral status are brought into existence, novel beings themselves could be both subjects and agents of domination. Novel beings could be subjects of domination if, once they emerge, they are kept as property either by corporations or individuals, as the owners would have the power to arbitrarily interfere in the novel being's life. On the other hand, novel beings could also be agents of domination if, once they emerge, we cannot effectively constrain their behaviour through commonly known and accepted rules. If this were to occur, novel beings could have the power to arbitrarily interfere in the lives of both other novel beings and humans, thereby dominating them.

In order to comply with the principle of non-domination, the exercise of power in all these potential relationships needs to be made non-arbitrary. As suggested above, one way of doing this is by ensuring public oversight over the rules that govern the relationship between the different parties through principles-based regulation. Here, however, we face even greater challenges to implementation. Given the uncertainty surrounding what novel beings will be like, we do not currently know how we could effectively constrain their behaviour to ensure they do not become agents of domination or, indeed, whether this would be possible after a certain point in their development.[86] The second challenge to implementing the principle of non-domination to govern the behaviour of novel beings is that, in virtue of their different embodiment, what constitutes domination for humans may not be domination for a novel being that is differently embodied.[87]

---

[86] Our thanks to the anonymous reviewer for this latter point.
[87] Roman Yampolskiy and Joshua Fox, 'Safety Engineering for Artificial General Intelligence' (2013) 32 *Topoi* 218.

To illustrate: suppose A, a human, is performing some mathematical calculations. B, another human, has the power to interrupt A's activities or thought processes and compel A to perform another action, without reason and whenever they like. This seems like a clear case of arbitrary interference and, hence, domination. Now, the fact that A is unable to perform his original actions in virtue of B asking him to do something else constitutes interference because A cannot do both at once. If A is compelled to do B's bidding, A's original activity must be delayed. The problem is this: the inability to perform more than one *conscious* action (or at most a few) at any one time seems to be a feature of human psychology which novel beings may not share.[88] Computer processors, unlike human minds, can perform multiple operations simultaneously (assuming there is sufficient processing power). It is, thus, not obvious that the same sorts of actions that constitute domination of humans will be the same as those that constitute domination of novel beings. Until this uncertainty surrounding what constitutes domination is resolved, it will be unclear how we ought to implement the principle of non-domination in a post-emergence world.

5.2   Responsibility

The second proposed principle for the regulation of novel beings is the principle of responsibility. The principle of responsibility holds that it should always be possible to hold some entity legally responsible for the negative consequences that might follow from the development and deployment of novel beings or their precursor technologies.

Although novel beings and their precursor technologies have the potential to deliver large benefits to humanity, as with other forms of technology, these benefits will not come without potential harms.[89] Ensuring that some party can be held legally responsible for harms is an important first step to controlling and mitigating them. This is because attributions of responsibility play two roles. First, attributions of responsibility have a prospective role in that they tell us who is required to take action to reduce the likelihood of harms materi-

---

[88]   Rene Marois and Jason Ivanoff, 'Capacity Limits of Information Processing in the Brain' (2005) 9 *Trends Cogn Sci* 296; Earl K. Miller and Timothy J. Buschman, 'Working Memory Capacity: Limits on the Bandwidth of Cognition' (2015) 144 *Daedalus* 112; Stanislas Dehaene et al., 'What Is Consciousness, and Could Machines Have It?' (2017) 358 *Science* 486, 489.

[89]   Dignum (n. 21) 215.

alising. Second, attributions of responsibility have a retrospective role in that they inform us who is liable for remedial action should the harms occur.[90]

In the context of precursor technologies, responsibility for any potential harms falls on the individuals who develop and deploy precursor technologies such as AI.[91] Here, as before, there are challenges to implementation. The first challenge is that many current AI systems operate as non-transparent, non-interrogable black boxes, making it hard to understand the cause of a fault (should one occur).[92] This problem is compounded by the complexity of the AI development process. AI systems (and other precursor technologies) are developed by large teams,[93] over an extended period of time, and will often require the use of inputs (e.g. training data sets) developed by other teams working for other organisations.[94] Together these features make it difficult to establish who is responsible for what.[95]

In other words, attributing responsibility for the functioning of an AI system is complicated by what is known as 'the problem of many hands'.[96] The problem is that, 'because many different individuals in an organization contribute in many different ways to the decisions and policies, it is difficult

---

[90]   Peter Cane, *Responsibility in Law and Morality* (Hart 2002) 31; H.L.A. Hart, *Punishment and Responsibility* (Oxford University Press 2008) 212–215; Karen Yeung, 'Responsibility and AI' (Council of Europe, Study DGI(2019)05) 48 <https://rm.coe.int/responsability-and-ai-en/168097d9c5> accessed 14 July 2021.

[91]   Institute of Electrical and Electronics Engineers (IEEE), 'Ethically Aligned Design: A Vision for Prioritising Human Wellbeing with Autonomous and Intelligent Systems' <https://ethicsinaction.ieee.org> accessed 14 July 2021; Wulf Loh and Janina Loh 'Autonomy and Responsibility in Hybrid Systems' in Patrick Lin, Keith Abney and Ryan Jenkins (eds) *Robot Ethics 2.0: From Autonomous Cars to Artificial Intelligence* (Oxford University Press 2017) 46.

[92]   David J. Gunkel, 'Mind the Gap: Responsible Robotics and the Problem of Responsibility' (2020) 22 *Ethics Inf Technol* 317; Mark Coeckelbergh, 'Artificial Intelligence, Responsibility Attribution, and a Relational Justification of Explainability' (2020) 26 *Sci Eng Ethics* 2057.

[93]   David Leslie, 'Understanding Artificial Intelligence Ethics and Safety' (The Alan Turing Institute 2019) 35. <https://www.turing.ac.uk/research/publications/understanding-artificial-intelligence-ethics-and-safety> accessed 20 October 2021; Brent Daniel Mittelstadt et al., 'The Ethics of Algorithms: Mapping the Debate' (2016) *Big Data and Society* 7.

[94]   Coeckelbergh (n. 92) 2057.

[95]   Our thanks to the anonymous reviewer for prompting us to expand our comment regarding the development of technologies by large teams and the problem of many hands.

[96]   Dennis Thompson, 'Designing Responsibility: The Problem of Many Hands in Complex Organizations' in Jeroen van den Hoven, Seumas Miller and Thomas Pogge (eds) *The Design Turn in Applied Ethics* (Oxford University Press 2017).

even in principle to identify who is responsible for the results'.[97] Individual team members in large organisations will often lack an understanding of (and control over) how their work might be used by other individuals in the organisation, making it difficult to consider them responsible.[98] This lack of control over outcomes is even more acute for organisations that produce component parts or provide services which third parties use to develop AI systems. The problem of many hands thus creates a 'responsibility gap',[99] which can make manufactured risks difficult to mitigate.[100]

There are three main responses to the responsibility gap. The first is to challenge the account of responsibility it relies on.[101] The responsibility gap arises only if one holds that control over an outcome is necessary for responsibility.[102] This may well be the case for moral responsibility, but it is less clear that it is the case for legal responsibility. Unlike moral responsibility, which focuses on apportioning moral blame, legal responsibility has traditionally 'been more sensitive to the interests of victims and of society in security of the person and property',[103] allowing for greater flexibility in who to hold responsible.[104] If we do not require control over outcomes for responsibility, we could assign responsibility for the actions of their subordinates to individuals higher up the corporate hierarchy, regardless of whether they themselves were personally involved in making the decisions or taking the actions that led to harm.[105] Implementing this solution, however, presents a challenge. As Lawrence and Morley point out, under current UK company law, it is unclear whether a company director's obligation to promote the success of the company 'stretches to include the responsible development of its products'.[106] Even if it does, and a claim can be brought under the Companies Act 2006, these claims are rarely successful in practice.[107]

---

[97] Ibid. 32.
[98] Ibo van de Poel et al., 'The Problem of Many Hands: Climate Change as an Example' (2012) *Sci Eng Ethics* 53; Andreas Matthias, 'The Responsibility Gap: Ascribing Responsibility for the Actions of Learning Automata' (2004) 6 *Ethics Inf Technol* 175; Mittelstadt et al. (n. 93) 10.
[99] Coeckelbergh (n. 92) 2055; Matthias (n. 98) 175; van de Poel et al. (n. 98) 50.
[100] Giddens (n. 25) 4.
[101] Yeung (n. 90) 49.
[102] Coeckelbergh (n. 92) 2056.
[103] Yeung (n. 90) 50.
[104] Ibid.
[105] Jacob Turner, *Robot Rules* (Palgrave 2019) 98; John Danaher, 'Robots, Law and the Retribution Gap' (2016) 18 *Ethics Inf Technol* 307.
[106] Lawrence and Morley (n. 3) 427.
[107] Ibid.

Another response to the responsibility gap argument is to create better systems for attributing responsibility.[108] As the problem of many hands arises because we do not know 'who did what' in group projects, it can be mitigated by establishing 'a continuous chain of human responsibility across the whole AI delivery workflow'.[109] This solution, however, may also be challenging to implement. Although the approach may be feasible for AI systems developed within an organisation, establishing a continuous chain of responsibility may be harder when inputs developed by other companies are used. In these cases, the chain of responsibility might have to be established contractually.[110] A third response to the responsibility gap might be to do away with fault requirements entirely, making the legal entity that puts the AI on the market strictly liable for harms caused by AI.[111]

Although fine-tuning the details of such an arrangement will be a complex and important task, 'these challenges all point to familiar solutions based in various ways of holding manufacturers liable'.[112] So whilst there are challenges to implementing the principle of responsibility to govern the development of precursor technologies, these do not appear to be insurmountable.[113]

Even stickier problems emerge when we try and implement the principle of responsibility in cases where we have already created novel beings with moral status, especially if we try and hold the novel being itself responsible for its own performance. The problem here is that it is far from clear what it would mean to hold a novel being responsible for their actions and how this could be achieved in practical terms. Given the current levels of uncertainty regarding what novel beings will be like if they emerge, it is unclear how novel beings would, for instance, pay compensation for harms they cause, or how one could punish a novel being for a lack of compliance with the relevant law and regulation.[114] Extracting compensation from novel beings would require them having resources that can be redistributed and effective punishment will depend on us being able to identify their interests and develop means of frustrating those

---

[108] Leslie (n. 93) 23; Joanna Bryson, 'The Artificial Intelligence of the Ethics of Artificial Intelligence: An Introductory Overview for Law and Regulation' in Dubber, Pasquale, and Das (eds) (n. 21) 6; Helen Nissembaum, 'Computing and Accountability' (1994) 37 *Communications of the ACM* 79; Mittelstadt et al. (n. 93) 13.

[109] Leslie (n. 93) 26.

[110] Turner (n. 105) 106.

[111] Nissembaum (n. 108) 79; Turner (n. 105) 91; David C. Vladeck, 'Machines Without Principals: Liability Rules and Artificial Intelligence' (2014) 89 *Washington Law Rev* 149; Danaher (n. 105) 307.

[112] Trevor N. White and Seth D. Baum, 'Liability for Present and Future Robotics Technology' in Patrick Lin, Keith Abney and Ryan Jenkins (eds) (n. 91) 69.

[113] Vladeck (n. 111) 141.

[114] Bryson, Diamantis, and Grant (n. 16) 288.

interests.[115] Given our current state of knowledge about what novel beings will be like, it is unclear how the principle of responsibility should be implemented to govern novel beings with moral status if and when they are created.

5.3   Explicability

The third proposed principle for the regulation of novel beings is the principle of explicability. The principle of explicability holds that people who are significantly affected by a decision are entitled to 'a factual, direct, and clear explanation of the decision-making process'[116] used to arrive at the outcome.

One of the novel features of current techniques in AI, such as machine learning or artificial neural networks, is that the workings of the system 'are often invisible or unintelligible to all but (at best) the most expert observers'.[117] If we are going to use AI systems to make (or support) important decisions, we need to understand how these systems work. If these systems operate as non-transparent, non-interrogable 'black boxes', then we cannot understand their decisions.[118] This is a problem because not being able to identify the causes of particular outputs will severely hamper both our ability to proactively mitigate the negative effects of using artificially intelligent systems and to ensure that these systems work safely.[119] This, in turn, could undermine trust in the system.[120]

In order for a system to satisfy the principle of explicability, the explanations produced need to be intelligible to humans. It is, therefore, not enough for the system to output a log of all of the processes followed and operations performed to arrive at a particular result.[121] These results need to be presented in a way that can be made sense of by humans.[122] The principle of explicability

---

[115]   White and Baum (n. 112) 71.

[116]   Luciano Floridi et al., 'AI4People – An Ethical Framework for a Good AI Society: Opportunities, Risks, Principles, and Recommendations' (2018) 28 *Minds Mach* 689, 702; MHRA, 'Good Machine Learning Practice for Medical Device Development: Guiding Principles' (MHRA 2021) Principle 9. Available at: <https://www.gov.uk/government/publications/good-machine-learning-practice-for-medical-device-development-guiding-principles> accessed 12 January 2022.

[117]   The Royal Society, 'Explainable AI: The Basics' (The Royal Society 2019) 8. <https://royalsociety.org/topics-policy/projects/explainable-ai/> accessed 14 July 2021.

[118]   Ibid. 4.

[119]   Ibid. 10.

[120]   Tim Miller, 'Explanation in Artificial Intelligence: Insights from Social Science' (2019) 267 *Artif Intell* 1.

[121]   Ibid. 11.

[122]   Luciano Floridi et al., 'How to Design AI for Social Good: Seven Essential Factors' (2020) 26 *Sci Eng Ethics* 1771, 1781.

thus mirrors standard requirements of public reason, which also hold that people are entitled to explanations they can understand, based on reasons they can accept, when decisions made by others significantly affect their interests.[123] To ensure that AI systems can meet this requirement, developers of AI need knowledge of what sorts of explanations humans want and what humans generally consider to be a good explanation.

Like the principle of domination, the principle of explicability can be applied both to the regulation of precursor technologies and to the regulation of novel beings with moral status. The difference between the scenarios is not *what* is owed in each case, but *who* holds the obligation and to whom it is owed. Prior to the emergence of novel beings with moral status, the human developers of AI systems have the obligation to ensure their systems can generate explanations comprehensible to humans. If, and when, novel beings with moral status are brought into existence, the obligation could plausibly be held by the novel being itself. Should novel beings with moral status emerge, we could demand an explanation for their decisions in a similar way to how we currently demand explanation from humans who make decisions. Given the uncertainty surrounding what novel beings would be like, precisely how this could be achieved in practice is not a question we can answer prior to their emergence.

Here, as before, there are likely challenges to implementing the principle of explicability. In the case of precursor technologies, the first challenge to implementing the principle is that it could conflict with the commercial interests of developers.[124] If the algorithm being designed and the data used to train it are proprietary, applying the principle of explicability could lead to the disclosure of commercially sensitive information. A second significant challenge with its implementation is the fact that ensuring explicability is significantly harder for complex systems than simple ones.[125] As more complex systems can often perform better, the demands of the principle of explicability can conflict with other valuable characteristics of an AI system, most notably accuracy.[126]

---

[123] Onora O'Neill, 'The Public Use of Reason' (1986) 14 *Political Theory* 529; Onora O'Neill, *Autonomy and Trust in Bioethics* (Cambridge University Press 2002) 91; Jonathan Quong, 'On the Idea of Public Reason' in J. Mandle and D. Reidy (eds) *The Blackwell Companion to Rawls* (Wiley-Blackwell 2014) 268; Onora O'Neill, *Constructing Authorities* (Cambridge University Press 2015) 67.

[124] Harry Surden, 'Ethics of AI in Law: Basic Questions' in Dubber, Pasquale, and Das (eds) (n. 21) 731.

[125] IEEE (n. 91) 27.

[126] Select Committee on Artificial Intelligence, 'AI in the UK: Ready, Willing and Able?' (HL 2017–19, 100) para. 99; The Royal Society (n. 117) 21; Bryson (n. 108) 8; Independent High-Level Expert Group on Artificial Intelligence, 'Ethics Guidelines for

Providing an account of how to trade off explicability against accuracy is a significant challenge here.

Harder challenges surface when we consider how to implement the principle of explicability in a post-emergence scenario. The problem is that, given that novel beings might be embodied differently to us, they are likely to perceive the world differently to us. This might make it hard for them to determine what counts as an appropriate explanation. As mentioned above, crafting appropriate explanations for decisions requires an awareness of what matters to humans.[127] The problem is that identifying what is salient to humans is notoriously difficult for artificial intelligent systems.[128] One potential solution to this problem would be to ask stakeholders what they would consider to be an appropriate explanation so that we can tell the AI what matters to us.[129] This, however, may not solve the problem if the resulting account of what matters cannot be formalised clearly enough for it to be communicated to an AI. This might be the case if, for example, what constitutes an appropriate explanation is subtly context-, socially-, or culturally dependent. It is, therefore, unclear whether novel beings which are embodied very differently will be able to satisfy the requirement of explicability.

5.4   Non-Harm

The fourth proposed principle is the principle of non-harm, which holds that the development and deployment of both precursor technologies and novel beings should not cause harm to others. The fact that an action would cause harm to others is generally considered to be a good reason for regulating or prohibiting the activity in question.[130] The non-harm principle proposed here is an application of this more general moral and legal principle to the regulation of new and emerging technologies.

In a pre-emergence scenario, human developers would hold the duty to ensure the systems they design and deploy do not cause harm to others. In other words, they need to ensure their systems perform the tasks they are intended to perform, in the expected fashion, in a consistent way, without causing risks to the health and safety of humans. Given that the world is unpredictable, to ensure that systems are safe, reliable, and robust, designers will

---

Trustworthy AI' (European Commission 2019) 18 <https://digital-strategy.ec.europa.eu/en/library/ethics-guidelines-trustworthy-ai> accessed 14 July 2021.

[127]   Leslie (n. 93) 35.

[128]   Miller (n. 120) 12.

[129]   Coeckelbergh (n. 92) 2064.

[130]   Joel Feinberg, *Harm to Others* (Oxford University Press 1984) 26; John Stuart Mill, *On Liberty* (Yale University Press 2003) 80.

need to ensure that they can manage unfamiliar events and unexpected scenarios in such a way as to avoid harms.[131] To do this, developers will need to
train their models on data that is sufficiently broad,[132] stress-test their systems
to see how they operate in unfavourable situations (e.g. by using adversarial
learning techniques or using simulations),[133] monitor their performance,[134] and
introduce 'fail-safe' measures.[135]

Implementing these requirements to govern the development of precursor
technologies presents some challenges. Ensuring that systems are rigorously
tested before release will likely increase the costs of development, as will
requirements to monitor and adjust the system once it has been deployed.
Enforcing these requirements will also present challenges for regulators, who
will need technical expertise to ascertain whether safety systems are up to task.

As with the other principles, things are more complicated when it comes to
applying the principle to a post-emergence scenario. If novel beings develop
moral status, the duty to satisfy the harm principle could theoretically be
transferred to the novel being itself. There are, however, a series of challenges
to implementing the principle in this way. The first problem is that, given the
uncertainty regarding what novel beings would be like, it isn't clear whether
a novel being's understanding of the purpose of what they are doing will match
that of humans. This problem is analogous to the main problem of implementing the principle of explicability: i.e. it is unclear whether novel beings will
share our understanding of what matters. Without an understanding of the
purposes humans are trying to achieve, the novel being might be unable to
recognise situations in which the sub-goals they are pursuing do not represent
appropriate means to the valued ends.[136] As a consequence, the deployment of
novel beings might lead to adverse events and unintended perverse outcomes.

The second problem concerns enforcement. As mentioned above, it is
unclear how we could enforce the duty to uphold the harm principle against
novel beings. The worry here is analogous to the challenges to implementing
the principle of responsibility: it is unclear how we could incentivise a novel
being to follow the principle of non-harm, or how we would punish or extract

---

[131] Commission, 'On Artificial Intelligence – A European Approach to Excellence
and Trust (White Paper)' COM(2020) 65 Final 20; Floridi et al. (n. 122) 1776.
[132] COM(2020) 65 Final 19; MHRA (n. 116) Principles 3 and 8.
[133] High-Level Expert Group on Artificial Intelligence (n. 126) 27; Floridi et al. (n.
122) 1777.
[134] Leslie (n. 93) 32; Independent High-Level Expert Group on Artificial Intelligence
(n. 126) 20; MHRA (n. 116) Principle 10.
[135] Robert Challen et al., 'Artificial Intelligence, Bias, and Clinical Safety' (2019)
28 *BMJ Qual Saf* 233.
[136] Leslie (n. 93) 33.

remedies from a novel being should the principle be violated.[137] Until these uncertainties are resolved, it is unclear how the principle could be implemented to govern the behaviour of novel beings.

6   CONCLUDING THOUGHTS: PRINCIPLES, UNCERTAINTY, AND NORMATIVE GUIDANCE

Our starting point in this chapter was to note that if novel beings come into existence, the law needs to be able to take account of such beings, as well as their precursor technologies. We suggested that the principal difficulty in trying to think about the regulation of (the emergence of) such beings is the high degree of epistemic uncertainty surrounding this possibility. We noted that there are (at least) four aspects to this: uncertainty regarding (1) whether novel beings will actually come to exist, (2) how this might happen if they do, (3) what the impacts of bringing such beings into existence might be, and (4) what such novel beings will be like (corporeally, cognitively, morally, and so on). Given this, we saw that one regulatory strategy is simply to wait and see. Although often favoured by regulators when it comes to uncertain technological developments, we made the case that this approach tends to lead to unsatisfactory reactive regulation later on. One consequence of this is that by waiting, the ability of regulators to influence the trajectory of technological development and deployment is significantly reduced. Equally, we noted that having a detailed regulatory regime early on would also be unsatisfactory. First, and most significantly, we simply do not have enough information to produce comprehensive and granular law and regulation to govern (the emergence of) novel beings. Second, given this, any *sui generis* regime drafted is likely to be out of date and obsolete pretty quickly. As such, what is to be done? Our suggestion in this chapter is that under conditions of significant uncertainty, a principles-based approach could offer a way to do something *now* and to offer appropriate normative guidance for the development of more concrete law and regulation *later*. Such an approach could keep our regulatory options open, helping to avoid the problem of crafting a detailed pre-emptive regulatory regime (which becomes obsolete or inapplicable as we gain more knowledge about novel beings and what they are like).

As noted by Black and colleagues, and we saw in section 4, 'The potential benefits claimed of using principles are that they provide flexibility, are more likely to produce behaviour which fulfils the regulatory objectives, and are easier to comply with.'[138] However, as we also noted, principles are not

---

[137] Yampolskiy and Fox (n. 87) 219.
[138] Black, Hopper, and Band (n. 41) 193.

a panacea. Significantly, a principles-based approach offers us high-level normative guidance and the flexibility needed to proactively regulate precursor technologies without hampering our ability to respond to new developments as they surface. Yet, as we saw in the previous section, implementing the principles of non-domination, responsibility, explicability, and non-harm, especially in a post-emergence scenario, would likely face a number of difficulties. Questions that would need to be answered to implement the principles outlined to govern the behaviour of novel beings include: what activities constitute arbitrary interference with a novel being? How do we ensure novel beings do not pose an unacceptable risk of harm to others? How could we hold novel beings responsible for any harms caused? How could they pay compensation? What would punishment of a novel being look like? And how could we ensure novel beings provide explanations for their decisions which are comprehensible to humans?

As well as these specific problems with each principle, there is also the more general problem of how to translate the principles into practice. Given the generality at which they are expressed, principles can be ambiguous and need to be interpreted for them to apply to the particular situations that confront regulators. As is usually the case in principles-based regulation, different organisations will interpret the different principles in different ways (usually to their own benefit or perceived benefit). Although this flexibility is necessary in light of the epistemic uncertainties we are facing, flexibility has the downside that we can end up with actions and outcomes which are undesirable or unsatisfactory and which were not anticipated at the time the principles were drafted.

Above we suggested four potential ways in which these problems could be mitigated. The first was to supplement each principle with a fuller explanation of their purpose to help future regulators interpret them appropriately. The second was to provide an account of the principles as a collective, helping reduce ambiguity over the normative direction of travel intended. The third was to combine general principles with more specific prescriptive rules that establish hard lines that should not be crossed in applying the principle. The fourth was to complement principles with a set of best practice examples. All four of these steps to mitigating the potential vagueness of a principles-based approach rely on making principles more specific, thereby constraining the way they can be interpreted by future regulators and regulatees.

The problem, however, is that mitigating concerns about indeterminacy in the application of principles necessarily involves reducing the flexibility of the regulatory regime. Meanwhile, the benefits of flexibility are connected to the problems of interpretation and application caused by the generality of the principles. We cannot have the benefits without the burdens. The best we can expect is a trade-off between our ability to react to novel developments with a flexible regulatory regime against the risk that the lack of specificity of the principles will lead to them being interpreted inappropriately. Our suggestion is that a principles-based approach to the regulation of (the emergence of) novel beings could strike a more plausible balance between flexibility and specificity than either adopting a 'wait and see' approach (which hampers our ability to influence the development of technologies) or the creation of a *sui generis* regulatory regime (which runs the risk of becoming obsolete as technology develops).

If carefully crafted, a principles-based approach has the potential to be both flexible enough to cope with future uncertainty and normative enough to be action-guiding. The four principles suggested in this chapter (non-domination, responsibility, explicability, and non-harm) are just that: suggestions. There may be others which are better suited, given the conditions of uncertainty under which we are operating. There are almost certainly others, which we have not had the space or time to consider here, and which could be added to round out our list. What is certain, however, is that no matter which principles are used, challenges will remain. Amongst other things, we will need to think about: how to resolve conflicts between principles;[139] who/which organisation would be best suited to take on the role of regulator when it comes to emerging technologies and novel beings; whether a single regulator could do the job, given the broad range of precursor technologies and potential novel beings possible; and if several regulators/regulatory agencies are to be involved, how we ought to ensure that there is not a diffusion of responsibility and a lack of coordination between agencies. We do not propose any answers to these questions here. What is needed to begin to answer these questions is likely some sort of in-depth 'legal foresighting' process such as that proposed by Laurie and colleagues for dealing with uncertainties regarding new technologies.[140] By this they 'mean the identification and exploration of possible and desirable future legal and quasi-legal developments aimed at achieving valued social and technological ends'.[141] We end, therefore, simply by noting that even if we can agree that a principles-based approach could help, and on which principles are entailed, this would only be the beginning of the process when it comes to the regulation and governance of (the emergence of) novel beings.

---

[139] Our thanks to the anonymous reviewer for prompting us to include this concern.
[140] Laurie et al. (n. 34).
[141] Ibid. 3. The authors propose an in-depth framework for doing this at 11–27 and look at its application in practice at 27–32.

7. The "ethical" regulation of "novel being" technologies: the potential role for patents as ethical drivers, blockers and guiders?

Aisling McMahon[1]

INTRODUCTION

> "Okay. Here it is. Klara, the fact is, there's growing and widespread concern about AFs right now. People saying how you've become too clever. They're afraid because they can't follow what's going on inside anymore. They can see what you do. They accept that your decisions, your recommendations, are sound and dependable, almost always correct. But they don't like not knowing how you arrive at them. That's where it comes from, this backlash, this prejudice. So we have to fight back. We have to say to them, okay, you're worried because you don't understand how AFs think..."[2] (Henry Capaldi to Klara (an android Artificial Friend (AF) companion) in Kazuo Ishiguro's *Klara and the Sun* (Faber and Faber, 2021))

This passage from Ishiguro's novel *Klara and the Sun* exemplifies some of the myriad of ethical issues raised by the potential future creation and existence of "novel beings" – technologies which are not-quite-human but which display characteristics akin to humans. In *Klara and the Sun*, we are introduced to a future dystopian world, where robots in the form of android technology

---

[1]   Some of the arguments in this chapter develop from earlier draft work presented at the following conferences/seminars: ATRIP Conference, Vanderbilt University, Nashville, Tennessee 26 August 2019; Durham CELLS Research Seminar, Durham University 30 October 2019; Patents and Emerging Technologies Workshop, Wellcome Trust, London, 19–20 November 2019; and the Health Law and Ethics seminar series, Queen's University Belfast 27 February 2020. I would like to thank participants at these events for their feedback. I would also like to thank the editors, Dr Sarah Morley and Dr David Lawrence, for the inspiration to consider the role of patents in regulating "novel being" technologies in this manner, and to thank Dr Karen Walsh, and also the anonymous reviewers for their helpful feedback.
[2]   Kazuo Ishiguro, *Klara and the Sun* (Faber and Faber, 2021) at 297.

act as routine companions for children and others. Klara is one such robot, a so-called artificial friend (AF), who in Ishiguro's imagined world displays characteristics akin to humans showing high levels of understanding and awareness.[3] Throughout the novel we see the complexity of a world with AFs, giving readers pause to reflect on questions about the status of AFs, their rights and needs, and how such beings could co-exist – in an ethical manner – with humans in such a future society.

Yet, this imagined world of Ishiguro's is not as futuristic as it may at first seem. Given contemporary technological developments, we are now at the cusp of being able to create such "novel beings". Already, we have debates around black box technologies,[4] algorithmic decision-making,[5] and artificial intelligence,[6] which often centre around a future potential for autonomous beings and the implications of this for law. Contemporary debates also explore how laws can be used to shape the development of such beings and their actions – including the role of law in limiting or pre-empting potential ethical or legal issues that could arise in such contexts.[7] In fact, emerging technologies, including artificial intelligence, neuro-technologies and advances in genetics and biotechnologies make it possible to imagine a (potentially near) future where it may be scientifically possible to create such "novel beings". Such beings may become a regular form of life and of human–societal interaction. As Lawrence and Morley have aptly argued:

> A vast range of technologies, including genomics, synthetic biology, advanced pharmaceuticals, neurotechnologies, and breakthroughs in computer science and artificial intelligence research promise to create new forms of sentient, even sapient

---

[3]   Ibid.

[4]   Frank Pasquale, *The Black Box Society: The Secret Algorithms That Control Money and Information* (Harvard University Press, 2015).

[5]   For example, see Rebecca Williams, "Rethinking Administrative Law for Algorithmic Decision Making" (2021) 42(2) *Oxford Journal of Legal Studies* 468, https://doi.org/10.1093/ojls/gqab032; The Law Society of England and Wales, "Algorithms in the Criminal Justice System: A Report by the Law Society Commission on the Use of Algorithms in the Justice System" (June 2019); Robert Brauneis and Ellen P. Goodman, "Algorithmic Transparency for the Smart City" (2018) 20 *Yale Journal of Law & Technology* 103; Jennifer Cobbe, "Administrative Law and the Machines of Government: Judicial Review of Automated Public-Sector Decision-Making" (2019) 39 *Legal Studies* 636.

[6]   Woodrow Barfield and Ugo Pagallo, *Research Handbook of the Law of Artificial Intelligence* (Edward Elgar Publishing, 2018).

[7]   Gerhard Wagner, "Robot, Inc.: Personhood for Autonomous Systems?" (2019–2020) 88 *Fordham Law Review* 591; Alice Guerra, Francesco Parisi and Daniel Pi, "Liability for Robots I: Legal Challenges" (2021) *Journal of Institutional Economics (First View)* 1–13.

intelligent life in the not too distant future, and perhaps change our understanding of life itself.[8]

For the purposes of this chapter, the term "novel being" is used as a broad term to refer to new forms of "beings" which may be created via many different types of technologies, for example, by using biotechnologies, artificial technologies, etc. Crucially, such beings are imagined as beings that display characteristics akin to humans, such as sentience, agency and autonomy. In other words, such beings are not-quite-human, but share commonality with humans, such as by demonstrating a level of understanding, cognitive ability, or sentience. As such technologies develop, there will be a (likely) spectrum of features which are seen as akin to human creativity,[9] sentience or cognisance that such "novel beings" display, with the level of shared human-like features likely differing depending on the "technology" in question, or the point in time of the technological development.

Alongside – and included within – the myriad of ethical questions raised by the potential for new forms of sentient or sapient life forms, a key question we must consider from a legal perspective is what is the role for law in *regulating* the development and use of such technologies in an "ethical" manner? The term "regulation" is used in this context, as will be discussed in further detail below, to denote actions which seek to *shape*, in this case, the development (and/or use) of "novel being" technology towards an intended outcome. Within this context, when considering questions of how technologies are shaped or developed, a key but often overlooked legal tool which can impact this is intellectual property rights (IPRs).[10] It is this potential role of IPRs and specifically, the role of patents in shaping the development and use of "novel being" technologies in an "ethical" manner that forms the focus of the chapter.

IPRs, such as patents, facilitate rightsholders in obtaining an exclusionary right over a technology for the duration of the right, which in turn enables

---

[8]   David Lawrence and Sarah Morley, "Novel Beings: Moral Status and Regulation" (2021) 30(3) *Cambridge Quarterly of Healthcare Ethics* 415.

[9]   For example, see the work of Ai-Da described as
the world's first ultra-realistic artist robot. She draws using cameras in her eyes, her AI algorithms, and her robotic arm. Created in February 2019, she had her first solo show at the University of Oxford, "Unsecured Futures", where her art encouraged viewers to think about our rapidly changing world … She continues to create art that challenges our notions of creativity in a post-humanist era. (https://www.ai-darobot.com/ accessed April 2022)

[10]   See also Aisling McMahon, "Biotechnology, Health and Patents as Private Governance Tools: The Good, the Bad and the Potential for Ugly?" (2020) 3 *Intellectual Property Quarterly* 161.

them to act as akin to gatekeepers over such technologies for the patent term.[11] This chapter aims to demonstrate that this control given to rightsholders could be – and in many cases is already – used to shape or dictate how patented technologies are developed and used by others downstream. I will argue that this could be used by rightsholders or third parties to play a role in the regulation of "novel being" technologies by seeking to shape or encourage their development and use in an "ethical" manner.[12]

There is now a developing body of literature which considers the role of patents in the governance of emerging technologies,[13] and in particular, a growing body of recent literature considering the role of patents in the governance of human genome editing technologies.[14] For example, in 2021, the World Health Organization Expert Advisory Committee on Human Genome Editing published a report which recognised the potential role of patent rights and licences in governing human genome editing.[15] In response to this report, a group of international patent scholars (of which I am a member) published

---

[11]   Aisling McMahon, "Accounting for Ethical Considerations in the Licensing of Patented Biotechnologies and Health-Related Technologies: A Justification" in Naomi Hawkins (ed.), *Patenting Biotechnological Innovation: Eligibility, Ethics and Public Interest* (Edward Elgar Publishing, 2022).

[12]   This builds on the author's earlier work, particularly McMahon, above n. 10; see also McMahon, above n. 11.

[13]   For example, see Shobita Parthasarathy, "Use the Patent System to Regulate Gene Editing" (2018) 562 *Nature* 486; Nienke de Graeff, Léon E. Dijkman, Karin R. Jongsma and Annelien L. Bredenoord, "Fair Governance of Biotechnology: Patents, Private Governance, and Procedural Justice" (2018) 18(12) *American Journal of Bioethics* 57–59; McMahon, above n. 10; McMahon "A Global Equitable Access to Vaccines, Medicines and Diagnostics for COVID-19: The Role of Patents as Private Governance" (2020) 47 *Journal of Medical Ethics* 142.

[14]   This includes: Jacob S. Sherkow, "Patent Protection for CRISPR: An ELSI Review" (2017) 4(3) *Journal of Law and the Biosciences* 565; Oliver Feeney et al., "Patenting Foundational Technologies: Lessons from CRISPR and Other Core Biotechnologies" (2018) 18(12) *American Journal of Bioethics* 36; Oliver Feeney, Julian Cockbain and Sigrid Sterckx, "Ethics, Patents and Genome Editing: A Critical Assessment of Three Options of Technology Governance" (2021) 3 *Frontiers in Political Science* No. 731505; Naomi Scheinerman and Jacob S. Sherkow, "Governance Choices of Genome Editing Patents" (2021) 3 *Frontiers in Political Science* No. 745898; Jacob Sherkow, Eli Y. Adashi and Glenn Cohen, "Governing Human Germline Editing Through Patent Law" (2021) 326(12) *Journal of the American Medical Association* 1149; Duncan Matthews, Abbe Brown, Emanuela Gambini, Aisling McMahon, Timo Minssen, Ana Nordberg, Jacob S. Sherkow, Jakob Wested and Esther van Zimmeren, "The Role of Patents and Licensing in the Governance of Human Genome Editing: A White Paper" (2021) Queen Mary Law Research Paper No. 364/2021.

[15]   WHO Expert Advisory Committee on Developing Global Standards for Governance and Oversight of Human Genome Editing, *Human Genome Editing a Framework for Governance* (WHO, 2021).

a paper which provides a detailed analysis of the legal issues, challenges and potential for patent grant and licensing to be used in the governance of human genome editing technologies.[16] This emerging and growing body of work highlights the potential role that patents could have in governing patented technologies.

This chapter differs from such existing literature, as it focuses at a broader conceptual level and in doing so, it provides novel insights in relation to the narrower question of the potential role that patents could play in acting specifically in a *regulatory* manner to shape and steer the "*ethical*" development and use of "novel being" technologies.[17]

In doing so, as will be developed further below, this chapter adopts a very specific conception of "regulation" as a narrower subset of governance which aims to steer the development of an object to an intended outcome.[18] That desired end may be one which is intended by the patent holder, in which case this chapter views this form of "regulation" as akin to a *self-regulation* – whereby, for example, a rightsholder may be seeking to limit certain uses of a technology in relation to which they have ethical concerns. The role of patents in a regulatory sense could also be employed by a third party such as a public entity (e.g. a governmental agency), including a regulatory body, to seek to achieve a public aim,[19] such as by encouraging the development or use of "novel being" technology in a certain "ethical" manner. In all such cases, the role of patents is considered here, specifically, in terms of how such rights (and how they are licensed), could be used as devices which seek to shape the "ethical" use and development of "novel being" technologies.[20]

---

[16]   Duncan Matthews et al., above n. 14.

[17]   The chapter is focused specifically on "novel being" technologies. Nonetheless, the arguments made in some cases will have broader resonance for the role of patents in a regulatory context for other technologies, and particularly, for the potential for patent rights/licences to be used to embed *ethical considerations* in the use and development of emerging technologies.

[18]   The chapter draws particularly on Julia Black, "Critical Reflections on Regulation" (2002) 27 *Australian Journal of Legal Philosophy* 1; John Braithwaite, Cary Coglianese and David Levi-Faur, "Can Regulation and Governance Make a Difference?" (2007) *Regulation and Governance* 1; see also T.T. Arvind and Aisling McMahon (forthcoming), *Social and Legal Studies, Special Issue: Contracts as Governance Instruments*.

[19]   For a detailed legal analysis of the potential governance role of patent rights and licences – including both public and private uses of patents/licences – in the human genome technology context, see Duncan Matthews et al., above n. 14.

[20]   Other ethical issues in terms of patent rights are also important, particularly around the role and impact of patent rights on access to patented technologies, and how to ensure "ethical" approaches to how patent rights are used that facilitate equita-

Importantly, for the purposes of this chapter, how "ethical" is defined in this context will depend on the entity (rightsholder(s) or third party) seeking to use the patent right (or licences) in such a directed regulatory manner.[21] However, the chapter does not aim to address the normative question of what the "ethical" development of "novel being" technologies should necessarily entail; instead, the chapter's contribution is to show how patents and how they are licensed could potentially be employed as a tool by rightsholders or third parties in an attempt to shape technological development and use in a way that they view as "ethical".

Moreover, at the outset, it should be noted that the chapter is not suggesting that patent law should act as a replacement for existing regulatory systems for "novel being" technologies; rather here the focus is on the extent to which patents could be used to complement, not substitute for, existing measures. Furthermore, reflecting on the themes within this edited collection, when considering patents within a regulatory approach to steer the "ethical" use and development of "novel being" technologies, patents could be used in both a proactive and reactive regulatory manner. For patents to be used in a proactive manner in this context, one would need to be able to anticipate how a technology may develop (and also to anticipate to what extent, and how, patents would act as a driver for the development of certain technologies) and then one could try to employ patent law to discourage or deter certain ethically contentious uses or developments of such technologies. For example, decisions could be taken at a policy level to deny patents entirely for certain technologies with the aim of seeking to deter development of such technologies.[22] Another avenue for proactive regulation in this context would be for a rightsholder to impose licensing restrictions over (or refuse to license entirely) a patented technology (or for a third-party regulatory body to recommend licensing restrictions) with the aim of deterring certain uses of that technology that they anticipate will be ethically contentious. The benefits and challenges with both approaches are considered below (Section 2). However, for many technologies, including for many "novel being" technologies, it will

---

ble access to patented "novel being" technologies. However, such issues are outside the scope of this chapter.

[21]   I have left the term "ethical" deliberately undefined, as different entities will have different perceptions of what this may entail in the "novel being" technology context. Moreover, an issue around seeking to use patents to shape technological developments towards ethical ends is defining what is meant by "ethical" and who should define this, which in itself raises ethical issues. This point will be alluded to throughout the chapter and is discussed in more detail in McMahon, above n. 11.

[22]   This could only occur where legally possible within the patent exclusions applicable in a jurisdiction, and in practice there are also challenges with this approach – a point returned to below.

likely not be possible to know how a technology will develop at the point a patent is granted or to know what types of ethical issues may arise related to its use. If a patent has already been granted before the ethical ramifications of certain uses of that "novel being" technology become evident, then two main reactive regulatory approaches using patents could arise, namely: depending on the context and jurisdiction, a patent could potentially be challenged at that point, where relevant legal grounds applied; or a patent licensing clause could be recommended by a third-party body or adopted by a rightsholder seeking to restrict ethically contentious future uses/developments of that technology by others. In considering patents' role in the regulation of "novel being" technologies, the fact that patents could be used in both a reactive and a proactive manner should be borne in mind.

In making such arguments the chapter is structured as follows: Section 1 outlines the scope and parameters of the arguments proposed. It expands further on what is meant by "regulation" for the purposes of this chapter, and then outlines the likelihood of patentability for many types of "novel being" technologies. Section 2 then examines the main avenues by which patents could potentially be used to regulate the development and use of "novel being" technologies in an "ethical" manner. It argues that patent rights/licences could be harnessed to act as drivers, blockers and guiders of "ethical" approaches to the development/use of "novel being" technologies by rightsholders, or by third parties as part of a broader regulatory approach. Section 3 concludes, arguing that the role of patents in the ethical regulation of "novel being" technologies has potential, but warrants much greater investigation.

1   PATENTS AND THE REGULATION OF "NOVEL BEING" TECHNOLOGIES: AN OVERVIEW

Importantly, there are many definitions and discussions on what it means to regulate,[23] and the purpose of this chapter is not to grapple with this conceptual question.[24] Rather, this chapter takes as its starting point a conception of "regulation" as a broad term which can encapsulate a device, action or tool that assists in the steering of behaviour towards achieving a particular outcome. More specifically, the chapter draws on Braithwaite, Coglianese

---

[23] For example, see Bronwen Morgan and Karen Yeung, *An Introduction to Law and Regulation* (Cambridge University Press, 2012); Peter Drahos (ed.), *Regulatory Theory: Foundations and Applications* (ANU Press, 2017); Ian Ayers and John Braithwaite, *Responsive Regulation: Transcending the Deregulation Debate* (Oxford University Press, 1992).

[24] For a broader discussion of regulation and the distinction between this and governance in the contractual context, see Arvind and McMahon, above n. 18.

and Levi-Faur's work, wherein regulation is viewed as a "large subset of governance that is about steering the flow of events and behaviour",[25] or as Drahos and Krygier observe, regulation could be conceived of as "influencing the flow of events".[26] Drawing on such understandings of regulation, as noted, regulation is discussed in this chapter in terms of to what extent patents could be used to steer or shape the development and use of "novel being" technology, specifically, in a particular "ethically" (intended) manner.

1.1   Potential of Patents as Regulatory Tools: An Introduction

When we consider the role and nature of a patent right, we can see it as a tool not only of an economic nature, as it is often traditionally conceived, but also as a tool which has a much broader control and potential governance function.[27] It is this broader function of the patent right, and particularly the exclusivity that underpins the patent right, that gives it potential to be used in a "regulatory" manner, i.e. a manner that can influence or change the flow of events or shape/steer an object towards a particular outcome.

A patent is an intellectual property right that is granted over an "invention" once that invention is deemed to have met the three main criteria for patentability, namely showing novelty, inventive step and industrial application.[28] One theory which is used as a justification for patent rights is the social bargain theory, whereby the grant of an exclusive right over a technology is seen as justified where it is given in return for the inventor producing a socially useful technology; the grant of a patent is in essence a quid pro quo.[29] Once granted, a patent allows a rightsholder the right to exclude others from using a technology for the duration of the patent (generally 20 years). Accordingly, rightsholders have considerable discretion to decide how a patented technology is

---

[25]   Braithwaite, Coglianese and Levi-Faur, above n. 18; Black, above n. 18. See also discussion in McMahon, above n. 11.

[26]   Peter Drahos and Martin Krygier, "Regulation, Institutions and Networks" in Peter Drahos (ed.), *Regulatory Theory: Foundations and Applications* (ANU Press, 2017), 17.

[27]   See, generally McMahon, above n. 10; for a discussion of the role of patents in the governance of human genome editing, see also Matthews et al., above n. 14; more generally, on patents' regulatory potential, see Parthasarathy, above n. 13.

[28]   Art. 27(1) TRIPS Agreement, 1995, as amended.

[29]   See discussion in Margaret Llewelyn, "Schrodinger's Cat: An Observation on Modern Patent Law" in Peter Drahos (ed.), *Death of Patents* (Lawtext Publishing, 2005). For a critique of this theory, see Shubha Ghosh, "Patents and the Regulatory State: Rethinking the Patent Bargain Metaphor After Eldred" (2004) 19(4) *Berkeley Technology Law Journal* 1315.

used, and by whom, during the patent term.[30] If a third party uses the patented technology without the permission (granted via a patent licence) of the rightsholder, they could potentially be liable for patent infringement. In such cases, the rightsholder could threaten patent infringement litigation and could seek, for example, an injunction to stop that party from using the patented technology, or an order for return of profits (depending on the applicable laws in the jurisdiction in question). In many cases, a threat of patent infringement may be sufficient to make a party stop using such a patented technology due to fear of legal sanction,[31] thereby acting as a deterrent against others using technologies without a rightsholder's permission.

In this way, a patent right gives rightsholders significant control over the patented technology for the duration of the patent, which can place rightsholders in a gatekeeping role over who can access, use and develop the patented technology.[32] Due to this role, it will be argued in Section 2 that there is a significant potential for patents to be used in a regulatory manner to steer "ethical" approaches to the development and use of "novel being" technologies.

1.2   Patents and "Novel Beings"

Prior to delving into the main ways in which patents have the potential to act in a regulatory manner (in Section 2), it is useful to briefly reflect on the likelihood of patents being granted over "novel being" technologies, if developed.[33]

Under the TRIPS Agreement, which is applicable in all World Trade Organization (WTO) states since 1995, patents must be made available under

---

[30]   The use of a technology is also affected by other regulatory systems, for instance a rightsholder may have a patent over a technology, but this does not mean they can use the technology – a patent is merely an exclusivity right, it is not a right of use per se. For example, even if a rightsholder had a patent over a technology which could be used for embryo research, they may be prohibited from using that technology for embryo research depending on the applicable laws governing embryo research in the country in which they are seeking to use it.

[31]   See discussion of this in the gene patent context in Aisling McMahon, "Gene Patents and the Marginalisation of Ethical Issues" (2019) 41(10) *European Intellectual Property Review* 608; in some cases, third parties may also ignore patents or exercise "wilful blindness", which can depend on the context; see discussion in Naomi Hawkins, "The Impact of Human Gene Patents on Genetic Testing in the United Kingdom" (2011)13 *Genetic Medicine* 320.

[32]   McMahon, above n. 10; McMahon, above n. 11.

[33]   For a detailed discussion of the potential patentability of novel being technologies, see Aisling McMahon, "Patents, Governance and Control: Ethics and the Patentability of Novel Beings and Advanced Biotechnologies in Europe" (2021) 30(3) *Cambridge Quarterly of Healthcare Ethics* 529.

Article 27 in *all fields of technologies*.[34] Accordingly, WTO states do not have discretion to impose a blanket refusal of patents over certain fields of technologies per se, for example, for biotechnologies or pharmaceuticals. There are specific exclusions from patentability at a regional level.[35] However, patent exclusions can be narrowed down via interpretation by courts or patent offices, or by carve-outs of such provisions within legislation. For instance, in Europe, under Art. 5(1) of the Biotechnology Directive, the human body itself is not patentable; however, technologies related to the body, but which exist in isolated form, are patentable; for example a patent is available on an isolated human gene in Europe.[36] Moreover, exclusions from patentability are often interpreted narrowly in practice, which can facilitate broader patentability than might first appear when one reads the legislative text of such patent exclusions. For example, in Europe, and some other regions and states, an invention is not patentable where its commercial exploitation is against morality or *ordre public*.[37] However, in practice this provision has been interpreted narrowly by the European Patent Office, such that it is rarely used to deny patents over emerging technologies.[38]

---

[34]   Art. 27(1) TRIPS Agreement.
[35]   For example, see Art. 6(2) Biotechnology Directive 98/44EC, which details specific exclusions applicable in Europe based on the morality provisions in Europe. Relevant applicable patent exclusions will differ depending on the field in question. For example, for a legal analysis of the main patent exclusions which could be considered in the human genome editing context, see Duncan Matthews et al., above n. 14.
[36]   Art. 5(2) Biotechnology Directive 98/44EC.
[37]   Art. 53 European Patent Convention; Art. 6(1) Biotechnology Directive 98/44EC.
[38]   As discussed in Aisling McMahon, "Institutions, Interpretive Communities and Legacy in Decision-Making" in Ted S. Dove and Niamh NicShuibhne (eds), *Law and Legacy in Medical Jurisprudences: Essays in Honour of Graeme Laurie* (Cambridge University Press, 2021); Aisling McMahon, "The Morality Provisions in the European Patent System: An Institutional Examination" (PhD Thesis, University of Edinburgh, 2016); there is considerable literature on the role of the morality provisions in European patent law; for example, see Derek Beyleveld and Roger Brownsword, *Mice, Morality and Patents* (Common Law Institute of Intellectual Property, 1993); Peter Drahos, "Biotechnology Patents, Markets and Morality" (1999) 21(9) *European Intellectual Property Review* 441; Oliver Mills, *Biotechnological Inventions: Moral Restraints and Patent Law* (revised edn, Ashgate Publishing, 2010); Aurora Plomer and Paul Torremans (eds), *Embryonic Stem Cell Patents: European Law and Ethics* (Oxford University Press, 2009); Margo Bagley, "Patent First, Ask Questions Later: Morality and Biotechnology in Patent Law" (2003–2004) 45 *William and Mary Law Review* 469; Lionel Bently and Brad Sherman, "The Ethics of Patenting: Towards a Transgenic Patent System" (1995) 3 *Medical Law Review* 275; Ana Nordberg, "Patents, Morality and Biomedical Innovation in Europe: Historical Overview, Current Debates on Stem Cells, Gene Editing and AI, and *de lege ferenda* Reflections", in Daniel Gervais (ed.), *Fairness, Morality and* Ordre Public (Edward Elgar Publishing, 2020); Justine

Furthermore, importantly, patents would not be excluded over "novel being" technologies, based on current interpretative practice, merely because the technologies displayed some characteristics of sentience or were living per se. This is demonstrated by the fact that, for example, transgenic animals may be patentable in Europe.[39] Thus, it is likely that patents would be available on many types of "novel being" technologies (depending on the technology in question), should they arise now or in the future in Europe, and much would depend on the nature of the technology and the extent to which that technology is generally patentable.[40]

Whether "novel being" technologies should be patentable is a different normative question that raises multiple ethical questions, particularly if "novel beings" in future developed high levels of sentience or cognition akin to humans. In such cases, if patents were granted over such "novel beings", this would arguably raise significant ethical issues and also practical legal questions.[41] However, the purpose of this chapter is not to delve into such normative issues. Instead, here the main aim is to highlight that "novel being" technologies may very likely be patentable in Europe if current interpretative practices prevail, and that being the case, the question of how patents over such technologies could be used in a regulatory manner to steer *ethical* use, and development of such technologies, and to complement broader regulatory frameworks for "novel beings", warrants greater scrutiny.

Pila, "Adapting the *Ordre Public* and Morality Exclusion of European Patent Law to Accommodate Emerging Technologies" (2020) 38 *Nature Biotechnology* 555; Karen Walsh and Naomi Hawkins, "Expanding the Role of Morality and Public Policy in European Patent Law" in Paul Torremans (ed.), *Intellectual Property and Human Rights* (4th edn, Wolters Kluwer, 2021); Duncan Matthews, Timo Minssen and Ana Nordberg, "Balancing Innovation, 'Ordre Public' and Morality in Human Germline Editing: A Call for More Nuanced Approaches in Patent Law" (2022) Queen Mary Law Research Paper No. 379/2022.

[39]   Aisling McMahon and David M. Doyle, "Patentability and De-extinct Animals in Europe: The Patented Woolly Mammoth?" (2020) 7(1) *Journal of Law and the Biosciences* lsaa017.

[40]   McMahon, above n. 33.

[41]   Ibid.

2 REGULATING "NOVEL BEING" TECHNOLOGIES: THE POTENTIAL FOR PATENTS AND (HOW THEY ARE LICENSED) TO ACT AS "ETHICAL" DRIVERS, BLOCKERS AND GUIDERS?

This section argues that patents could be used in a regulatory manner, specifically, to steer "ethical" approaches to the use and development of "novel being" technologies in three main ways: (1) at patent grant stage: at a policy level the grant or denial of a patent could be used in a regulatory manner, as whether a patent is granted can potentially act as a means to *drive* certain types of technological developments; (2) after a patent is granted, rightsholders could seek to refuse patent licences to third parties in an attempt to use the patent in a *blocking* manner to block third-party use or development of patented "novel being" technologies where in their view ethical issues arise; (3) relatedly, patent licensing clauses could be used in a more tailored manner by rightsholders or recommended by third parties for adoption by rightsholders, with the aim of seeking to *ethically guide* "novel being" technologies by restricting specific uses of such technologies via "ethical licensing clauses". In this latter context, patents have considerable potential to be used within a broader regulatory framework, including for "novel being" technologies.

2.1 Patents as Ethical Drivers: Shaping the Development of "Novel Being" Technologies?

In terms of regulatory uses of a patent right, if there was agreement that the development of a certain "novel being" technology was ethically contentious, there could be an attempt to use the patent system to deny patents over such technologies, for example, under the morality provisions,[42] to seek to discour-

---

[42] The morality provisions under Article 27(2) TRIPS state:
Members may exclude from patentability inventions, the prevention within their territory of the commercial exploitation of which is necessary to protect *ordre public* or morality, including to protect human, animal or plant life or health or to avoid serious prejudice to the environment, provided that such exclusion is not made merely because the exploitation is prohibited by their law.
In the European context, see Art. 53(a) EPC, and Art. 6 of the Biotechnology Directive 98/44EC.
Importantly, the chapter is not arguing that the morality provisions should never be used to deny patentability where ethical concerns around the *use* of a technology arise. It is the author's view that there will be cases where this is clearly warranted. However, the main point here is that using patents alone to seek to discourage use of technology could have unintended consequences, as will be discussed below. Moreover, in some

age the development/use of such technologies. However, this section argues that in practice the implications of adopting such an approach to discourage the development (and/or use) of certain technologies, including for "novel being" technologies, is not always straightforward and warrants greater consideration.[43]

As noted, a patent confers a time-limited exclusivity right on the rightsholder, which allows rightsholders to develop an income stream from a technology, as, for example, rightsholders can require payment for licences to use that technology for the duration of the patent.[44] Thus, the ability to obtain a patent right is a factor that may often be considered within the strategic development of new products, and in some contexts, commercial and other entities may be more likely to invest in research and development, if there is the potential for a patent (or other IPR) to derive a return on the development of the technology if successful. Accordingly, having a patent can, in some cases, be seen as encouraging the development of certain inventions. If certain types of "novel being" technologies were deemed patentable, this could act as an incentive for research and development of such technologies by certain entities. As a corollary, where certain types of technologies are not patentable (such as where patents are excluded over technologies under applicable law, e.g. excluded under the morality provisions where such provisions are applicable) this *may* discourage certain types of technological developments,[45] or may limit the applicable incentives, in certain contexts.

However, in practice the picture is more complex, as patents (or other IPRs) are not the sole incentive for the development of technologies nor are they necessarily an efficient incentive for all technological development. Arguably, much depends on the nature of the technology in question and also on the actor that is developing the technology. For instance, in some contexts, such as for many vaccines, IPRs, including patents, are often an insufficient

---

cases ethical issues may arise over the patent right (as opposed to the use of the technology) over a technology including, for example, the implications of the patent right for access to that technology. In such latter contexts, it is the author's view that there will also be cases where denial of the patent right based on morality provisions is warranted.

[43]   For a discussion of the role of morality provisions to deny patents in the human genome editing context, which calls for a more nuanced approach, see Matthews, Minnsen and Nordberg, above n. 38.

[44]   See discussion in McMahon, above n. 10.

[45]   See discussion in the gene-editing context in Ana Nordberg et al., "Cutting Edges and Weaving Threads in the Gene Editing (Я)evolution: Reconciling Scientific Progress with Legal, Ethical, and Social Concerns" (2018) 5(1) *Journal of Law and the Biosciences* 35; Matthews et al., above n. 14 at 2.3.2; Matthews, Minnsen and Nordberg, above n. 38.

incentive alone for technological development for various reasons.[46] Relatedly and arguably, the types of invention more likely to be incentivised by IPRs are inventions from which potential rightsholders could generate a profit, which may not necessarily be the type of invention that is most needed in society.[47] Moreover, other drivers of scientific discovery and technological development include, for example, scientific curiosity, or a public interest motivation (e.g. to cure disease, to develop new knowledge, etc.) and thus removing a patent incentive does not necessarily mean there are no other incentives to develop a technology.

Furthermore, and importantly, from a regulatory perspective the denial of a patent does not mean a technology cannot be used.[48] In fact, if a technology is unpatentable this could lead to more use and development of that technology because, in the absence of patent rights applying,[49] the development of that technology by others may become easier for many reasons, including the fact that if no patents apply this would remove the potential blocking effect patents may have on other parties working in a field and the threat of patent infringement litigation.[50]

Accordingly, in considering how to discourage the development and use of ethically contentious "novel being" technologies, it is not as straightforward as suggesting that if we deny patents over certain "novel being" technologies,

---

[46]   Ana Santos Rutschman has argued:
    In practice, however, the patent system on its own is incapable of incentivizing sustained R&D on many types of vaccines we collectively need, including vaccines for which the required scientific knowledge exists prior to the outbreak of an infectious disease. It should be noted that, apart from the historically ingrained pervasiveness of patent regimes in contemporary innovation infrastructure, there is no particular reason why vaccine R&D should be best incentivized through intellectual property incentives.
See Ana Santos Rutschman, "Property and Intellectual Property in Vaccine Markets" (2021) 7 *Texas A&M Journal of Property Law* 110 at 120–121.

[47]   For example, some diseases which primarily affect low-income countries urgently need research and development to devise better treatment or other health-care options; however, the ability to patent such products is often not a sufficient driver for invention, at least in part because of the likelihood of low financial gain even if such a product is developed.

[48]   See also discussion in Matthews et al., above n. 14; McMahon, above n. 11; Matthews, Minssen and Nordberg, above n. 38.

[49]   For example, see discussion in Michele Boldrin and David K. Levine, *The Case Against Intellectual Property* (Cambridge University Press, 2008); see also discussion in Siva Thambisetty, "Why Patent Law Doesn't Do Innovation Policy" (2013) LSE Legal Studies Working Paper No. 20/2013.

[50]   Shawn Harmon, Graeme Laurie and Aidan Courtney, 'Dignity, Plurality and Patentability: The Unfinished Story of *Brustle v Greenpeace* (Case Comment)' (2013) 38(1) *European Law Review* 92.

we will have fewer technological developments in a field; the reality is more complex. Arguably the most that can be said is that granting patents to a technology can act as a potential driver for some technologies by some entities, but the extent to which patents are incentives will depend on many factors, including the type of entity one is dealing with, the type of field one is in, and the type of technology one is developing.[51] Greater empirical investigation would be needed around the potential impact of denial of a patent on this basis – which is also specific to the technological field and different entities working in such fields – to understand the potential practical effect that the denial of patents could have in discouraging the development of ethically contentious "novel being" technologies.[52]

Furthermore, if we are looking at the potential regulatory role of patents at grant stage for "novel being" technologies, beyond considering whether a denial of a patent right could act as a means to discourage technological development on the basis of limiting the commercial incentive, we must also consider what the grant or denial of a patent signifies. Under the social bargain theory underpinning patent law, the grant of a patent is seen as justified because the inventor has developed a technology that is beneficial to society. Thus, the grant of a patent could be seen by some as denoting that the technology is one which the government wants to encourage the development of. Under this theory, it is questionable whether patents should be granted for inventions, which many in society may have concerns about or do not wish to encourage.[53] Indeed, at a policy level, the refusal of a patent, for example, on the basis of the morality provisions, could send a message about what technologies are being encouraged/discouraged which may also be used to drive or shape technological development.[54] Considering this in the "novel being" context, some types of "novel being" technology may be socially desirable, while other types of "novel being" technology may not be, or may give us pause for thought, depending on how technologies develop. In this latter context, from the perspective of the social bargain theory, it is questionable whether patents should be granted. Nonetheless, again in such contexts, the likely effects of denial of a patent need to be investigated further, if one is seeking to use patent grant/

---

[51] For instance, the patentability of a platform technology (depending on how the rightsholder used this right) could have a strong blocking effect on others using that technology to develop other products.

[52] For World Trade Organization member states, the ability to exclude inventions from patentability depends on whether they fall within the scope of patent exclusions under the TRIPS Agreement, which, as noted, are often narrowly interpreted.

[53] See discussion in Mills, above n. 38.

[54] See also discussion in the context of human genome editing in Matthews, Minnsen and Nordberg, above n. 38 at 21.

denial to encourage/discourage technological developments, as it could have unintended outcomes.

Moreover, ideally, in such contexts, the patent system would align with broader regulatory systems, and such systems would work together to deny patents and to introduce broader regulatory restrictions on technological development/use in the "novel being" context where certain "novel being" technologies were deemed ethically contentious. Nonetheless, a further complexity is that in some cases certain uses of a "novel being" technology may be ethically contentious, whereas other uses may not be, in such instances denying a patent over the technology in its entirety may be too broad a tool to use,[55] and other approaches such as using "ethical licensing", discussed below, can be used to have a more targeted effect in such contexts.

2.2   Patents as a Blocking Tool: Shaping the Ethical Downstream Use and Development of "Novel Being" Technologies

I now turn to consider the potential regulatory role of patents at post-grant stage for "novel being" technology. Once a patent has been granted over a technology, the patent right could potentially be used by the rightsholder to block technological use and development. As discussed above, if others use that patented technology without a rightsholder's consent, they could be liable for patent infringement, and in such cases, rightsholders can apply for an injunction or other legal remedy (depending on the jurisdiction) requiring that third party to desist in the alleged infringing activity. There are certain exceptions under which a third party could use a patented technology without the rightsholder's permission, for example where the use fell within the scope of the research exemption in patent law,[56] or where a compulsory licence is issued. Nonetheless, such exemptions to patentability tend to be interpreted narrowly in Europe, whilst compulsory licensing is not used on a routine basis in practice, and thus, for the duration of the patent rightsholders have a largely

---

[55]   This is discussed in McMahon, above n. 11, in terms of why "ethical licensing" approaches may offer a more nuanced role in guiding "ethical" uses of emerging technologies. See also discussion in Matthews, Minnsen and Nordberg, above n. 38.

[56]   For a recent discussion of the research exemption in the context of human genome editing, see Matthews et al., above n 14 at 2.3.3.1; however, the research exemption is often interpreted narrowly in practice, and in many jurisdictions, including the UK, this would not apply if the use of the product was to develop technologies for future commercial purposes; see Aisling McMahon, "Patents, Human Biobanks and Access to Health Benefits: Bridging the Public–Private Divide" in Jessica Lai and Antoinette Maget Dominicé (eds), *Intellectual Property and Access to Im/Material Goods* (Edward Elgar Publishing, 2016).

unfettered discretion over how the patented technology is used and by whom.[57] Accordingly, rightsholders have a significant gatekeeping function controlling how patented technologies are used and developed and by whom.[58] In theory, rightsholders could potentially use this function, where they had an ethical concern about the use of the technology they were developing, to apply for a patent with the intention of using that patent (if granted) to block others from using or developing a patented "novel being" technology by refusing a licence to such parties for that technology, and threatening or using patent infringement proceedings where the technology was used without their permission.

This potential for patents to be used in this way is demonstrated, for example, by considering Jeremy Rifkin and Stuart Newman's application for a patent in the US in 1997 over a human–animal hybrid, or chimera – specifically, a being which would be comprised of human DNA mixed with some DNA from another animal.[59] This case became known by many as a patent for a "humanzee" (resembling the notion of a human–chimpanzee hybrid being).[60] The applicants submitted the patent application in a context where they had not produced the technology, but where such developments were in their view increasingly scientifically plausible.[61]

It was reported that a key motivation for the applicants in seeking the patent was to prevent others from using or creating chimeras for the duration of the patent, i.e. 20 years.[62] This suggests that the applicants may have viewed patent rights as encompassing a potential to be used as a tool to restrict how a patented technology could be used, i.e. to regulate the development, use and

---

[57] McMahon, above n. 10. It is conceded a use of a technology could be prohibited by specific scientific regulations in a field/jurisdiction, in which case, as noted, no one can use the technology in that way, regardless of its patentability status.

[58] Aisling McMahon, "Global Equitable Access to Vaccines, Medicines and Diagnostics for COVID-19: The Role of Patents as Private Governance" (2021) 47 *Journal of Medical Ethics* 142.

[59] Brock Heathcotte and Jason Scott Robert, "The Strange Case of the Humanzee Patent Request" (2006) 6(1) *The National Catholic Bioethics Quarterly* 51.

[60] Stephen Munzer, "Human–Non-Human Chimeras in Embryonic Stem Cell Research" (2007) 21(1) *Harvard Journal of Law & Technology* 123, available at http://jolt.law.harvard.edu/articles/pdf/v21/21HarvJLTech123.pdf.

[61] Ibid.

[62] Heathcotte and Scott Robert, above n. 59, who state (at 52) that "Newman, supported by anti-biotechnology activist Jeremy Rifkin, aimed to secure the patent and then restrict the application of this technology for a period of twenty years, during which they hoped to foster a social debate about moral boundaries", citing Stuart A. Newman, "The Human Chimera Patent Initiative" (Winter 2002) *Lahey Clinic Medical Ethics Journal* 9(1) 4, 7; Mark Dowie, "Gods and Monsters" (January–February 2004) *Mother Jones* 48–53, 84. See also "Human/Non-Human Chimeras", *Stanford Encyclopaedia of Philosophy* available at https://plato.stanford.edu/entries/chimeras/.

access to technologies under patent. Ultimately, their patent application was rejected by the US Patent and Trademark Office (USPTO).[63] Thus, they were unable to use patent rights to restrict other parties' use of such technology. However, the fact that applicants sought to do this is the key point for the purposes of this chapter, as it suggests the potential for patent applicants to seek to use a patent right to restrict downstream development/use of a technology for the patent term. Indeed, the potential for patents to be used in such a blocking manner over technological use has also been referred to in other contexts. For example, it is sometimes argued that those opposed to abortion technologies, for ethical or other reasons, could seek to patent such technologies to restrict their use by others.[64]

However, the likelihood of patents being used in such a directed blocking manner, wherein applicants apply for patents with the intention of using that right (if granted) to restrict *all* uses of a technology due to ethical objections to that technology is arguably unlikely (or likely to be rare) for several reasons. First, there is an obligation within patent law in many national systems to work a patent.[65] Where this applies, in theory depending on the circumstances, and the scope of the national laws applicable, not practising or using an invention at all over a long period of time could ultimately lead to the patent being challenged. It is conceded on this point that it is questionable how likely, or easy, it would be to bring such a challenge. Moreover, not all systems have this requirement, and in recent times far less attention has been paid to the requirement at an international level.[66]

Second, for a patent to be applied for with the intention of using it to block downstream uses of that technology, an entity would have to be in a position to develop or invent a technology that they did not wish to use, then apply for a patent on it, and then seek to maintain this patent (by paying patent renewal fees, potentially in multiple jurisdictions if they wished the patent to have

---

[63] See discussion in David Dickson, "Legal Fight Looms over Patent Bid on Human/Animal Chimaeras" (1998) 392 *Nature* 423; Rick Weiss, "Patent Sought on Making of Part-Human Creatures", *Washington Post* (2 April 1998): Ryan Hagglund, "Patentability of Human–Animal Chimeras" (2012) 25 *Santa Clara High Technology Law Journal* 51; Editorial, "Hybrid Too Human to Patent" (2005) 4 *Nature Review Drug Discovery* 270, available at https://doi.org/10.1038/nrd1710.

[64] Kara W. Swanson, "Patents, Politics and Abortion", Northeastern University School of Law Research Paper No. 161-2013, available at https://ssrn.com/abstract =2337062 accessed 31 July 2021; Scott A. Allen, "Patents Fettering Reproductive Rights" (2012) 87(1) *Indiana Law Journal* 445; Mindy J. Lees, "I Want a New Drug: RU-486 and the Right to Choose" (1990) 63 *Southern California Law Review* 1113.

[65] Marketa Trimble, "Patent Working Requirements: Historical and Comparative Perspectives" (2016) 6 *UC Irvine Law Review* 483.

[66] Ibid.

broad international application). The likelihood of this happening is questionable in any context, including for "novel being" technology, given the level of time, financial resources and research and development which would be needed. It may be more likely that an entity opposed to a patented technology's use would seek to license patent rights over such a technology on an exclusive basis after a technology was developed and patented. However, even that scenario is arguably unlikely, and even if an entity were interested in doing that, it is questionable whether the rightsholder(s) of a technology would be willing to agree to such a licence if they were aware that the intended licensor sought to prevent use of the invention.

Third, and relatedly, a "novel being" technology, such as an artificial intelligence companion, is likely to be composed of multiple technologies with multiple patents (and potentially other intellectual property rights) over each of these elements that may be held by many different rightsholders. Therefore, if one rightsholder refused to license or use its patented technology, this would have a (potentially – depending on the technology) limited blocking effect over the "novel being" technology more generally, unless all relevant rightsholders refused licences for all the technological components of that technology.

It is arguably more likely that a technology may be developed and at a later stage that ethical concerns around how that technology could be used could become apparent. It is at least plausible, if a rightsholder later discovers that *many* uses of their patented technology are ethically contentious in their view, that they may at that point seek to refuse all patent licences over the technology, even as a temporary measure, to halt uses of it by others until more is known or until broader regulatory systems review the technology. It is also arguably even more likely that after a technology is developed, certain specific plausible uses of the technology may give rise to ethical concerns, and rightsholders may seek to use licensing conditions to block such specific uses, but still allow other uses of that technology. This in turn brings us to consider the role of "ethical licensing" clauses.

2.3   Patents as Ethical Guiders: Ethical Licensing Clauses to Shape the "Ethical" Development and Use of "Novel Being" Technologies?

In this context, aside from patents being used in an outright blocking manner (where all licences of the patent are refused), a patent licence could be used in a more tailored manner to discourage specific "ethically" contentious uses of a technology. Once a patent is granted, as noted earlier, a rightsholder can grant permission to others to use that technology by licensing the patented technology. Licences are contractual agreements within which the licensee and licensor agree terms of use of the patented technology. However, alongside facilitating the uses of a technology by third parties, licences could also be used to specify uses which are not permissible or not covered under the licence. In this way, so-called "ethical licensing" clauses could be used in a tailored manner to seek to prohibit or restrict certain uses of a patented technology, including in the case of patented "novel being" technologies.

Recently, there have been several examples of rightsholders using ethical licensing clauses to restrict or prohibit specific uses of a patented technology.[67] For example, the Broad Institute included tailored licensing clauses within its licence for uses of CRISPR gene-editing technology for agricultural purposes, prohibiting three specific uses of the technology due to safety/ethical concerns.[68] If an entity who had a licence were to use such technology for that prohibited purpose, they would be in breach of the licence, and could face legal penalties in that context; whilst, if a third party who did not have such a licence were to use the technology in the restricted manner, they could be found to be infringing the patent. Using an ethical licensing clause such as this could be viewed as a regulatory use of the patent right/licence – in the sense that the licensor is seeking to restrict certain uses of a patented technology via the patent licence. This could be used if "novel being" technology were developed, and there was a desire by the rightsholder to limit certain specific uses for ethical or other reasons – this could be seen as a form of self-regulation as a condition imposed by the rightsholder on the uses of that patented technology.

In terms of the likely usefulness of rightsholder-led "ethical licensing" approaches from a regulatory perspective, it is important to bear in mind again that multiple patents which may be held by multiple rightsholders may apply over any given "novel being" technology. Moreover, patents are territorial so who holds a patent, or whether something is patentable, will differ depending on the jurisdiction in question.[69] This can mean that the effectiveness of rightsholder-led ethical licensing clauses may depend on how a technology is patented, how many patents apply over it, and whether there is agreement amongst relevant rightsholders over how it should be used, and over what, if any, restrictive ethical licensing clauses should be imposed on how a technol-

---

[67] For a discussion, see McMahon, above n. 10; Christi J. Guerrini, Margaret A. Curnutte, Jacob S. Sherkow and Christopher T. Scott, "The Rise of the Ethical License" (2017) 35(1) *Nature* 22; Sherkow, above n. 14; Feeney et al., above n. 14.

[68] The clause prohibited uses for the purposes of creating gene drive, to create terminator or sterile seeds, and uses of the technology to modify tobacco for any use other than "(i) In the context of a model organism for research not directed to the commercialization of tobacco, and (ii) for manufacturing purposes of non-tobacco products". See https://www.broadinstitute.org/news/licensing-crispr-agriculture-policy -considerations; see discussion in McMahon, above n. 10.

[69] See discussion in Matthews et al., above n. 14.

ogy is used. Such issues and the legal issues which arise in these contexts are discussed in detail elsewhere.[70] Whether rightsholders are the most appropriate entities to devise such clauses is also questionable in some contexts given the power such clauses may have to shape downstream uses and development of a patented technology. In such contexts, rightsholders' actions may be entirely well-intentioned; however, unless there is broad scientific consensus around the restrictions adopted (such as existed in the context of the Broad Institute example given above), how clauses are decided upon, whose input is used in deciding upon them, and how compliance with these clauses is monitored, if at all, in practice need greater consideration.[71] Nonetheless, it is conceivable that rightsholders who are concerned about certain uses of a technology giving rise to ethical issues could use such "ethical licensing" clauses to flag these uses, and in doing so, this could send a message to others, including regulators, of their concerns around such uses of the technology – this could be used as a means, for example, to prompt greater investigation of such uses from a regulatory perspective.

Another avenue for ethical licensing clauses to be used, beyond a patent holder-led model, is for policy or international regulatory entities to make recommendations on the types of ethical clauses that should apply to emerging technologies,[72] such as in the novel being technology context. Such clauses could be used as a complement to other regulatory systems, as an additional tool which aims to deter specific uses and developments of a patented technology, or within a field of technology where ethical concerns arise. The use of ethical licensing in this way has several potential advantages from a regulatory perspective, including: such clauses, or recommendations for them, are malleable and could be tailored to specific uses of a technology which are deemed contentious; the patent system is often the first point at which technologies come under external scrutiny, so using licensing clauses as a means to seek to restrict or send a message about which uses are restricted could be a key point in a technology development in which restriction of contentious uses is desired; such clauses are contractual so could be expediently adopted, and potentially be varied over time, as needed, as more becomes known about that

---

[70]   See McMahon, above n. 11; Matthews et al., above n. 14.
[71]   Such issues are discussed in detail in McMahon, above n. 11; McMahon, above n. 10; see also WHO Expert Advisory Committee on Developing Global Standards for Governance and Oversight of Human Genome Editing, *Human Genome Editing: A Framework for Governance* (World Health Organization, 2021) para. 84; Matthews et al., above n. 14. See also Naomi Scheinerman and Jacob S. Sherkow, "Governance Choices of Genome Editing Patents" (2021) 3 *New Frontiers in Political Science* at 5; Feeney, Cockbain and Sterckx, above n. 14 at 5.
[72]   This is discussed in detail in McMahon, above n. 11.

technology.[73] For example, a regulatory body for artificial intelligence (AI), could recommend such clauses as part of a policy on the ethical approaches to uses of AI that if such technologies are patented, ethical licensing clauses would be adopted by rightsholders to preclude certain specified uses. To formulate "ethical licensing clauses", the regulatory body could engage with stakeholders and interdisciplinary experts, and, for example, such clauses could be made subject to review and operate for a temporary period until more is known about a technology. In this manner, arguably, ethical licensing clauses have potential to be a significant additional policy tool for regulatory bodies to guide "ethical" uses of emerging "novel being" technologies.

CONCLUSION

Patent law is often viewed as a technical, esoteric and even a value-neutral field.[74] Yet in practice, patents have significant implications for the use, development and access to emerging patented technologies. The development of "novel being" technology has the potential to be a defining moment for humanity. It is vital in this context that the role of patents and other IPRs that have potential – both currently and in the future – to act as a mechanism to shape such technology's development, access and use are given greater scrutiny. Patents are already allowing rightsholders to exercise a governance role which needs further probing in this context, both in terms of the extent of control rightsholders have and how this is monitored.[75] Greater scrutiny is also needed over how this control might be used in a directed *regulatory* manner to shape the ethical development and use of technologies, both by rightsholders concerned about how technologies they develop are used, and as a means to complement existing regulatory approaches for "novel being" technologies.

In this context, this chapter has argued that patents (and how they are licensed) could act as ethical drivers, blockers and guiders in the development and use of "novel being" technologies. The grant or denial of a patent on the basis of the morality provisions (where jurisdictions have such provisions) may potentially drive technology development, as this could increase/decrease the commercial (and potentially other) incentives for certain technological development. However, the chapter has argued that how the grant or denial of a patent encourages or discourages the development of a technology is a complex picture that requires much greater investigation. At best one could

---

[73]   In the context of patent holder-led approaches, the flexibility advantage associated with ethical licensing clauses is discussed in Feeney, Cockbain and Sterckx, above n. 14.

[74]   Bently and Sherman, above n. 38.

[75]   McMahon, above n. 10.

say that patent grant may encourage certain types of invention in certain fields by certain actors, and it is not necessarily the case that denial of a patent would result in fewer inventions in a field or in less use of such technologies. Put simply, if patent grant/denial was intended to be used at a policy level as part of a broader regulatory approach to shape ethical uses and/or developments of "novel being" technologies, much greater empirical investigation is needed to determine the likely effect of denial of a patent for ethical reasons on the development/use of such technologies.[76]

Furthermore, patents, and specifically how they are licensed, could act as a *blocker* of technological development and/or use where rightsholders have ethical concerns or objections to a specific technology. In such contexts, rightsholders may seek to patent a technology and refuse to license that technology to third parties due to ethical concerns about the use of that technology. This could be used to restrict uses of that technology for the duration of the patent term, but as the chapter has highlighted, the likelihood of such an approach being used is rare and could be challenged.

Finally, patent licences could act as an *ethical guider* of uses of "novel being" technologies, as rightsholders could tailor patent licensing clauses to seek to restrict specific uses in relation to which they have ethical concerns. In this latter licensing context, third parties such as regulatory bodies could also recommend ethical licensing clauses for adoption over certain uses of "novel being" technologies to deter such uses where ethical concerns arose. Such an approach, in particular, has significant potential to complement broader regulatory approaches for "novel being" technologies.

Thus, in short, how patents are granted and licensed has significant potential to complement existing regulatory systems to shape ethical uses and development of "novel being" technologies. However, to harness this potential, there needs to be a greater normalisation of a conception of patents as having much more extensive and nuanced functions, beyond the mere economic role they are traditionally seen as occupying, towards conceiving of patents as occupying a much broader governance role for "novel being" and other emerging technologies.[77]

---

[76] In the context of genome editing technologies, see discussion in Matthews, Minnsen and Nordberg, above n. 38; Matthews et al., above n. 14.

[77] McMahon, above n. 10.

8. A phased approach to protection of artificial beings

Colin Gavaghan and Mike King

The prospect of self-aware machines – artificially intelligent software and, most commonly, robots – has long been a staple of science fiction.[1] In recent years, it has re-emerged in popular culture, via television series,[2] films[3] and literary fiction.[4]

The question of how we should behave towards such entities has also received a degree of academic attention. Most commentators seem to agree that, were an artificial being (AB) ever to attain relevant moral properties, we would owe certain duties towards them. What precisely those duties would be would depend significantly on what properties the AB possessed. Qualities like sentience, consciousness and personhood are frequently invoked in discussions about what we owe to various entities, and what is owed might depend on which of those qualities is present.

At a minimum, though, we consider it relatively uncontentious that a being with these properties would merit *some* degree of direct moral consideration. They would matter, to some extent, for their own sake, and not just because of effects on other people. The fact that they are manufactured rather than born is not enough to disqualify them from the realm of beings that we ought to care about, and neither is the fact that their physical substance is non-organic. As Eric Schwitzgebel and Mara Garza have said:

> It shouldn't matter to one's moral status what kind of body one has, except insofar as one's body influences one's psychological and social properties. Similarly, it shouldn't matter to one's moral status what kind of underlying architecture one has,

---

[1] Isaac Asimov claimed to have started his first 'robot story' in 1939; *The Complete Robot* (Granada Publishing Limited 1982).

[2] HBO's *Westworld* reimaging has probably been the most high-profile example, but the Swedish series *Real Humans* (*Äkta människor*) and the Russian-made *Better Than Us* also merit mention.

[3] *Ex Machina* (Universal 2014).

[4] Ian McEwan, *Machines Like Me* (Jonathan Cape 2019); Kazuo Ishiguro, *Klara and the Sun* (Faber and Faber 2021).

except insofar as underlying architecture influences one's psychological and social properties.[5]

Whether machines will ever attain such properties and status is a matter for speculation. As best as we can tell, though, no such beings presently exist, and most experts seem to agree that we are still some way from their creation.[6] We share the view of most writers that, were ABs with morally considerable properties ever to emerge, we would owe some sorts of duties to them, though we take no view on the likelihood or timescale for such a development. In this chapter, though, our focus is on two phases of development that would precede any such emergence.

While we may still be many years from creating self-aware ABs, we have certainly entered a stage in technology where we can create machines that look and to some extent act in a manner that is humanlike, or at least lifelike.[7] And the capacity for these ABs to mimic the behaviour of actual living beings is becoming increasingly convincing. The Boston Dynamics BigDog or Spot (large quadruped robots) have physical capabilities, such as self-stabilising, that can uncannily resemble those of a sentient mammal. Another example is the Child with Biomimetic Body (CB2) robot, which mimics an average two-year-old human infant in physical and cognitive development, learning from visual and sensory input, developing its expressive and physical capabilities, such as learning to walk.

These developments needn't be restricted to embodied ABs. New Zealand AI company Soul Machines has developed 'Human OS – a cloud-based Autonomous Animation Platform that allows stunningly life-like CGI characters to both learn from and interact with real people – in very human ways'.[8]

This is what we refer to as Phase One. Although Phase One ABs cannot feel, think or care about what happens to them, an emerging body of scholarship is considering the question of whether there should nonetheless be limits (moral and possibly legal) on how we can behave towards them. According to these

---

[5]   Eric Schwitzgebel and Mara Garza, 'A Defense of the Rights of Artificial Intelligences' (2015) 39(1) *Midwest Studies in Philosophy* 98.

[6]   Toby Walsh asked over 300 colleagues working in AI to give a best estimate of how long it would take before artificial general intelligence became a reality. For 90% probability, median estimate was 2112; for 50% probability, median estimate was 2062. The last figure became the title for Walsh's book, *2062: The World That AI Made* (La Trobe University Press 2018).

[7]   Some robots are specifically designed to resemble non-human animals. The PARO therapeutic robot, for example, is designed to look like a seal cub. http://www.parorobots.com.

[8]   https://www.soulmachines.com/technology.

arguments, they may be owed a degree of *indirect* moral consideration. In the first part of this chapter, we consider some of these arguments.

Looking beyond Phase One, we can anticipate that we will eventually enter a period of uncertainty around the properties possessed by ABs. We simply will not know whether they can think or feel. Some people will be persuaded, others highly sceptical, and the evidence will be inconclusive. This is what we refer to as Phase Two, and this will be our focus in the second part of the chapter. This is a situation of potential moral risk. What moral and legal duties might arise in that context? What should be our default setting when we cannot be sure what (if anything) it feels like to be an AB? And what sort of evidence should we be looking for?

Of course, there may well be considerable temporal overlap between those phases. We may have reason to wonder about the moral properties of some ABs, while being entirely sure that others lack them entirely. The picture becomes more complex yet if we consider the situation where we are fairly sure that some ABs possess such properties – what we would call Phase Three. This chapter focuses on Phases One and Two, but in the conclusion we share a few reflections on the subsequent phase.

PHASE ONE

Phase One describes the situation we have at present. Artificial beings are increasingly able to display lifelike or humanlike responses and behaviours, to an extent that would be convincing to many people at least for a short time. In some cases – such as the AI personal assistant Google Duplex,[9] which can famously make believably human-sounding appointments over the telephone – the human interacting with it may never suspect they have been talking to an AI.

In other cases, the human will know rationally that they are dealing with an AB, but may find themselves reacting in a manner that doesn't reflect this. They may sympathise with the AB, for instance, or they may become angry with it – not as one becomes angry with a defective tool, but in a manner more suited to the attribution of intentionality to the AB. In some cases, people may become emotionally or even romantically attached to the AB, even in the knowledge that it cannot reciprocate those feelings.[10]

---

[9]   Yaniv Leviathan and Yossi Matias, 'Google Duplex: An AI System for Accomplishing Real-World Tasks Over the Phone', Google AI Blog, 8 May 2018, https://ai.googleblog.com/2018/05/duplex-ai-system-for-natural-conversation.html, accessed 8 March 2022.

[10]   Examples abound, but for probably the most detailed and startling treatment to date, see David Levy's *Love and Sex with Robots: The Evolution of Human–Robot Relationships* (HarperCollins 2007).

This is the situation in which we find ourselves now, and it's highly likely that we will progress further down this road as ABs more accurately mimic lifelike or humanlike behaviours or responses. What sorts of concerns arise in this first phase? Are any of these concerns of a nature that may attract legal or regulatory responses?

The most obvious issue to arise in this context is whether there should be any sort of protection for lifelike or humanlike ABs. To repeat, in Phase One, we are entirely confident that there are no ABs capable of subjective experiences such as feeling pain, fear, loneliness, humiliation or boredom. The question of how and indeed whether we can know this with confidence will be addressed in the second part of this chapter. However, we are proceeding on the basis that we can, at present, be sure that at least the ABs with which we interact have no subjective experiences, and that this is true also of their past and future.[11] Whether the capacity exists to develop ABs with such capacities at present is not something we can dismiss, but such attributes are certainly beyond the chatbots and cobots[12] that we are likely to encounter.

Our assumption, then, is that any 'mistreatment' visited upon an AB will not be a cause of suffering or any other unpleasant sensation for the AB itself. Boston Dynamics' Spot robot may in some vague sense resemble a dog or other quadruped;[13] but very much unlike a dog, it doesn't feel anything when it is kicked around in stress tests.[14]

Our first question, then, is whether there is any plausible basis to protect at least some ABs from at least some kinds of harsh treatment. What sort of reasons might justify our taking such a position?

---

[11]   We assume that there can be good reasons to treat beings on the basis of their past or future interests, as when we give effect to wishes after death or act so as to safeguard the well-being of future persons.

[12]   The term 'cobot' is a shortening of 'collaborative robot', robots 'meant to operate in conjunction with, and in close proximity, to humans to perform their tasks'. Kathleen Walch, 'You've Heard of Robots; What Are Cobots', *Forbes*, 15 December 2019, https://www.forbes.com/sites/cognitiveworld/2019/12/15/youve-heard-of-robots-what -are-cobots/?sh=599413f34862, accessed 8 March 2022.

[13]   https://www.bostondynamics.com/spot.

[14]   'Google's Robot Spot Stays Standing After Kick', BBC News, 10 February 2015, https://www.bbc.com/news/av/technology-31372447, accessed 8 March 2022.

Observer Distress

Kate Darling has written extensively and insightfully on the social and ethical issues raised by lifelike robots. In a 2016 chapter, she considered one possible basis for restrictions on how they can be treated:

> [V]iolent behavior towards robotic objects feels wrong to many of us, even if we know that the 'abused' object does not experience anything. We may be hardwired to respond instinctively to cues like simulated pain or need. If this discomfort becomes stronger with increasingly sophisticated technology, how should we deal with it? Should we encourage or discourage it? Might we even reach a point where we want rules in place governing the treatment of our robot companions?[15] (Darling 2006, 223)

Darling considers various reasons for introducing rules around our treatment of social robots. One reason relates to the potential impact on young children of seeing 'cruelty' to social robots:

> [P]rotecting social robots more generally would ensure that societal standards are set and prevent children from witnessing or adopting undesirable behavior elsewhere. It could protect children from potentially traumatizing experiences, for instance seeing older children or adults 'torture' a robotic toy, the likes of which the child has developed an emotional relationship to at home.[16] (Darling 2006, 224)

Exposure of young children to potentially distressing images seems like a valid basis for moral concern, and maybe even for legal intervention. Whether this requires 'protecting social robots more generally' is more questionable. We would usually consider it an overreaction to prohibit altogether anything on the basis that it may distress young children. A more proportionate response, and one more in line with analogous concerns in other areas, would be a rule preventing such things happening where younger children can see them. For instance, films with adult themes are certified for viewing only by age-appropriate audiences, and some venues are accessible only to adults. Perhaps it could be an offence intentionally to allow young children to witness such things, as is the case with sexual acts.[17]

---

[15] Kate Darling, 'Extending Legal Protection to Social Robots: The Effects of Anthropomorphism, Empathy, and Violent Behavior Towards Robotic Objects' in Ryan Calo, Michael A. Froomkin and Ian Kerr (eds), *Robot Law* (Edward Elgar Publishing 2016).

[16] Ibid.

[17] Most obviously, some jurisdictions have offences relating to engaging in sexual activity in the presence of a child; e.g. Sexual Offences Act 2003, s. 11 (England and Wales).

Or perhaps people who want to beat up or 'kill' lifelike robots – or watch them do that to one another – should have to go to designated adults-only venues to do so. This would also go some way to addressing potential offence or upset to adults who find themselves in the position of being reluctant spectators. Much as we currently do with adult cinemas, sex shops and paintball arenas, the offence concern could be addressed by confining violence to and by robots to Westworld-type theme parks or Robot Wars fighting pits.

There is a lot written on the question of whether and when offence justifies a legal response, and as we should expect, opinions vary widely. We are sympathetic, however, to those opinions which regard activities to which we can easily avoid exposure as presenting a much weaker claim for legal action than those to which we are reluctantly and unavoidably exposed. So-called 'bare knowledge' offence – that is, offence caused by mere awareness that certain activities are taking place out of our sight and hearing – presents a still weaker claim.[18]

There could, of course, be fuzzy edges around the rules in this regard, and questions still to be asked. Should it, for example, be against the law for parents or older children to harm social robots in front of children? How might such a law be enforced? Such issues, though, do not seem obviously more intractable than in the case of showing age-inappropriate films to young children or allowing them to drink alcohol. It may be difficult to monitor compliance, certainly, but that is rarely seen as a justification either for dispensing altogether with a rule protecting children, or for banning such things even for adults.

A related question would be whether the law should respond differently when someone damages someone else's companion AB. Should this be treated in the same way as any other property crime, or is there a case for the law reflecting the extra emotional significance that many people might attach to this particular form of property? To put it another way, if many people view Phase One ABs as more than property, should the law do likewise? Insofar as the law should reflect and protect the important interests people actually have, there is a certain appeal to such an approach, though as we discuss at the end of this section, possibly also a danger were the law to proceed in this direction.

---

[18]   A. P. Simester and Andreas von Hirsch, *Crimes, Harms, and Wrongs* (Hart 2014) 111. Cf. Joel Feinberg, *The Moral Limits of the Criminal Law: Volume 2: Offense to Others* (Oxford University Press 1988) 58 – though he would certainly set a high bar for the bare knowledge offence, he wouldn't entirely rule it out.

Danger to Real People or Others Who Matter for Their Own Sake

More serious than the prospect of offence is the concern that abuse of ABs could heighten physical risks to actual humans. One way in which this could come about could be if lifelike, embodied robots came to be confused for actual humans or other living beings that matter for their own sake, such as some animals. If harming of robots is permissible, we might falsely believe that we're maltreating a robot when in fact we're harming a sentient being. In the HBO television series *Westworld*, the 'host' robot Angela responds to William, a guest who is unsure whether she is human or robot: 'Well if you can't tell, does it matter?'[19] Assuming (as we do) that humans and many other living things possess morally relevant qualities that are absent in Phase One ABs, it seems that this distinction should matter. But if we can't reliably distinguish human from robot, then that might provide a good reason not to maltreat something that we *think* is a robot, but which just might be human.

Following on from our previous suggestion, the risk could be lessened by restricting harmful behaviour to premises approved for such purposes, with humans and robots clearly identified and distinguished within those premises. This would not, however, entirely negate the possibility of accidents happening outside such contexts, and the law would need to consider how to respond to such incidents.

Culpability for mistakes that result in death or injury is hardly an issue unknown to the law, both criminal and civil. Often, how the law responds will depend on the nature of that mistake – was it genuine, reasonable, careless, reckless, etc. Occasionally, the usual burden of proof can be reversed, and the defendant will need to prove some fact about the mistake. In rare circumstances, entire forms of defence can be removed from the law altogether. From a more regulatory perspective, it would be possible for the law to insist that lifelike ABs were built so as to be readily distinguishable from living beings (though it is not difficult to imagine potential complications even with such a strategy, such as humans pretending to be robots!).

Whether such a literal blurring of lines between humans and robots could ever present a major social danger, it seems to present no particular problem in legal terms. A considerably more challenging concern, though, is that 'mistreatment' of lifelike robots may weaken our reservations about cruelty to actually living things, perhaps even humans. The main concern here is, of course, that cruelty to robots might somehow blunt or weaken our aversion to

---

[19]   *Westworld*, Season 1 Episode 2: 'Chestnut' (HBO Entertainment 2016).

cruelty to living things, including humans, or perhaps reinforce or normalise tendencies towards cruelty or casual violence. As Sven Nyholm explains it:

> The idea is that if someone spends a lot of time being cruel to robots, this might corrupt and harden the person's character. The person might then go on to treat human beings in cruel ways.[20]

This concern has received particular attention in the context of sex robots. Kathleen Richardson, one of the founders of the Campaign Against Sex Robots, has argued that

> the development of sex robots will further reinforce relations of power that do not recognise both parties as human subjects. Only the buyer of sex is recognised as a subject, the seller of sex (and by virtue the sex-robot) is merely a thing to have sex with.[21]

On this basis, sex robots risk contributing to the commodification of sex and dehumanisation of persons (and particularly of women[22]) in the eyes of many of its consumers. Although sex robots are a common focus for such concerns, it's possible that they could also arise with other forms of ABs. AI assistants are frequently created with female/feminine voices, which has led some to speculate about the impact of reinforcing the perception of women in subservient roles. And workplace robots could contribute to the perception of human workers as instruments rather than persons.

Perhaps the most visceral context for this concern, though, lies with robots that are designed specifically to be abused. John Danaher has speculated about the creation of robots designed to be 'raped' or to allow the acting out of child abuse scenarios.[23] If we are able to visit all manner of violence and indignity on lifelike ABs, how will that affect our relations with living beings? Will it normalise our baser urges? Render us callous and indifferent to their suffering?

---

[20] Sven Nyholm, *Humans and Robots: Ethics, Agency, and Anthropomorphism* (Rowman & Littlefield International 2020) 184.

[21] Kathleen Richardson, 'The Asymmetrical "Relationship"': Parallels Between Prostitution and the Development of Sex Robots' (2015) 45(3) *SIGCAS Computers & Society* 290.

[22] The belief that sex robots will have a particularly gendered effect may derive from the assumption that most sex robots will be of female appearance, and most consumers male. Alternatively, it may derive from what some commentators fear will be an exacerbation of existing conditions wherein female bodies are disproportionately sexualised and commodified. For further discussion, see Sinziana M. Gutiu, 'The Roboticization of Consent' in Calo, Froomkin and Kerr (eds), (n. 15).

[23] John Danaher, 'Robotic Rape and Robotic Child Sexual Abuse: Should They Be Criminalised?' (2017) 11 Criminal Law and Philosophy 71–5.

As with the offence concern, this seems like a new manifestation of an old worry. The idea that depictions of violence can make real violence more likely has been played out in the context of violent films, cartoons and comics, children's toys and, more recently, violent computer games. Pornography – either in general or in certain forms – has long been a particular focus for this sort of concern. Despite many decades of study and scrutiny, however, no consensus has ever been reached about the causal effects of any of these media. As Rob Sparrow has said:

> The relationship between film and television violence and real violence, and the relationship between videogame violence and real violence, have been debated ever since the relevant technologies came into widespread use. Similarly, there is a long history of controversy about the relationship between pornography and sexual violence and/or sexism. Despite decades of argument and thousands of academic studies, consensus on these questions remains elusive.[24]

It seems unlikely that the evidence around mistreating ABs in any of the ways we consider will be any more conclusive. How should the law respond to such uncertainty?

Roger Brownsword has written about the 'regulatory tilt' that should be adopted when dealing with new technologies whose effects are as yet uncertain.[25] This is the default position that would be adopted when evidence is inconclusive. Regulators and lawmakers might adopt a precautionary tilt, which would see them default to restrictive approaches; or a permissive tilt, which would default in the other direction. A precautionary response to abuse of ABs might favour restricting practices that have a plausible causal connection to actually abusive behaviours, even if the evidence of such a link is inconclusive. Such an approach is most appropriate when, as here, the potential harm is very serious, though even then, some sort of evidence is likely to be required, and as Brownsword has observed, 'there is scope for endless argument about just how strong the evidence needs to be before precaution kicks in'.[26]

Moralism

Let's assume, though, that we were not convinced of a causal link between abuse of ABs and abuse of living things, or perhaps no more convinced than

---

[24] Robert Sparrow, 'Robots, Rape, and Representation' (2017) 9(4) *International Journal of Social Robotics* 465, 471.

[25] Roger Brownsword, *Rights, Regulation, and the Technological Revolution* (Oxford University Press 2008) 21.

[26] Ibid., 106.

we are by other practices that we currently allow, such as violent computer games. Might there nonetheless be a reason why we should be concerned about AB abuse? Even if we can't show that such conduct causes harm, might it nonetheless be *wrong*? And if so, does that provide a good enough reason for the law – perhaps even the criminal law – to become involved?

There is a long history and extensive literature of debates about the permissible limits of the law. For those on the liberal/libertarian side of that debate, it is no proper purpose of law to punish mere immorality. Rather, some additional justification is required. In the classic Millian version, this criterion would be conduct that causes (or at least risks or threatens) harm to others.[27] Later liberal theorists have tentatively extended the qualifying condition to include some limited instances of *offence* to others,[28] while a plausible case could also be made for widening the strict 'harm' threshold to encompass offending against the rights or dignity of others.

What the liberal approaches have in common, though, is that conduct which is considered immoral is not a valid target for law, and particularly for criminalisation, unless it impacts adversely (or threatens to do so) upon the interests, rights, dignity, etc. of people or other living things. As Andrew Simester and Andreas von Hirsch say, 'the legitimate grounds for coercive state intervention arise only when conduct directly or indirectly affects people's lives'.[29]

For legal moralists, on the other hand, moral wrongness can at least sometimes be a sufficient reason for the imposition of criminal sanctions.[30] What Danaher describes as 'the moralistic premise' holds that 'It can be a proper object of the criminal law to regulate conduct that is morally wrong, even if such conduct has no extrinsically harmful effects on others.'[31] If certain kinds of AB abuse (he gives the examples of robotic acts of rape and child sexual abuse) can be said to 'fall within the class of morally wrong but extrinsically harmless conduct', then on this view it can be a proper object of the criminal law to prohibit such conduct.

---

[27]   John Stuart Mill, *On Liberty* (first published 1859, Penguin Classics 1982).
[28]   Feinberg (n. 18).
[29]   Simester and von Hirsch (n. 18) 29. Depending on one's approach to morality, of course, it may make no sense to refer to conduct as being wrongful if it does not affect other people's lives.
[30]   There is an important distinction between 'negative' legal moralism, which sees wrongdoing as a necessary condition for criminalisation, and the 'positive' variety which sees it as sufficient. The former would supplement a harm-based approach, requiring that conduct be both harmful and wrongful. Our focus here, though, is on those cases where the conduct is not harmful, and where moral wrongfulness is therefore being posited as a sufficient rather than a necessary condition. See R. A. Duff, 'Towards a Modest Legal Moralism' (2014) 8 *Criminal Law and Philosophy* 217.
[31]   Danaher (n. 23)

For the positive legal moralist, the fact of an action's moral wrongness can be sufficient reason to criminalise it (though considerations of proportionality and pragmatism can count against actually doing so in certain cases). Not all legal moralists, though, believe that just any wrongful act could justifiably be criminalised. Duff has defended a 'modest' account of legal moralism, according to which 'the criminal law is ... properly concerned not (even in principle) with every kind of moral wrongdoing, but only with wrongs that should count as "public" rather than "private"'.[32]

For Duff, such 'public' moral wrongdoing can even occur in a private setting. He gives the example of '"extreme" pornography that graphically depicts the humiliation or torture of members of one sex or group as a source of sexual gratification for readers or viewers'. For Duff,

> What makes it plausible to see these as public wrongs (even when, in the case of pornography, they are perpetrated in the 'privacy' of the person's home) is that they are serious violations of the respect that we owe each other, and thus denials (at least implicitly) of the moral status of those who are their objects.[33] (Danaher 2017, 89)

Danaher applies a similar approach to the question of sex robots. He argues that

> those who engage in acts of purely robotic rape and child sexual abuse either demonstrate an immoral desire for the real world equivalents of those acts, and/or a disturbing moral insensitivity to the social meaning of those acts.[34]

In a similar vein, Rob Sparrow has argued that

> If the rape of a robot represents and simulates the rape of a real woman then performing the first act implicates the agent in a relationship with the second. The precise nature of this relationship may be difficult to capture but it's hard not to think that it is something akin to complicity. To return to the analogy with advertising: even if the rape of robots does not succeed in promoting – in the sense of increasing – the rape of women, it exhorts and endorses it.[35]

Central to this argument, then, is the claim that 'robot rape' is indicative of endorsement or complicity (Sparrow), or at least moral insensitivity towards (Danaher), real rape. Acceptance of some such claim would be required to support Danaher's *wrongness premise*: that robotic acts of rape and child abuse are morally wrong even when they are extrinsically harmless.

---

[32] Duff (n. 29) 222.
[33] Ibid., 232.
[34] Danaher (n. 30).
[35] Sparrow (n. 23) 471.

But need this be so? Is it really the case that fantasy, role play and representation necessarily imply acceptance or endorsement of the practice being pretended? There is a danger here of oversimplifying the sometimes fairly complex psychological states that lie behind, e.g., sexual role play and BDSM practices. The claim seems even further strained if we extend it to other fantasy and game-playing, including violent computer games, paintball and laser tag, and the myriad other ways that we entertain and stimulate ourselves by pretending to be and do things that would repel us if done to real people in the real world.

It is surely possible that someone could consider real acts of rape or other violence to be morally abhorrent, precisely because of their harmful impacts on real people, but see no analogous objection to a pretence that contains no such ingredient. They might, after all, argue that abusing a robot is not morally adjacent to abusing a human or animal, precisely because it is a *robot*, with none of the attributes (sentience, autonomy, dignity, etc.) that make abuse of humans so wrong. And while abuse of a robot may display certain kinds of urges or appetites that we may find distasteful, it is a large step to make any stronger claim about endorsing, trivialising, or even expressing a desire for abuse of humans.

Other versions of the argument are concerned less with apparent endorsement of the abuse, and rather that mistreating 'a very humanlike robot ... can appear to be a way of failing to act with due respect for human beings and our humanity'.[36] But again, we might wonder whether what matters most about 'our humanity' is not our appearance, but the moral properties we possess. On that analysis, we may have less reason to worry about mistreating humanlike robots that entirely lack these properties, and (as we discuss in our conclusion) more reason to worry about treatment of ABs that are not humanlike but which nonetheless may possess them.

Even were we to accept the wrongness premise, however, it is not entirely clear what should be the appropriate legal or regulatory response. This would involve accepting Danaher's *moralistic premise*: that it is the proper business of the law to address conduct that is immoral but harmless. Scrutinising that claim in detail would lead us into the thickets of legal theory, but for present purposes, it is perhaps enough just to introduce the contrary suggestion, that 'there must remain a realm of private morality and immorality which is, in brief and crude terms, not the law's business'.[37] And if such a realm is deemed to exist at all, then it seems plausible that it exists most obviously when we are

---

[36] Nyholm (n. 20) 185.
[37] The Wolfenden Committee, 'Report of the Departmental Committee on Homosexual Offences and Prostitution' (1957) 24.

indulging in our private sexual or other fantasies, on our own, away from other people. Even if such conduct does express deplorable views about matters of morality, it would be a considerable reach for the criminal law to extend to the views we express while alone, or even to the thoughts we are merely entertaining.

REGULATORY STRATEGIES FOR PHASE ONE

There are a number of reasons, then, why we might feel justified in applying some kinds of legal limits to how we can treat lifelike ABs, even when we are confident they have no morally significant properties of their own, and cannot be harmed or wronged in themselves. This is not to say, however, that we regard any of these reasons as entirely persuasive. There is much to be said for a permissive or liberal regulatory tilt, which takes as its starting point that the burden of justification lies with anyone seeking to use the law to limit anyone else's choice.[38] History suggests that we be at least somewhat cautious about imposing our values and tastes on others if we lack a clear moral mandate for doing so, and intuitive distaste has not invariably been an accurate guide on such matters.

If we were persuaded by any of these reasons, though, how might such protection be afforded? What would be the regulatory target of any new laws? Monitoring how people treat their domestic robots in their own homes is likely to prove practically difficult, though not impossible; it's just about possible to imagine a design solution whereby, for example, domestic or companion robots automatically report being kicked. Such a degree of intrusion into how we deal with our personal possessions in the privacy of our own homes would be almost, if not entirely, novel for the law, and we suspect very difficult to justify given the speculative nature of the risk that provides its justification.

A more plausible regulatory target might be the supply of robots that are designed for the purpose of maltreatment. (Technically, it could be argued that if they are being used in the manner for which they were designed, this cannot be 'maltreatment', but we are using that term to denote conduct that would constitute maltreatment were it done to a living being.) Sex robots designed to display reluctance or resistance offer a particularly vivid example, but it's possible to imagine robots and even non-embodied ABs designed to be 'abused' in other ways; to cry out or cringe when slapped or kicked, or to react 'emotionally' when verbally abused, for example.

---

[38]   Douglas Husak, *Overcriminalization: The Limits of the Criminal Law* (Oxford University Press 2008) 103; Simester and von Hirsch (n. 18) 31.

Unlike how we treat our legally owned private property, there is already a wide array of rules restricting what can be imported, manufactured, bought, sold and even possessed. In New Zealand, it is an offence to make, copy, import, possess, distribute or display 'objectionable material'.[39] This is defined as a publication that

> describes, depicts, expresses, or otherwise deals with matters such as sex, horror, crime, cruelty, or violence in such a manner that the availability of the publication is likely to be injurious to the public good.[40]

This specifically includes any publication that 'promotes or supports'

- the exploitation of children, or young persons, or both, for sexual purposes;
- the use of violence or coercion to compel any person to participate in, or submit to, sexual conduct;
- bestiality;
- acts of torture or the infliction of extreme violence or extreme cruelty.[41]

A 'publication' is defined for these purposes as including films, books, pictures, etc., but also includes an electronic or computer file.[42] This would seem to extend to software that programmed an AB to respond to cruel or abusive treatment with simulated pain, fear or resistance.[43]

An AB designed to be 'tortured' for titillation, or a robot programmed to be 'raped' in the manner imagined by Danaher and Sparrow, would seem like an obvious candidate for inclusion in such a ban. But it would not, presumably, have anything to say about abuse of ABs that were not designed for that purpose. Kicking a robot dog, or even violently abusing a humanlike robot, would be considerably out of scope, provided those robots were not designed to facilitate or encourage such treatment.

There is a fairly good pro tanto reason, we think, for making sure the law's treatment of Phase One ABs is consistent with its treatment of subjects like violent computer games and pornography. Insofar as there are good reasons

---

[39] Films, Videos, and Publications Classification Act 1993, s. 123 and s. 124.

[40] Films, Videos, and Publications Classification Act 1993, s. 3.

[41] Rather curiously, the provision also includes 'the use of urine or excrement in association with degrading or dehumanising conduct or sexual conduct', an inclusion that arguably seems more influenced by reactions of disgust rather than concern with what is injurious to the public good.

[42] Films, Videos, and Publications Classification Act 1993, s. 2.

[43] Further discussion of the possible application of this legislation to sex robots can be found in Hannah Atkinson's 2020 Honours dissertation, '"Regulated or Not, Here I Come": Regulating Sex Robots in New Zealand', https://www.otago.ac.nz/law/research/journals/otago828536.pdf.

to restrict access to those (and of course, debate is to be expected about that) those reasons might well apply also to Phase One ABs. But there is also a good reason to be cautious about expanding the rules around ABs much beyond those.

The idea that humans may abuse Phase One ABs has received considerable coverage, both in the academic literature and in popular culture. More recently, though, attention has begun to turn to the opposite danger: that humans may care *too much* about such things. The prospect of becoming invested emotionally, perhaps even romantically, in ABs that lack the capacity to reciprocate that investment, is hardly far-fetched. David Levy has recounted numerous colourful examples of people developing strong emotional attachments even to fairly basic and only vaguely lifelike ABs like Tamagotchi.[44] Some of the most startling examples have been of battle-hardened soldiers who became strongly attached to robots, begging engineers to save their fallen 'comrades' when they were damaged. A test of a centipede-like robot designed to clear minefields had to be abandoned in 2007 when the officer in command of the exercise ordered it to be stopped: 'The colonel just could not stand the pathos of watching the burned, scarred and crippled machine drag itself forward on its last leg. This test, he charged, was inhumane.'[45]

This concern is amplified when we consider the potential to design robots specifically to induce sympathetic emotional responses. The nature of the concern here is well explained by Woodrow Hartzog:

> Robots, particularly embodied ones, are uniquely situated to mentally manipulate people. Robots can mimic human socialization, yet they are without shame, fatigue, or internal inconsistency. Robots are also scalable, so the decision to design a robot to manipulate humans will impact hundreds, if not thousands or millions of people.[46]

This advanced capacity for manipulation has led Hartzog to conclude that 'at some point, it seems clear that our tendency to emotionally invest in robots is a vulnerability worth regulatory attention'.

Kate Darling has expressed similar concerns:

> If people develop attachments to their robotic companions, can the companies who control the hard- and software exploit this attachment? Should companies be

---

[44]   Levy (n. 10).

[45]   Joel Garreau, 'Bots on the Ground', *Washington Post* (6 May 2007), https://www .washingtonpost.com/wp-dyn/content/article/2007/05/05/AR2007050501009.html, accessed 8 March 2022.

[46]   Woodrow Hartzog, 'Unfair and Deceptive Robots' (2015) 74(4) *Maryland Law Review* 785, 804.

allowed to make use of the fact that individuals might have a massively increased willingness to pay for technology upgrades or repairs?[47](Darling 2006, 221)

If this capacity of Phase One ABs to 'hack' our emotional responses to the extent of leaving us vulnerable to exploitation becomes sufficiently serious, it may be that some direct regulatory response will be required. Some jurisdictions have already introduced laws requiring chatbots to disclose their true nature. While this may address certain concerns, it is not clear that it would insulate us from the dangers that concern Hartzog and Darling. After all, these can arise in contexts where the human *knows* that they are dealing with a Phase One AB.

More likely, the best protection we (or the generations after us) will have against such manipulation will lie in cultivating capacities that allow us to fine-tune our emotional responses in the face of ABs designed to exploit them. This will not be a straightforward matter. The emotional processes being exploited have evolved over millennia, and for the most part serve us well.[48] The tendency to care about and empathise with Phase One ABs is likely an offshoot of tendencies that are generally worth preserving and cultivating.

Nonetheless, some fine-tuning may be a necessary defensive strategy. Rationally, we know that the AI chatbot trying to sell us its wares doesn't actually care if we buy them; that the robot dog isn't really sad if we don't play with it (or refuse to buy it an expensive robot brother or sister!); that the robot minesweeper isn't actually a fallen comrade worth risking human lives to save. But knowing it won't be enough. The trick will be in training ourselves to *feel* it as well, and to act accordingly.

That doesn't, of course, mean that we have to go out of our way to treat Phase One ABs badly. It doesn't mean that we have to kick and push them around, like in the Boston Dynamics stress tests, or abuse them in the manners Danaher and Sparrow imagine will happen to sex robots. But it might mean that there are reasons to be wary of introducing moral taboos or legal rules that further blur the distinction between the living and the merely lifelike; between genuine claims on our moral concern, and false or manipulative claims on our insufficiently tuned instincts.

We are presently agnostic as to whether this concern outweighs the reasons to be concerned about abuse. It is, however, a factor that we believe properly

---

[47]   Darling (n. 15).
[48]   Though arguably not *perfectly* well. There is a school of thought that our evolved tendencies see us prioritise the well-being of those who are close to or similar to ourselves to a degree that is morally indefensible. Paul Bloom, *Against Empathy: The Case for Rational Compassion* (Penguin Vintage 2016).

belongs on the scales when any decision is being made about how to treat lifelike Abs.

PHASE TWO

In this phase, we are concerned with novel beings that *may* be deserving of direct moral consideration. We will call these Phase Two ABs. Just like Phase One ABs, they may be indirectly considerable, in as much as their treatment may affect others. Or actions regarding them may themselves be intrinsically morally wrong. To the extent that this is the case, the reasons for protecting novel beings from certain kinds of use or treatment that we have already discussed also apply to them. However, unlike Phase One ABs, Phase Two ABs could be due *direct* moral consideration. To put it simply, they might matter for their own sake.

Moral Status of ABs[49]

What would it take for an AB to have the sort of moral status we are concerned with here?

This is fertile ground for ethical inquiry. It continues to be so in domains outside, and much older than, the ethics and law of ABs, such as environmental and animal ethics, and in relation to the edges of human life (embryos and the permanently unconscious, for instance). There, different features of living and non-living things are defended as grounds for attributing or recognising moral status, including sentience, consciousness, psychological agency, personhood, goal-directedness or biological function arising from merely being alive.[50] For some, what matters is that they have the capacity for well-being and that it is therefore possible for their existence to go well or badly for them, for them to be harmed or benefited by what happens to them. If this were the case, then that fact alone generates a pro tanto ethical reason not to harm them, and perhaps even a reason to benefit them by protecting them from harmful treat-

---

[49] What we describe here owes much to the account of moral status described by David DeGrazia in 'Moral Status as a Matter of Degree?' (2008) 46(2) *Southern Journal of Philosophy* 181; and David DeGrazia, 'An Interest-Based Model of Moral Status' in Steve Clarke, Hazem Zohny and Julian Savulescu (eds), *Rethinking Moral Status* (Oxford University Press 2021) 40.

[50] John Danaher, 'What Matters for Moral Status: Behavioral or Cognitive Equivalence?' (2021) 30(3) *Cambridge Quarterly of Healthcare Ethics* 472; David DeGrazia, *Taking Animals Seriously: Mental Life and Moral Status* (Cambridge University Press 1996) 36–74; Marc G. Wilcox, 'Animals and the Agency Account of Moral Status' (2020) 177(7) *Philosophical Studies* 1879; Paul W. Taylor, 'The Ethics of Respect for Nature' (1981) 3(3) *Environmental Ethics* 197.

ment. These reasons don't necessarily justify ethical or legal obligations all things considered, but they at least give us a reason to care about these beings for their own sake.

Similar arguments have been made for recognising the moral status of some ABs.[51] Generally speaking, these focus on determining whether ABs have anything at stake regarding how they are treated, a view with which we agree. For the purposes of this chapter, we assume the plausible view that moral status will depend on intrinsic properties such as sentience or consciousness, a sense of identity, or agency.

Although these accounts will overlap on some ABs possessing moral status, most accounts of moral status are exclusive – affirming their own propositions entails denying those of competing accounts. This means that we are faced with two kinds of uncertainty here: uncertainty about which properties give rise to moral status; and uncertainty about whether a Phase Two AB possesses those properties. Obviously answering the second question is contingent on being able to answer the first: we can't determine whether an AB possesses the relevant properties if we can't even agree about what these properties are.

While complete consensus on the first question is likely to prove elusive, it doesn't follow that no progress is possible. For instance, we would expect a wide degree of agreement around the claim that a being capable of experiencing unpleasant states like pain and fear has an interest in avoiding those states. Of course, things get trickier when we move to the higher-level questions, and properties like consciousness and personhood enter the discussion. But while the capacity to suffer doesn't give us anything like a complete answer to the question of moral status, it would be a strange claim that denied it was relevant at all.

Assuming we are right that hardly anyone would deny that the capacity to suffer is at least somewhat relevant, this takes us into the second area of uncertainty. How can we be confident about whether a Phase Two AB has that capacity? If an AB behaves as if it is in pain, is that a good enough reason to believe that it really feels that way? Or (potentially a different question) a good enough reason to treat it as if it does?

---

[51] DeGrazia, 'An Interest-Based Model of Moral Status' (n. 48); Henry Shevlin, 'How Could We Know When a Robot Was a Moral Patient?' (2021) 30(3) *Cambridge Quarterly of Healthcare Ethics* 459; J. Shepherd, 'Moral Status: Machines and Post-Persons' in *Consciousness and Moral Status* (Routledge 2018) 89; Walter Sinnott-Armstrong and Vincent Conitzer, 'How Much Moral Status Could Artificial Intelligence Ever Achieve?' in Clarke, Zohny and Savulescu (eds) (n. 48) 269.

John Danaher has defended an 'ethical behaviourist' approach, according to which

> if a robot consistently behaves like another entity to whom we afford moral status, then it should be granted the same moral status. So if a robot consistently behaves as if it is in pain, and if the capacity to feel pain is a ground of moral status, then a robot should be granted the same moral status as any other entity to whom we ascribe moral status on the grounds that they can feel pain.[52]

For Danaher, a behaviourist approach should be favoured because 'it respects our epistemic limits'. Behaviour, he argues, is 'for practical purposes, the only insight we have into the metaphysical grounding for moral status'. In other words, it is not that the behaviour itself gives us a good reason to attribute moral status to ABs, but rather that it's likely to be the best evidence we have access to about what it feels like to be an AB. It is, as Danaher notes, an ethical version of the famous Turing Test.[53]

Perhaps the most obvious reservation about such an approach is that it leaves us vulnerable to being 'spoofed' by convincing fakes. As Harry Shevlin writes, Danaher's behaviourist approach

> is at risk of being 'gamed': given some criterion for behavioral equivalence (say, avoidance behavior), a dedicated computer scientist may be able to produce a robot or system with the capability of producing the relevant behavior yet doing nothing else.[54]

In some contexts, we might argue, computer scientists are already there. Google's Duplex assistant is already capable of fooling people on the other end of the phone line into believing that it is a human. While it's probably unlikely to be able to withstand prolonged or detailed scrutiny, a great deal of work is underway to create ABs that even more convincingly mimic the behaviour of humans or other animals.

Danaher anticipates some of these objections. His approach does not rely on a superficial 'first impression' evaluation of behaviour, according to which an AB programmed to cry or laugh would be assumed to really be feeling a particular emotion. Rather, his notion of behaviour 'is not limited to external

---

[52]　John Danaher, 'Welcoming Robots into the Moral Circle: A Defence of Ethical Behaviourism' (2020) 26 Science and Engineering Ethics 2026.

[53]　Graham Oppy and David Dowe, 'The Turing Test' in Edward N. Zalta (ed.), *The Stanford Encyclopedia of Philosophy* (Winter 2021 Edition), https://plato.stanford.edu/archives/win2021/entries/turing-test/.

[54]　Shevlin (n. 50) 465.

physical behaviours (i.e. the movement of limbs and lips); it includes all external observable patterns, including functional operations of the brain'.[55]

This, we might think, stretches the concept of 'behaviour' considerably beyond its everyday usage; what Danaher seems to be proposing is a 'best evidence' approach, according to which we make our best guess as to the presence of mental states by looking at all observable indicators. With that caveat added, there is probably not much to argue against in his approach.

Nonetheless, there are likely to be instances where the observable evidence is highly ambiguous. And the possibility exists that future ABs may possess internal mental states that don't manifest themselves in a familiar way at all. The possibility of 'false negatives' – assumptions that an AB has no moral status just because it doesn't behave in the sort of manner we are used to – is also one we should keep in mind.

In any event, it seems likely that there will be a fair number of borderline cases, where the observable evidence is not determinative either way. What sorts of rules should govern that situation? Here, the notion of regulatory tilt arises again. What should be our default setting when the evidence is ambiguous? Susan Schneider has suggested a precautionary approach to attribution of moral status and associated legal protection: 'if we have some reason to believe an AI may be conscious, even in absence of a definitive test, a precautionary stance suggests that we should extend the same legal protections to the AI that we extend to other sentient beings'.[56]

As with the question of risk in the context of Phase One ABs, though, this leaves open the question of what we mean by 'some reason to believe'. If the epistemic bar were set low, this would include ABs who we are *fairly sure but not entirely certain* lack moral status. Whether extending legal protections to such beings is justified, all things considered, will depend on a range of factors that we consider later.

Degree of Moral Status

Let's set the problem of knowing whether a being has moral status aside to some degree, and imagine that we were pretty confident that some ABs had moral status. This is the situation we find ourselves in with respect to non-human animals. We're pretty confident, perhaps equally so, that mice have moral status, that buffalo do, that cats and dogs do, and that bonobo monkeys and gorillas do, among others. Does that mean that there is the same

---

[55]   Danaher (n. 51) 2028.
[56]   Susan Schneider, *Artificial You: AI and the Future of Your Mind* (Princeton University Press 2019) 67.

degree of moral resistance to forms of treatment that would set back the interests of these animals? It is common to find that reasonable people believe that
there is more moral resistance to harming some of these compared to others.[57]
Sometimes this belief can be related to an account of moral status – such as
that there is stronger reason not to use companion animals in harmful research
because of their social role and relationships with people, or that morally relevant intrinsic properties, such as personhood, are unequally distributed among
mice and non-human hominids. [58]

The Kantian view that possession of some capacities, such as personhood, conveys moral status is defended by Buchanan: 'According to the
respect-based account stemming from Kant's moral philosophy, all beings
that possess certain capacities have an intrinsic moral worth that in some sense
confers inviolability.'[59] The capacity can include that of mutual accountability
arising from shared rationality (i.e. being reasonable – reason-advancing, and
reason-responsive) and arguably relational properties such as social embed-
dedness. In Buchanan's respect view, possession of the relevant capacity
meets a threshold that confers equal, full, moral status, such as the moral status
that human persons hold. Other beings don't possess the relevant capacity, and
are therefore of lower and variable moral status on other bases.

DeGrazia challenges the purported egalitarianism among those above the
threshold.[60] His argument is that the capacity for mutual accountability is var-
iably distributed, and could be widely so, depending on the type of beings that
are brought into existence. There is no reason to think that enhanced beings
could not one day be as far advanced relative to human persons in the degree to
which they possess the capacity of mutual accountability as human persons are
relative to non-human animals. If so, higher moral status beings would be entitled to more than lower moral status beings and there would be moral reason to
favour them when their interests are in competition with those of others.

DeGrazia has described both equal and unequal moral status views based
on the possession of interests.[61] Skating over a lot of complexity here, equal
moral status arises when beings have interests of similar prudential value (e.g.

---

[57]   Catherine A. Schuppli, 'Decisions about the Use of Animals in Research: Ethical
Reflection by Animal Ethics Committee Members' (2011) 24(4) *Anthrozoös* 409;
David DeGrazia, 'Moral Status as a Matter of Degree?' (n. 48) 181.
[58]   See Schuppli for evidence of the former and DeGrazia for discussion of the latter.
[59]   Allen Buchanan, 'Moral Status and Human Enhancement' (2009) 37(4)
Philosophy & Public Affairs 346.
[60]   David DeGrazia, 'Genetic Enhancement, Post-Persons and Moral Status:
A Reply to Buchanan' (2012) 38(3) *Journal of Medical Ethics* 135.
[61]   See David DeGrazia, 'Equal Consideration and Unequal Moral Status' (1993)
31(1) *Southern Journal of Philosophy* 17; DeGrazia, 'Moral Status as a Matter of
Degree?' (n. 48).

the interest in avoiding pain) and these deserve equal consideration. Unequal moral status arises when the prudentially comparable interests of different beings merit unequal consideration, or because their interests are of unequal prudential value. The nuances of these accounts need not concern us here; what matters is that, like the view of Buchanan and others, moral status is dependent on the morally relevant qualities of beings, and admits of degrees whether there is a threshold or not.

As suggested above, the moral status of a being matters. This is not surprising, since moral status is *what it is to matter*. Much ink has been spilled in defending and critiquing different accounts of moral status, in part defensively because of the moral threat that creation of beings with higher moral status than humans would pose. As Douglas notes, it may be desirable for humans for an account of moral status not to admit of higher status beings than humans, but this does not mean that such an account is correct.[62] If a being has moral status, the degree of moral status will in part determine the degree to which we protect that being's interests, whatever they may be, even if setting them back could be to our advantage.

Like possession of moral status, the picture we see with respect to degree of moral status is more uncertainty, particularly with respect to beings about which we lack knowledge – particularly knowledge of their capacities, and their interests. And the importance of interests raises a further question – how do we understand the welfare of ABs?

What Is Good for Artificial Beings?

Ethics is significantly concerned with interests, their nature and how they are affected by actions and circumstances. This is to say that ethics is concerned with well-being. Although there is disagreement about the grounds of moral status and their degree, it seems that most reasonable views among these would accept that any AB that has the capacity for well-being will likely have at least some moral status.

Law is also significantly concerned with interests, and harm in particular – setbacks to interests.[63] Given this, we need to understand the ways that ABs can be harmed, and, of course, benefited. Both are questions of prudential value – what is good for the AB. An example will help to illustrate the complexity of understanding good for ABs.

---

[62] Thomas Douglas, 'Self-Serving Bias and the Structure of Moral Status' (2012) 38(3) *Journal of Medical Ethics* 141.

[63] Joel Feinberg, *The Moral Limits of the Criminal Law Volume 1: Harm to Others* (Oxford University Press 1987).

Excentia is a company using its 'Centaur Chemist' AI platform for drug compound discovery, and 'Centaur Biologist' platform to identify targets for these compounds.[64] The company currently have one cancer immunotherapy molecule in a Phase One clinical trial, which is the first AI-designed molecule of this type. Creating this method of drug discovery is an achievement of both the company, and of those that designed the AI. If nefarious actors had interfered with their work, and prevented them from achieving this, it is reasonable to say the company, and those working within it, would have had an important interest set back. This is the interest in achieving the creation of their drug discovery platforms.

How should we understand this interest? On a plausible objective list account of well-being, achievements are good for the achievers.[65] On a desire satisfaction account of well-being, achievements are good for achievers if they are desired. On a hedonist account, the pleasure of achievement is good for achievers. And on a perfectionist account, creation of the drug discovery platforms is (instrumentally) good if it furthers the development and perfection of the nature of those involved, which is (intrinsically) good for them. These are mutually exclusive accounts, cashing out well-being in fundamentally different ways. We can see that answering whether the prevention of this achievement is a harm depends on the nature of those involved, the nature of the achievement, and which account of well-being is right. Since we have first-hand knowledge of the first two things, the largest doubt is the philosophical one, and often these accounts will overlap on standard elements of human life.

However, if the drug is a success, it seems plausible that this is, at least in part, an achievement of the AI platforms themselves. If the AI's achievements were frustrated, perhaps by hackers who interfered with their computations, is this a harm to these ABs? Here we find significant questions about the nature of the ABs, which we have already discussed. Do they have minds, and are they capable of hedonic mental states, or intentional desires (desires that are *about* something)? Do they have a nature that they develop towards perfection though certain acts? In the case of Centaur AIs, the answer is plausibly that they are not capable of any of these – they are Phase One ABs. But if this were

---

[64] Neil Savage, 'Tapping into the Drug Discovery Potential of AI', Biopharma Dealmakers, 27 May 2021, https://www.nature.com/articles/d43747-021-00045-7, accessed 8 March 2022; Kit-Kay Mak, Madhu Katyayani Balijepalli and Mallikarjuna Rao Pichika, 'Success Stories of AI in Drug Discovery – Where Do Things Stand?' (2022) 17(1) *Expert Opinion on Drug Discovery* 79.

[65] For more on each of these accounts, see Roger Crisp, 'Well-Being' in Edward N. Zalta (ed.), *The Stanford Encyclopedia of Philosophy* (Winter 2021 Edition), https://plato.stanford.edu/archives/win2021/entries/well-being/.

not the case, they would be Phase Two ABs and we might have moral reason to be concerned about them directly.

There are also significant questions about the nature of the achievement, in particular, its value. The Centaur AIs enabled an anti-cancer drug discovery to be achieved in eight months that would normally take four to six years. The AIs themselves did not perform all of the tasks in this process; however, in a very short time they sorted through and compared the properties of millions of molecules and determined their targets, identifying a small number that should be synthesised, tested and developed. This would be a huge achievement for humans. Is it a huge achievement for AI? Nick Agar explores the value of achievement when considering radical human enhancement.[66] Quite plausibly, he argues that our valuing of achievements is informed by our achievement-relevant capacities. Consider an AB with AI that has the capacity to realise the value of its achievements according to the correct account of well-being (whatever that may be). Given its immense capacity for computational work, perhaps the drug discovery is a relatively trivial feat and of little prudential value. If that is so, then it may not have been harmed at all by its success being thwarted.

This assumes that ABs are similar enough to us that our accounts of well-being apply to them. These accounts have been developed primarily with humans in mind, and are arguably limited by our appreciation of value. Is achievement a concept that applies to ABs given their potentially radically different natures, not just from us, but also from each other? They may expose the need for a new account of well-being that has the scope to include them. Less radically, an objective list theory can account for such difference by populating the list with the relevant objective goods that ABs can realise in their lives. But what are these goods? Perhaps ABs will one day explain them to us. But if they do, they would not be Phase Two ABs. For Phase Two ABs, this is one of the many relevant aspects of them that we would be uncertain about.

What Is Right, Legally and Morally, for Phase Two Artificial Beings?

Harms are pro tanto bad. But that doesn't in itself mean that doing or allowing harm is always wrong, far less that it's always the proper place of the law to try to prevent it. To establish that, we might need to be satisfied of certain other things. As we saw earlier in this chapter, many legal philosophers believe that to be a suitable subject at least for criminal prohibition, an act must not only

---

    [66]   Nicholas Agar, *Truly Human Enhancement: A Philosophical Defense of Limits* (MIT Press 2014).

cause harm, but also be wrongful. That is, it must violate someone's rights or other legitimate moral entitlement.

But lawmakers will also want to consider the degree of harm caused, and weigh that against the harms and costs involved in legislating or regulating. All protections impose some costs, or prevention of benefit, for others, and therefore require justification. Actions that are likely to cause a great deal of suffering, or that wrong their victims in important ways, are therefore more plausible candidates for legal attention than those which are more trivial; and we might think that very trivial harms or wrongs are no proper business of law (or perhaps even morality) at all. If we are less confident that protections deliver a benefit for the subject or that the subject has moral status of some degree, then this weakens the justification because it is a reason to discount that benefit on epistemic grounds.

Using this understanding, we can start to sketch what would inform a regulatory response to Phase Two ABs. It should be informed by: (a) our confidence that the AB has a particular moral status (that it possesses, for example, the capacity to suffer), and (b) the likely impact of the proposed act upon them if they do. These considerations are of course related; the badness of 'torturing' an AB will depend substantially (though as we saw in the first part of this chapter, perhaps not exclusively) on the capacity of the AB to suffer.

Drawing on these considerations, we propose a *gradualist* approach to protecting Phase Two ABs. On this view, moral and legal reasons to protect ABs from harm gradually grow stronger in proportion to our epistemic confidence about their status. Roughly speaking, this resembles probably the most influential approach to protection of the interests of early human life. Here, like ABs, we are bringing new individuals into existence, and we are uncertain when they gain moral status or become subjects of well-being, and what the nature of harms or wrongs to them are as a result. Michael Selgelid advances an argument on the basis of uncertainty for gradualism regarding moral concern for the developing embryo and fetus, which, he argues, justifies gradualist legal protections regulating its treatment.[67] On this view there is less reason to be concerned about the human zygote for its own sake than it is for the near-term fetus, because of the greater uncertainty about whether a zygote has moral status than there is about the fetus. It is also possible to defend gradualism on other grounds, such as because of a belief that the embryo gains moral status over its development, which justifies greater consideration and protection – uncertainty is not a consideration.

---

[67] Michael J. Selgelid, 'Moral Uncertainty and the Moral Status of Early Human Life' (2012) 30(1) *Monash Bioethics Review* 52.

Our gradualist proposal is compatible with both of these. In Phase Two ABs there may be different levels of moral status, and different levels of certainty about this moral status.

Let's consider an example. All things considered, we are moderately uncertain about whether a particular AB has the capacity for welfare. Even after applying Danaher's behaviourist test, there is insufficient evidence to convince us either way about whether it can feel pain or fear, or experience any mental states at all. Should we extend protections to that AB from certain kinds of treatment? Although we are uncertain if it can suffer, we can say with confidence that *if* it can, then certain kinds of treatment (including some of those discussed in the first part of the chapter) would be very bad for it; our closest human or animal analogy to this would be torture. The degree of moral badness involved in torturing a sentient being is very high, and this gives us a strong reason to prevent the treatment. But this is discounted by our uncertainty about whether the AB is really the sort of thing that can suffer when tortured. The better our reasons for thinking that it can, the stronger the case for regulating to protect it.

In view of our earlier comment about costs, it probably shouldn't come as a surprise that we believe a third criterion should inform this decision: (c) we should be willing to take more of a risk of harming the AB if this is being done for a very good reason. The risk of subjecting an AB to painful or unpleasant stimuli might be more justified if, for example, this were being done while researching a serious human disease than if it were being done just for the gratification or amusement of the torturer. There could, of course, be a range of uses about which people might disagree (what about ABs being created and destroyed for military training?). Such disagreements, while challenging, are not unfamiliar in regulatory contexts; consider, for example, debates about the acceptable use of animals in research, entertainment or food production.

Moderate uncertainty, however, is a fairly simple case. Let's imagine that we have low certainty that putting an AB in a waste disposal grinder while both are in operation is equivalent to violently murdering the AB (we will set aside the potential assault of the waste disposal unit). We have high certainty that it's equivalent to grinding a carrot. We are torn – both are reasons that are considerable under our gradualist approach, both are true beliefs, and holding them both is coherent. Is this a problem for our approach? We think not. There are many possible options here. Should only one belief be used, or all reasonable beliefs? If only one, should it be that about which we have the greatest epistemic certainty, or that which assesses moral badness highest? If all reasonable beliefs are used, how should multiple results be dealt with? We think that it is likely that all of these approaches would yield a roughly similar result. The highest epistemic certainty belief is about a low level of badness, and the highest level of badness belief has a low epistemic certainty. We think these are roughly equivalent. Therefore, one or both could be used and it would make little difference. In this case, there is little ethical reason not to grind up the AB, and little reason to protect it from being ground up through law and policy.

Given the high level of uncertainty about almost every feature of ABs and actions regarding them that is relevant for determining the moral badness of any action, we do not see any reason for a cautious approach to be taken towards legal protection of ABs currently, or in the near future. However, much of the uncertainty we discuss may be resolved by progress in ethical and jurisprudential reasoning. This will make clearer whether there are reasons to protect ABs for their own sake, and which we should be concerned about.

CONCLUSION

Whether or not we eventually succeed in creating ABs that possess an 'internal' life – that can feel and think and care about what happens to them – we will certainly have ABs that can behave as if these things are true. Some will be designed specifically for that purpose; either benignly, to meet our needs and desires, or with a view to manipulating us. In other cases, their lifelike properties will be an unintended by-product of the abilities for which they were designed, or of our innate tendency towards anthropomorphism.

For a variety of reasons, we might want to consider introducing rules that prevent such beings from being subjected to certain kinds of treatment. Although they are not morally considerable in themselves – they do not make direct moral claims against us – our conduct towards them may risk offence or even harm to humans or other living things. Furthermore, some would argue that certain kinds of treatment (robotic rape or torture, for example) are inherently wrong, in a way that could justify their prohibition.

Whether we are persuaded by such arguments will depend on whether we are persuaded by certain factual claims, for example about whether abusing an AB is more likely to lead to abuse of humans, or about whether abuse of ABs necessarily involves endorsing certain abhorrent acts or attitudes. It will also depend significantly on what we think about the justifiable role of the law in preventing acts that might be immoral or risky, even when they do not directly harm or wrong anyone.

Regardless of how we feel about those matters, we have suggested that, when considering new rules (moral and certainly legal) governing our conduct towards ABs, we should be cautious of blurring the line between morally significant beings, and those which merely mimic that status. Responding to the 'maltreatment' of Phase One ABs as if it were even remotely of the same moral nature as maltreatment of sentient, conscious or autonomous lifeforms might risk losing sight of what matters in our conduct to those lifeforms, and leave us more vulnerable to impersonation and manipulation by the mimics.

It may be inevitable that we will anthropomorphise ABs that behave in a lifelike manner, even when we know rationally that they are not alive. In some contexts, this will be harmless; in others, possibly even beneficial (as in the case of companion ABs for the chronically lonely). But there are significant dangers, both from ABs designed to hijack our sentiments (such as robot pets that persuade us to pay for expensive repairs and upgrades), and from those that divert our attention from others who properly deserve it (such as battlefield robots whose 'lives' are viewed as worth risking humans for). We should be at least somewhat cautious that regulatory responses to such beings could exacerbate our tendency to see them and treat them as if they were actually living beings, and also be somewhat cautious of what risks that may pose.

Phase Two ABs are those whose moral status is uncertain. They might behave as if they can think and feel, experience joy and pain and fear, but we cannot be sure whether this is genuine or just clever technical mimicry. How should we behave towards such beings? What rules should govern our conduct towards them? Should they protect such ABs from certain kinds of treatment?

We have suggested an approach that seeks to balance epistemic and moral considerations. It asks us to consider how likely it is, based on all observable evidence, that the AB has moral status (the epistemic criterion). Since it's likely that such enquiries will leave considerable room for uncertainty, we also ask how bad it would be for the AB to be subject to the treatment in question, if in fact it was the sort of being capable of being harmed or wronged thereby (the badness criterion). A third consideration asks about the costs and trade-offs of any protective intervention (the cost criterion).

Such an approach will not provide a clear or simple way to decide how a particular AB should be treated. But it does start to sketch a framework for approaching questions about how we should behave towards Phase Two ABs. Let's imagine we were deciding whether to try to rescue an AB from a burning building. Looking at the badness criterion, being burned up in a fire would involve terrible harm for any being capable of experiencing that fate. This gives us a pro tanto reason to rescue the AB. But the epistemic criterion might negate that reason, if we were very confident that the AB was not even minimally sentient. And the cost criterion could outweigh it even if we were less certain, if the only way to save the AB was by risking our own life, or failing to rescue those who are definitely moral subjects.

Our approach, then, is cautious about implementing rules protecting ABs. This derives in part from what we see as the danger of regulatory overreach into the realm of private conduct and morality; and in part from the possible dangers of overly anthropomorphising the sorts of ABs we have at the moment, and are likely to have in the future.

There is, however, another possible approach to this matter. It involves taking seriously the possibility that there will one day be ABs that really can think, feel, care and possess other morally relevant properties; and further, accepting our assumption that, were we to be fairly sure such beings exist, we would owe moral duties to them. Whether or not those beings are organic, whether they are created in a laboratory rather than born, and whether they happen to resemble humans or other recognisable animals, will matter much less than the morally salient capacities they possess, and what (if anything) it feels like to be them.

Ideally, we would be able to fine-tune our emotional responses such that we could behave towards a range of different beings in a manner that is appropriate to the capacities and status they actually possess. Given the imperfect nature of our emotional responses, though, that may prove challenging or even impossible for many of us. Perhaps, then, there is something to be said for embarking now on a (probably) long course of moral training, familiarising ourselves with the idea that beings which differ from us in very obvious ways should matter to us all the same. It's not unthinkable that such training could start now, with how we behave towards lifelike, but not living, ABs.

Getting used to the idea that inorganic 'life' forms may matter morally may be an important step, but so too is the idea that it may not resemble human or animal life. An artificially intelligent AB may not be embodied at all, but may still possess capacities that render it directly morally considerable. An approach, then, that favours those ABs that resemble humans or other animals in superficial ways may, from this perspective, be counterproductive.

9. Concluding remarks

This collection cannot be thought of as any kind of empirical study on the weighting of attitudes to one side or the other within the proactive/reactive regulation debate. Rather, it is the product of discussions held amongst some of the many members of our wide research network on our concept of 'novel beings'. It should be said, though, at the close, that we originally envisioned (and expected) a more equal balance of chapters in the two sections. Sadly, this was not to be the case due to the knock-on effects of the global pandemic that still threatens to spark back to life as we write these remarks. Several excellent colleagues were unfortunately forced to pull out of the collection through illness and through the cumulative workload pressures that our academic readers will be more than familiar with. As it happens, our discussions with them and their early work on their chapters indicate that the likelihood is that these pieces would have fallen largely on the 'reactive' side of the debate. This would have perhaps redressed the balance between Part I and Part II of this collection. We thank those missing contributors for their early efforts, and lament that they could not be included alongside the excellent chapters you have read.

However, we, the editors, don't see the imbalance within these pages as especially meaningful. All the chapters included, despite the positions they take and despite the part they are in, acknowledge that a multifaceted approach will be required for meaningful regulation of novel beings and the technologies that may lead us to them. This is perhaps most clearly stated in the chapter by Gavaghan and King, which was the subject of some debate between us as to whether it ought to have a part of its own. Ultimately that chapter's emphasis on caution about acting too soon won out, but the fact that we struggled to place it was instructive. It seems there is less of a clear binary between approaches to emerging technology regulation than we expected.

TO WAIT AND SEE, OR TO ACT DECISIVELY?

Several events,[1] held as part of our wider research into novel beings, revealed a preference for a 'wait and see' approach amongst the lawyers and legal aca-

---

[1] We have held a number of events under the various grants that have supported our research into novel beings, including 'Regulating the Tyrell Corporation: Company Law and the Emergence of Novel Beings', 26–27 October 2018, Wellcome

demics in attendance, along with the computer scientists who were with us to provide their expertise on AI. The rest of the attendees, including applied philosophers, geneticists, neuroscientists, and social scientists, tended to favour a more active regulatory strategy. This disciplinary divide was not universal, but quite distinct, although we had not the foresight at the time to record it empirically.

Given the weighting of this collection towards legally focussed contributions, it was our expectation that the majority of chapters would prefer a reactive style of regulation for novel beings. It was argued by a number of legal colleagues that many principles capable of effectively regulating novel beings already existed within the law; under contract law, consumer protection, equity, tort, and criminal law. Any harm that potentially could be caused by emerging technology could, therefore, be covered by adapting these already settled principles – we don't need to reinvent the wheel. The same idea was held to be true of existing laws in certain areas. For example, the Consumer Protection Act 1987 (and Consumer Rights Act 2015) could be used to address defective AI that causes harm, where that harm can be traced back to the developer or designer. A highly convincing argument of this nature is provided by McMahon, who in her chapter suggests that intellectual property rights under patent law could play a key role in regulating novel beings, and other emerging technology, as a driver, blocker and ethical guide for technological development and use.

A 'wait and see' approach would also allow us to react to the real-world developments of emerging technology (and novel beings) to provide an appropriate and effective solution to the problems that these technologies actually create. This would allow us to better adapt existing legal principles or create new regulations with a minimum of upheaval and without speculation. This view is broadly reflected in Roberts and Quigley's chapter, but – reflecting the emergent theme of multifaceted approaches – they too acknowledge that a wait and see approach is not always ideal.

Interestingly, despite our differing expertise (one lawyer and one ethicist), we are both firmly in favour of the proactive approach. Our research into, and development of, the broad concept of novel beings over several years has led us to the conclusion that the question is ultimately one of moral impetus; can we allow harm to come to entities that we ourselves have created? Creating sentient or sapient life without regard for its future seems like a great moral ill, and so we find our viewpoints influenced towards prevention, rather than cure.

Collection, London, UK; and 'Novel Beings Network: Navigating the Proactive/ Reactive Regulatory Debate for Emerging and Future Technologies', 24 March 2021, held online due to the global COVID-19 pandemic.

Even if the law does currently provide some useful tools to regulate novel beings, it does not address some of these more fundamental questions about the creation of new life and the rights and protections that such lives may warrant. Many areas of existing law are not fit for purpose here, including the foundations of human rights law, but more particularly legislation around AI and biotechnologies. These instruments broadly, if understandably, maintain a narrow focus, and do not set out to engage with questions that could upset many of their core assumptions.[2]

For our purposes, it may be necessary to ask questions beyond the remit of these statutes and other proposed regulations, questions that are likely to be vital to the maintenance of our society – including whether we want novel beings to exist at all, and if so, for what purpose. These questions are currently being left to large multinational corporations to answer. As Morley argues in her chapter, corporations are self-regulating their development of this technology and as such have the effective freedom to choose how they operate it. There are already problems emerging with this approach – scandals with Uber, Facebook (now Meta), Google and Microsoft demonstrate that these corporations are not equipped to deal appropriately with these issues – particularly as they are driven by their own interests and to increase shareholder wealth.[3] We must consider the broader social construction of the humans who plan and develop this technology in their own interest, as Dignam argues in this volume. Therefore, regulation should consider mitigating or guiding the human choice behind the technology.

During our prior work on this topic, our scientific and industry colleagues referred to codes of practice, ethical stances, and closely held principles that guide their research to ensure that human interest or bias is mitigated. Indeed, a field of research already exists that addresses these issues: responsible research innovation (RRI), which considers how to direct technology and inno-

---

[2]   These 'legislative gaps' are engaged with in more detail in David R. Lawrence and Sarah Morley, 'Regulating the Tyrell Corporation: The Emergence of Novel Beings' (2021) 30 *Cambridge Quarterly of Healthcare Ethics* 421–434. There, we have a particular focus on the law of England and Wales, but similar arguments can be made regarding instruments from other jurisdictions.

[3]   Examples abound, but particularly egregious are Google's now-terminated 'Project Dragonfly' (Madhumita Murgia and Siddarth Shrikanth, 'How Big Tech is Struggling with the Ethics of AI', *Financial Times* (28 April 2019) <https://www.ft.com/content/a3328ce4-60ef-11e9-b285-3acd5d43599e> accessed 13 April 2022), and the actions of Cambridge Analytica in connection with Facebook (see Digital Culture, Media and Sport Committee, 'Disinformation and "Fake News"' (Final Report, HC 1791, 2019)).

vation towards socially desirable ends.[4] However, we cannot solely rely on RRI or other self-regulatory codes of conduct to regulate behaviour alone. The famous 1975 Asilomar Conference, which instituted procedural guidelines to avoid a self-imposed global moratorium on recombinant DNA research, was hailed as a resounding success for the self-regulation of science. This is fair praise – the freedom that it bought led to important advances in genetics. However, elsewhere we have seen resounding failures – perhaps the most significant in recent years being the birth of Lulu and Nana, the 'CRISPR Babies', twin girls born through heritable genome editing technology, deployed recklessly and counter to the global consensus on safety. No code, no ethical position, prevented this extreme risk being taken. If we are to avoid somewhat predictable scenarios such as this, legislative action before they are realised seems necessary.

A WILL TO ACT PROMPTLY?

Proactive regulation (or proposals for it) relies on speculation and requires flexibility so as not to preclude unforeseeable scenarios. The concern then is that any attempt to proactively regulate may be subsumed by the understandable desire for certainty of outcome. As Lawrence discusses in his chapter, emerging biotechnologies such as those likely to play a role in any novel being are likely to be viewed with a certain suspicion – if not fear – in public debate. This type of reaction lends itself to either reliance on harsh reactive regulation or calls for wholesale bans on developing technologies, as they at least appear to provide surety of resolution (or indeed prevent the feared possibilities from ever materialising). This can have the effect of preventing serious discussion in the legislature about the realities of what is usually a nuanced situation, something that warrants lengthy exploration before any action can be taken. Proactive regulation is a more difficult 'sell' in the policy sphere – one which is, perhaps understandably, most concerned with pragmatism and concrete, immediate problems. This is exemplified well in that it is only in the last several years that serious conversations are being held regarding the rights of sentient and potentially sapient animals, with a string of high-level court cases in the US and Argentina.[5] We have long known that some animals may warrant moral status, and yet it has never been a legislative priority.

---

[4] See Richard Owen and others, 'A Framework for Responsible Innovation' in Richard Owen, John Bessant and Maggy Heintz (eds), *Responsible Innovation: Managing the Responsible Emergence of Science and Innovation in Society* (John Wiley & Sons, 2013).

[5] Most notably including the orangutans Cecilia (Expte. Nro. P-72.254/15 *Presentación Efectuada por A.F.A.D.A Respecto del Chimpancé 'Cecilia' – Sujeto No*

Reflecting on the points made by Tigard in this volume, this kind of reluc-tance to act with an eye to future challenges has, in a very real sense, led to direct harms and even deaths. We can point, for instance, to the fatal incidents involving 'self-driving' cars.[6] Whilst countries around the world are now scrambling to put laws in place to properly regulate the deployment and public testing of these vehicles,[7] it does not seem far-fetched to suggest that with some foresight, some of these deaths may have been avoided.

Something similar can be said in the biosciences. In recent years, for example, there has been a scramble to legislate for the advent of mitochondrial replacement therapies, which were made legal under licence in 2015,[8] to great controversy in public opinion. However, the technology was known and dis-cussed in scientific circles for quite some time beforehand;[9] and it bears saying that it is possible that cases of mitochondrial disease – with the potential for

---

Humano [2016]; Expte. A2174-2015/0 *Asociacion de Funcionarios y Abogados por los Derechos de los Animales y Otros Contra GCBA Sobre Amparo* [2016]); and Sandra (Expte. A2174-2015/0 *Asociacion de Funcionarios y Abogados por los Derechos de Los Animales y Otros Contra GCBA Sobre Amparo*); see also: 'Orangutan Granted Controlled Freedom by Argentine Court', CNN (23 December 2014) <http://edition .cnn.com/2014/12/23/world/americas/feat-orangutan-rights-ruling/> accessed 13 April 2022.

    Additionally, the chimpanzees Tommy (*The Nonhuman Rights Project, Inc., On Behalf of Tommy v Patrick C. Lavery*, 518336, State of New York Supreme Court [2014]); and Hercules and Leo (*Matter of Nonhuman Rights Project, Inc. v Stanley*, N.Y. Slip Op 31419, State of New York Supreme Court [2015]); see also: Jesse McKinley, 'Judge Orders Stony Brook University to Defend Its Custody of 2 Chimps', *New York Times* (22 April 2015) <http://www.nytimes.com/2015/04/22/nyregion/ judge-orders-hearing-for-2-chimps-said-to-be-unlawfully-detained.html> accessed 13 April 2022.

    [6] Such as the 2018 death of Elaine Herzberg. Daisuke Wakabayashi, 'Self-Driving Uber Car Kills Pedestrian in Arizona, Where Robots Roam', *New York Times* (19 March 2018) <https://www.nytimes.com/2018/03/19/technology/uber-driverless -fatality.html> accessed 13 April 2022.

    [7] See, for instance, the calls made in the Law Commission report: *Automated Vehicles: Joint Report* (Law Com No. 404, 2022).

    [8] The Human Fertilisation and Embryology (Mitochondrial Donation) Regulations 2015 No. 572.

    [9] Newcastle University having applied for a research licence in 2004: James Randerson, 'Scientists Seek to Create "Three-Parent" Babies', *New Scientist* (19 October 2004) <https://www.newscientist.com/article/dn6547-scientists-seek-to-create -three-parent-babies/> accessed 12 April 2022.

terrible suffering – could have been avoided in the four-year interim between the technology being deemed 'ready'[10] and the first licence being granted.[11]

A POSSIBLE ROUTE FORWARDS

Given the problems and difficulties on either side of the proactive/reactive divide, and the somewhat unexpected tendency towards a middle ground in this volume, perhaps we glimpse a route forwards. We suggest that the regulation of novel beings, and perhaps emerging technologies more generally, will require a combined approach of hard and soft regulation. There are too many important issues that require addressing for it to be left entirely to self-regulation, as highlighted above; however, there are valid concerns about certainty and flexibility that hard law does not always address well.[12] We propose that both approaches are taken.

Discussions within research events, along with arguments made in this volume, have made it clear that while we cannot act too drastically based on prediction, we may wish to act proactively to enshrine in hard legislation a range of core principles. These would be values that we may wish to protect, no matter exactly how the technology develops. The final pages of this collection are not the place to establish these 'cornerstones' – to do so will require extensive work across disciplines and with the involvement of a huge range of stakeholders. We might imagine that we must begin by asking about the type of beings that should exist – and what duties we might owe to anything we create.

Whatever specifics it includes, this baseline will ensure that developers, owners and operators of technology have agreed-upon guidelines to follow and, most importantly, the use of hard law means that if the guidelines are breached, those people can be held accountable. We know that self-regulation lacks the enforcement mechanisms required to prevent the types of harm novel beings and related technologies have the potential to engender, and so it is important that this hard law has sufficient teeth to effectively guide behaviours.

---

[10] Steve Connor, 'UK Becomes First Country in World to Approve IVF Using Genes of Three', *The Independent* (28 June 2013) <http://www.independent.co.uk/news/science/uk-becomes-first-country-in-world to-approve-ivf-using-genes-of-three -parents-8677595.html> accessed 13 April 2022.

[11] James Gallagher, 'Three-Person Baby Licence Granted', BBC News (16 March 2017) <http://www.bbc.co.uk/news/health-39292381> accessed 13 April 2022.

[12] Deryck Beyleveld and Roger Brownsword, 'Emerging Technologies, Extreme Uncertainty, and the Principle of Rational Precautionary Reasoning' (2012) 4 *Law, Innovation and Technology* 35.

Some hard principles with which to work will also provide certainty as to who we would hold accountable in specific situations, such as where the likely determination of traditional torts might feel counterintuitive. For instance, harms done by an AI capable of reason and self-determination, of true choice, seem intuitively different from the probable liability situation relating to a current self-driving car.

However, as noted, we cannot entirely cross the epistemic gap in emerging technology. Any hard law should therefore be accompanied by soft law regulation – which can utilise the benefits of self-regulation. Codes can be developed and adapted reactively to the specifics of the technology at hand; this can flesh out the proactive baseline and provide the detail for hard law, and ideally, allow matters to be approached on a case-by-case basis. But the limitations that we usually see with soft law must be avoided – for it to be effective, there must be mechanisms in place to assess adherence to any code or ways in which to punish those who breach it.

This will only be practicable if we have an independent and specialist regulator to provide oversight. The regulator could be a mix of full-time and part-time staff – including industry experts who are on secondment from technology firms, scientists, commercial scientific research groups, or academia. In order to be effective, the regulator will need to be granted the power to create rules that adapt to the emergence of novel beings, and also pre-empt future problems we cannot now foresee. They will also require powers to investigate complaints or breaches, and to apply appropriate sanctions to ensure compliance.

We are aware that in the aforementioned policy climate, it is unlikely that such an agency, or such a complex regime, will ever be a priority – at least until the technologies in question are undeniable realities. Before it could ever be considered pragmatic, this brief proposal will clearly require significantly more thought and detail. The implications of how this system would work in practice, including costs of such a system and how it might be funded, are as yet unanswered questions. We hope to address them in the future, alongside our expanding network of researchers in many fields – academics, policymakers, industry actors, and interested members of the public – who recognise the imminent and expansive challenge of the dawn of the novel being.

Index